W9-APL-100

新SAT
阅读真题对应词汇

郭松坡 编著

化学工业出版社
·北京·

《新SAT阅读真题对应词汇》包含阅读词汇、历史词汇、抽象词汇和态度词汇4个部分。阅读词汇是主体部分，大概有2100个词汇，来源于新SAT官方指南、可汗、PSAT和2016年－2018年真题，总计55 List。这些词汇标注了音标、词性和由10年SAT阅读一线名师亲自精挑细选的最常考词义。历史词汇618个，来源于从OG到可汗，从PSAT到2018年12月份以前所有的历史文章中比较常考的或者比较熟词僻义的单词。书中从100套老SAT阅读中约4800道选项里和新SAT 45套阅读（包含了OG、可汗、PSAT和2016年－2018年的真题）中约2300道选项中整理了非常具有代表性的抽象词（725个）和态度词（598个），并配上了英文释义，可以有针对性地帮助学生解决抽象词和态度词词义辨析的难题。

本书是一本非常实用的SAT词汇备考书，可供参加SAT考试的学生备考参考、使用。

图书在版编目（CIP）数据

新SAT阅读真题对应词汇 / 郭松坡编著 .—北京：化学工业出版社，2019.6

ISBN 978-7-122-34212-6

Ⅰ.①新… Ⅱ.①郭… Ⅲ.①英语—词汇—高等学校—入学考试—美国—自学参考资料 Ⅳ.①H313

中国版本图书馆CIP数据核字（2019）第057571号

责任编辑：陶艳玲　　　　装帧设计：史利平

责任校对：宋　夏

出版发行：化学工业出版社（北京市东城区青年湖南街13号 邮政编码100011）

印　　装：大厂聚鑫印刷有限责任公司

710mm×1000mm　1/16　印张17¾　字数400千字　2019年6月北京第1版第1次印刷

购书咨询：010-64518888　　　售后服务：010-64518899

网　　址：http://www.cip.com.cn

凡购买本书，如有缺损质量问题，本社销售中心负责调换。

定　　价：59.00元　　　　　　　　　　　　　　　版权所有　违者必究

前　言

编写理念

随着中国经济形势渐行渐佳，中国人的生活水平也在逐步提高，越来越多的中国人希望送子女去国外留学深造。由于美国大学在全世界享有卓越声誉，越来越多的中国学生选择赴美留学，2018 年，约 20 万中国学生赴美留学，并且，留学人数正在逐年递增。

如果希望就读美国的大学本科，中国学生除了需要参加托福考试外，同时，还需要参加一个类似于中国高考的"美国高考"，即 SAT 考试。2014 年，编者针对当时 SAT 考试的情况，编写出版了《SAT 填空词汇速记 3500》。从 2016 年 3 月开始，美国考试委员会（CB）已对 SAT 考试进行改革。由于改革后的 SAT 考试取消了句子填空题，这类题目经常会考一些特别偏僻的单词，比如，besmirch（v. 诽谤，中伤）、evanescent（adj. 昙花一现的）等，这些词汇甚至连大部分美国人也不一定认识。因此，在考试取消了这种题型之后，中国学生急需一个新的 SAT 词汇书，既不需背诵以前那些很偏僻的单词，又要学习对新 SAT 阅读有针对性的单词。因此我及时编撰了《新 SAT 阅读词汇速记 2000》（第 2 版），在 2016 年 8 月出版。目前市面上针对新 SAT 的词汇书还比较少，并且良莠不齐，甚至很多学生仍然继续在背诵针对老 SAT 的"巴郎 3500"，为了急学生之所急，经过三年多的教学积累，对新 SAT 有了更多的了解，我在第 2 版的基础上重新整理，编纂了这本《新 SAT 阅读真题对应词汇》。书中，每个 Word List 对应相应的真题。历史词汇对应历史文章，抽象词汇对应主旨题和目的题选项，态度词汇对应小说文章和选项。

词汇来源

笔者从事留学考试培训十年以上，在 SAT 考试培训方面都有着丰富的研究和教学经验，已经出版过国外考试书籍 7 本，培训过上万人次的学生，数千学生老

SAT 2200 分以上或新 SAT 1500 分以上，能很好地把握 SAT 考试的难度和深度，非常专业地选出词汇在阅读文章中最常考的意思，尤其是历史文章中的"熟词僻义"。

阅读考试是新 SAT 考试的重中之重，也是中国学生需要攻克的最大难关。而阅读的最基本的前提条件就是单词。本书分以下几个部分进行词汇归纳：阅读词汇、历史词汇、抽象词汇和态度词汇。

本书的阅读词汇是主体部分，大概有 2100 个词汇，这些单词来源于新 SAT 官方指南（OG 4 套）、可汗（相当于 12 套题目）、PSAT（6 套）、2016 年 – 2018 年真题（合计 33 套），总计 55 套（list）。至于 2019 年后的真题，考虑到在没有背诵单词的情况下模考才更具有真实性，因此没有收录，主要是拿来模考使用。学生在模考完毕后可自行整理背诵。

本书的阅读词汇在收录时剔除了托福，四、六级和初、高中词汇（这些词汇约 8000 个）。因此，准备新 SAT 阅读大概需要的词汇量合计在 10000 个左右。这些单词是保障同学们能考到 1500 分的前提和基础。书中的这些词汇标注了音标、词性和由 10 年 SAT 阅读一线名师亲自精挑细选的最常考词义。这些英文释义都是笔者根据牛津或韦氏词典精心挑选的针对考试中阅读文章的释义，因此，该词表的部分释义和普通词典上的释义并不完全雷同，更具有针对性。

同时书中还整理了 618 个历史词汇，这些词要么比较古老，要么是在法律或历史文献等特定文章里表现为特殊释义，在平时背诵的时候可能就没有注意到这个释义，比如 act（n. 法案）、observe（v. 遵守法律）等。因此书中整理了从 OG 到可汗，从 PSAT 到 2018 年 12 月份以前所有的历史文章中常考的或者熟词僻义的历史词汇，好让大家集中歼灭。

从笔者多年一线授课的经验来看，还有些单词虽然简单，但是比较难以理解。即使你认识它们，或即使给出中文释义，也不一定能够一下子反应出它在文中到底是什么意思，比如 claim（v. 宣称）、proclaim（v. 声称）。常有很多类似的抽象词和态度词出现在选项里，特别是正确选项里。很多同学在没有深入"理解"这些单词的情况下，很难辨析词义，在排除选项的时候，往往会比较纠结。因此，为了有针对性地帮助学生解决抽象词和态度词词义辨析的难题，书中从 100 套老 SAT 阅读中约 4800 道选项中和新 SAT 45 套阅读（包含了 OG、可汗、PSAT 和 2016 年 – 2018 年的真题）中约 2300 道选项中整理出了非常具有代表性的抽象词（725 个）和态度词（598 个），并配上了英文释义，尤其是对主旨题、双篇题和目的题特别有效。这些单词也经常出现在"词汇题"里，说明考试官方出题人对这些词有比较强烈的考察要求。即使同学们认识这些单词，也希望同学们能够好好"体会"这些词的内涵，这样在考试排除选项时就会事半功倍。对于这些单词，重点不是背诵，而是仔细"体会"。

背词方法

对不同的单词，有不同的背诵要求，因此，书中根据不同的单词类型设计了不同的内容形式。阅读词汇配了音标、词性和最精准的中文词义以及对应的英文释义（书中部分大写英文单词为同义词）；历史词、抽象词和态度词主要背诵英文释义。最终希望本书能使同学们既节约时间，又能有针对性地准备单词，起到事半功倍的效果，把宝贵的时间留在分析文章而不是无聊的背单词上。

背诵单词一般分为 3 个境界：1. 认出单词即可；2. 需要了解单词的精准释义；3. 需要在比较合规的英文环境下（比如在写作和对话中）应用这些单词。对于大部分 SAT 单词，在 SAT 阅读考试中，只要能够快速认出单词的意思即可。对于书中前部分 Word List 中的约 1700 个单词，比如 obsolete（adj. 荒废的），preposterous（adj. 不合理的），需要先背诵出来，待背诵 3 轮（注意，不是 3 遍）之后，或者能够记住 90% 以上之后，则达到了背诵单词的第一境界。然后，则需要读英文释义来理解这些单词的精准释义，或者在做阅读题的时候，根据对应的 List 来"体会"原文中的意思，以达到背诵单词的第二境界。

对于阅读词汇，第一遍每天背诵 300 个，第二天复习前一天的 300 个，外加新背 300 个，6 天背完一轮。然后开始第二遍的复习，每天复习 700 个，3 天复习完毕。再 3 天复习一遍。背 3 轮之后就可以开始读英文释义或对照着做题来进行语境词汇的把握，对单词认识得更加精准。历史词汇中有部分和前面 Word List 中的词汇是重合的，但也有部分比较简单的但考熟词僻义的单词不在前面的单词范围里，可以结合它们的英文释义在专门刷历史文章的时候对照使用。

对于主要针对目的题、主旨题和双篇题选项的抽象词和主要针对小说文章以及主旨题选项的态度词，则需要仔细"体会"英文释义。抽象词大家可能大部分都认识，但不一定知道精确的英文释义。在背诵的时候，如果英文释义和你理解的一致，才算真正认识；如果不一致，就需要反复细读英文释义，直到真正理解一致为止。态度词有很多意思比较难，并且差异比较细微，因此需要专门背诵，在背诵的时候也要和抽象词一样仔细"体会"它们的英文释义。

本书是一本非常实用的词汇备考书。"工欲善其事，必先利其器"，希望此书能够帮助莘莘学子在准备 SAT 考试时事半功倍，取得理想的成绩，从而顺利地踏上赴美留学之路。

由于时间仓促，编者水平有限，书中难免有疏漏和不足之处，恳请广大读者和同行提出宝贵意见，以便日后再版时做出修订，使本书更加完善。

编著者

2019 年 3 月

目　录

新 SAT 阅读真题对应词汇

Word List 1 OG1

scuttle ['skʌtl]	v. 急跑 to run with quick and short steps
deferential [ˌdefə'renʃl]	adj. 恭敬的 showing that you respect someone and want to treat them politely
unseemly [ʌn'si:mlɪ]	adj. 不合适的 not polite or suitable for a particular situation
preposterous [prɪ'pɒstərəs]	adj. 不合理的 completely unreasonable or silly
frantically ['fræntɪklɪ]	adv. 疯狂地 emotionally out of control
relish ['relɪʃ]	v. 欣赏 to get great pleasure from sth ; to want very much to do or have sth
dread [dred]	v. 担忧 fear of something bad that might happen or is going to happen
construe [kən'stru:]	v. 理解 to understand the meaning of a word, a sentence, or an action in a particular way
restrictive [rɪ'strɪktɪv]	adj. 限制的 strictly limiting or controlling someone or something
permutation [ˌpɜ:mju'teɪʃn]	n. 排列 any of the different ways in which a set of things can be ordered
procession [prə'seʃn]	n. 游行 a line of people or vehicles moving slowly as part of a ceremony
mount [maʊnt]	v. 登上 to get up on something above the level of the ground
ascend [ə'send]	v. 登上 to rise ; to go up ; to climb up

preach [pri:tʃ]	v. 布道 to give a religious talk in a public place, especially in a church during a service
transact [træn'zækt]	v. 交易 to do business with a person or an organization
solemn ['sɒləm]	adj. 严肃的 performed in a serious way
esthetic [es'θetɪk]	adj. 审美的 of, relating to, or dealing with aesthetics or the beautiful
queer [kwɪə (r)]	adj. 奇怪的 strange or unusual
stir [stɜ: (r)]	v. 激起（感情） to make sb excited or make them feel sth strongly
convene [kən'vi:n]	v. 召集 to arrange for people to come together for a formal meeting
prospect ['prɒspekt]	v. 寻找 to search an area for gold, minerals, oil, etc.
venture ['ventʃə (r)]	n.（有风险的）企业 a business project or activity, especially one that involves taking risks
flurry ['flʌrɪ]	n. 一阵风 an occasion when there is a lot of activity, interest, excitement, etc. within a short period of time
glut [glʌt]	v. 充斥；贪婪 to fill beyond capacity, especially with food ; satiate
barren ['bærən]	adj. 贫瘠的 not good enough for plants to grow on it

新 SAT 阅读真题对应词汇

Word List 2 OG2

baffle ['bæfl]	v. 使困惑 to confuse sb completely
rust [rʌst]	n. 生锈 a reddish-brown substance that is formed on some metals by the action of water and air
pen [pen]	v. 囚禁；把…关入栏中 to make someone feel they cannot escape from a situation；to shut an animal or a person in a small space
intimate ['ɪntɪmət]	v. 暗示 to let sb know what you think or mean in an indirect way
distress [dɪ'stres]	n. 悲痛 a feeling of great worry or unhappiness；great suffering
tumult ['tju:mʌlt]	n. 骚乱 a confused situation in which there is usually a lot of noise and excitement，often involving large numbers of people
pant [pænt]	v. 渴望 to long demonstratively；yearn
fetish ['fetɪʃ]	n. 痴迷 the fact that a person spends too much time doing or thinking about a particular thing
sever ['sevə (r)]	v. 隔断 to cut sth into two pieces
antipathy [æn'tɪpəθɪ]	n. 反感 a strong feeling of dislike
trifle ['traɪfl]	n. 不重要的事 something that is not valuable or important
liable ['laɪəbl]	adj. 有 ... 倾向的；有义务的 likely to do sth；legally responsible for paying the cost of sth

mortify ['mɔːtɪfaɪ]	v. 使羞愧 to make sb feel very ashamed or embarrassed
prowl [praʊl]	v. 暗中寻觅 moving quietly and carefully，hunting or looking for sth
pry [praɪ]	v. 刺探 to try to find out information about other people's private lives in a way that is annoying or rude
malignity [məˈlɪgnɪtɪ]	n. 恶毒 intense ill will or hatred
sneer [snɪə(r)]	v. 嘲笑 to show that you have no respect for sb by the expression on your face or by the way you speak
empathy [ˈempəθɪ]	n. 共鸣 the ability to understand another person's feelings，experience，etc.
raid [reɪd]	v. 袭击 to attack a place without warning
commandment [kəˈmɑːndmənt]	n. 戒律 a law given by God，especially any of the Ten Commandments given to the Jews in the Bible
queasy [ˈkwiːzɪ]	adj. 恶心的 feeling sick
phony [ˈfəʊniː]	adj. 假冒的 not real or true；false，and trying to deceive people
quirk [kwɜːk]	n. 怪癖 a strange thing that happens，especially accidentally
welter [ˈweltə(r)]	n. 混乱 a state of wild disorder
underpin [ˌʌndəˈpɪn]	v. 支持 to support or form the basis of an argument，a claim，etc.
inductive [ɪnˈdʌktɪv]	adj. 归纳的 using known facts to produce general principles
reverberate [rɪˈvɜːbəreɪt]	v. 回响 to be repeated several times as it bounces off different surfaces

revamp [ˌriːˈvæmp]	v. 改进 to make changes to the form of sth, usually to improve its appearance
verdict [ˈvɜːdɪkt]	n. 裁定 the finding or decision of a jury on the matter submitted to it in trial
undulate [ˈʌndjuleɪt]	v. 波动 to go or move gently up and down like waves
conjugate [ˈkɒndʒəgeɪt]	v. 使结合；列举词形变化 to become joined together ; to give the different forms of a verb, as they vary according to number, person, tense, etc.
bulk up	v. 变大 to become bigger and heavier
fierce [fɪəs]	adj. 凶猛的 angry and aggressive in a way that is frightening
amendment [əˈmendmənt]	n. (宪法) 修正案 a statement of a change to the Constitution of the US
suffrage [ˈsʌfrɪdʒ]	n. 选举权 the right to vote in political elections
aggrandize [əˈgrændaɪz]	v. 夸大 to make great or greater
slaughter [ˈslɔːtə (r)]	n. 大屠杀 the cruel killing of large numbers of people at one time, especially in a war
persecute [ˈpɜːsɪkjuːt]	v. 迫害 to treat someone extremely badly or refuse them equal rights, especially because of their race, religion, or political beliefs
temper [ˈtempə (r)]	v. 缓和 to dilute, qualify, or soften by the addition or influence of something else
disfranchise [ˌdɪsˈfræntʃaɪz]	v. 剥夺选举权 to deprive of a privilege, an immunity, or a right of citizenship, especially the right to vote ; disenfranchise
dilution [daɪˈljuːʃn]	n. 削弱；稀释 to make a quality, belief etc., weaker or less effective ; to make a liquid weaker by adding water or another liquid

appall [əˈpɔːl]	v. 使惊骇 to make someone feel very shocked and upset
mourn [mɔːn]	v. 哀悼 to feel or express grief or sorrow
exalt [ɪgˈzɔːlt]	v. 赞扬 to praise someone or something very much
subjugate [ˈsʌbdʒugeɪt]	v. 征服 to defeat sb/sth
vain [veɪn]	adj. 徒劳的；自大的 that does not produce the result you want ; in an irreverent or blasphemous manner
staggering [ˈstæɡərɪŋ]	adj. 巨大的，惊人的 large , shocking or surprising that it is difficult to believe
scenario [səˈnɑːriəʊ]	n. 设想；剧本 a description of how things might happen in the future ; a written outline of what happens in a film/movie or play
salinity [səˈlɪnətɪ]	n. 盐分 consisting of or containing salt
strait [streɪt]	n. 海峡 a narrow passage of water that connects two seas or large areas of water
plunge [plʌndʒ]	v. 跳下 to fall quickly from a high position
proficient [prəˈfɪʃnt]	adj. 熟练的 able to do sth well because of training and practice
curator [kjʊəˈreɪtə (r)]	n. 馆长 a person whose job is to be in charge of the objects or works of art in a museum or art gallery , etc.
compile [kəmˈpaɪl]	v. 汇编 to compose out of materials from other documents
patron [ˈpeɪtrən]	n. 赞助人 a person who gives money and support to artists and writers
obsolete [ˈɒbsəliːt]	adj. 废弃的 no longer used because sth new has been invented

ornate [ɔːˈneɪt]	adj. 装饰的 decorated with complicated patterns or shapes
marvel [ˈmɑːvl]	v. 惊奇 to be very surprised or impressed by sth
stock [stɒk]	v. 把…装满；adj. 乏味的 to fill sth with goods, food, etc.; not thinking of anything more interesting or original
painstaking [ˈpeɪnzteɪkɪŋ]	adj. 煞费苦心的 very careful and thorough
sparse [spɑːs]	adj. 稀少的 of few and scattered elements
voracious [vəˈreɪʃəs]	adj. 贪婪的 eating or wanting large amounts of food
devour [dɪˈvaʊə (r)]	v. 吞食 to eat all of sth quickly especially because you are very hungry
sequester [sɪˈkwestə (r)]	v. 使隔绝 to cause to withdraw into seclusion
austere [ɒˈstɪə (r)]	adj. 简朴的；严厉的 simple and plain; stern and cold in appearance or manner
reinforce [ˌriːɪnˈfɔːs]	v. 加强 to make a feeling, an idea, etc. stronger
brainchild [ˈbreɪntʃaɪld]	n. 独创 an idea, plan, organization etc. that someone has thought of without any help from anyone else
perpetuate [pəˈpetʃueɪt]	v. 使持久 to make a situation, attitude, etc., especially a bad one, continue to exist for a long time
inaugural [ɪˈnɔːgjərəl]	adj. 开幕的，就职的 an inaugural speech is one made by someone to celebrate the start of an important new job
municipal [mjuːˈnɪsɪpl]	adj. 市政的 connected with or belonging to a town, city or district that has its own local government
affiliate [əˈfɪlieɪt]	v. 使连接 to become closely connected or associated

新 SAT 阅读真题对应词汇

Word List 3 OG3

sullen [ˈsʌlən]	adj. 闷闷不乐的 gloomily or resentfully silent or repressed
besiege [bɪˈsiːdʒ]	v. 围攻 to surround sb/sth in large numbers
impose [ɪmˈpəʊz]	v. 强加于，征税 to establish or apply by authority (impose a tax)
apparition [ˌæpəˈrɪʃn]	n. 幽灵 a ghost or an image of a person who is dead
meek [miːk]	adj. 温顺的 quiet，gentle，and easily persuaded by other people to do what they want
correctitude [kəˈrektɪtjuːd]	n. 得体 correctness or propriety of conduct
colloquial [kəˈləʊkwiəl]	adj. 对话的 used in informal conversation rather than in writing or formal language
allude [əˈluːd]	v. 暗示 to make indirect reference
discomfiture [dɪsˈkʌmfɪtʃə (r)]	n. 尴尬 a feeling of being embarrassed
patroness [ˌpeɪtrənˈes]	n. 女资助人 a female PATRON
abject [ˈæbdʒekt]	adj. 可怜的 without any pride or respect for yourself
ignominious [ˌɪgnəˈmɪniəs]	adj. 可耻的 marked with or characterized by disgrace or shame
squalid [ˈskwɒlɪd]	adj. 脏的 very dirty and unpleasant

decrepit [dɪˈkrepɪt]	adj. 衰老的 very old and not in good condition or health
lurch [lɜːtʃ]	v. 突然倾斜 to make a sudden, unsteady movement forward or sideways
wrestle [ˈresl]	v. 费力处理；摔角 to struggle to deal with sth that is difficult ; to fight sb by holding them and trying to throw or force them to the ground, sometimes as a sport
levitate [ˈlevɪteɪt]	v. 漂浮 to rise or float in or as if in the air especially in seeming defiance of gravitation
whisk away/off	v. 飞快带走 to take sb/sth somewhere very quickly and suddenly
ramify [ˈræmɪfaɪ]	v. 使分叉 to split up into branches or constituent parts
incredulous [ɪnˈkredjələs]	adj. 怀疑的 unwilling to admit or accept what is offered as true : not credulous
locomotion [ˌləʊkəˈməʊʃn]	n. 运动 movement or the ability to move
ingenious [ɪnˈdʒiːniəs]	adj. 聪明的 marked by inventive skill and imagination
ramp [ræmp]	n. 斜坡 a slope that joins two parts of a road, path, building, etc. when one is higher than the other
scramble [ˈskræmbl]	v. 攀登 climb with difficulty
balk [bɔːk]	v. 犹豫 to be unwilling to do something or let something happen, because you believe that it is wrong or that it will cause problems
fatigue [fəˈtiːg]	n. 疲劳 a feeling of being extremely tired, usually because of hard work or exercise
circadian [sɜːˈkeɪdiən]	adj. 生理节奏的 connected with the changes in the bodies of people or animals over each period of 24 hours

ailment ['eɪlmənt]	n. 小病 an illness that is not very serious
funnel ['fʌnl]	v. 通过（小孔） to move or make sth move through a narrow space
curfew ['kɜ:fju:]	n. 宵禁 a law that does not allow people to go outside between a particular time in the evening and a particular time in the morning
lucrative ['lu:krətɪv]	adj. 有利可图的 bringing a lot of money
blaze [bleɪz]	v. 燃烧；开辟路径 to burn brightly and strongly ; to be the first to do something new and important
decree [dɪ'kri:]	v. 颁布（法令） to decide, judge or order sth officially
sanction ['sæŋkʃn]	v. 批准 to give permission for sth to take place
incontestable [ˌɪnkən'testəbl]	adj. 无可辩驳的 that is true and cannot be disagreed with or denied
strenuous ['strenjuəs]	adj. 费力的 needing great effort and energy
onerous ['əunərəs]	adj. 繁重的，费力的 needing great effort ; causing trouble or worry
summon ['sʌmən]	v. 召集，召唤 to call together ; convene
invoke [ɪn'vəuk]	v. 引经据典 to use a law, principle, or theory to support your views
denomination [dɪˌnɒmɪ'neɪʃn]	n. 教派；面额 a branch of the Christian Church ; a unit of value, especially of money
usurp [ju:'zɜ:p]	v. 篡夺 to seize and hold (as office, place, or powers) in possession by force or without right to do this
immure [ɪ'mjʊə (r)]	v. 监禁 to shut someone in a place so that they cannot get out

infestation [ˌɪnfeˈsteɪʃn]	n. 群袭 to spread or swarm in or over in a troublesome manner
postulate [ˈpɒstjuleɪt]	v. 假设 to suggest or accept that sth is true so that it can be used as the basis for a theory, etc.
pathogen [ˈpæθədʒən]	n. 病菌 something that causes disease
panacea [ˌpænəˈsiːə]	n. 万能药 something that will solve all the problems of a particular situation
fragrant [ˈfreɪɡrənt]	adj. 芳香的 having a pleasant smell
aroma [əˈrəʊmə]	n. 芳香 a pleasant, noticeable smell
homage [ˈhɒmɪdʒ]	n. 尊敬 something that is said or done to show respect for sb
stately [ˈsteɪtli]	adj. 庄严的 impressive in size, slow, formal and gracefml
scarlet [ˈskɑːlət]	n. 猩红色 bright red in colour

新 SAT 阅读真题对应词汇

Word List 4 OG4

consummation [ˌkɒnsəˈmeɪʃn]	n. 圆满成功 the fact of making sth complete or perfect
sustenance [ˈsʌstənəns]	n. 给养，生计 food that people or animals need in order to live
litter [ˈlɪtə (r)]	v. 乱丢 to be spread around a place，making it look untidy
trot [trɒt]	v. 慢跑 to move forward at a speed that is faster than a walk and slower than a CANTER
volition [vəˈlɪʃn]	n. 决心 the power or ability to decide something by yourself and take action to get what you want
ephemeral [ɪˈfemərəl]	adj. 短暂的 lasting or used for only a short period of time
egotism [ˈeɡətɪzəm]	n. 自大 the belief that you are much better or more important than other people
surrender [səˈrendə (r)]	v. 投降 to yield to the power，control，or possession of another upon compulsion or demand
census [ˈsensəs]	n. 人口普查 a usually complete enumeration of a population
stampede [stæmˈpiːd]	v. 使冲动行事 to make sb rush into doing sth without giving them time to think about it
albeit [ˌɔːlˈbiːɪt]	conj. 尽管 although
inversion [ɪnˈvɜːʃn]	n. 倒转 a reversal of position，order，form，or relationship

blunt [blʌnt]	adj. 钝的；adj. 直言不讳的 without a sharp edge or point ; very direct ; saying exactly what you think without trying to be polite
affluent [ˈæfluənt]	adj. 富裕的 having a lot of money and a good standard of living
condo [ˈkɒndəʊ]	n. 独立产权的公寓 CONDOMINIUM
bust [bʌst]	v. 打破 to break sth
proxy [ˈprɒksɪ]	n. 代理人，代议制 the agency, function, or office of a deputy who acts as a substitute for another
fiscal [ˈfɪskl]	adj. 财政的 connected with government or public money, especially taxes
incur [ɪnˈkɜː(r)]	v. 招致（不好的） to experience something unpleasant as a result of something you have done
enclave [ˈenkleɪv]	n. 被包围的领土，飞地 an area of a country or city where a particular group of people live
pharmaceutical [ˌfɑːməˈsuːtɪkl]	adj. 药学的 connected with making and selling drugs and medicines
therapeutic [ˌθerəˈpjuːtɪk]	adj. 治疗的 designed to help treat an illness
obstinacy [ˈɒbstɪnəsɪ]	n. 固执 the quality of being unwilling to be reasonable and change your behavior, plans, or ideas
subversion [səbˈvɜːʃn]	n. 偷偷颠覆 the action of trying to destroy a government or an established belief, especially by attacking it indirectly in written or spoken material
pious [ˈpaɪəs]	adj. 虔诚的 having or showing a deep respect for God and religion
rashly [ræʃlɪ]	adv. 鲁莽的 marked by or proceeding from undue haste or lack of deliberation or caution
dissolve [dɪˈzɒlv]	v. 使解散；溶解 to become dissipated or decomposed ; to make a solid become part of a liquid

subservient [səb'sɜ:viənt]	adj. 次要的；卑躬屈节的 less important than sth else；willing to obey other people
perish ['perɪʃ]	v. 死亡 to die，especially in a sudden violent way
contingent [kən'tɪndʒənt]	adj. 依情况而定的 dependent on sth that may or may not happen
insolent ['ɪnsələnt]	adj. 无礼的，侮慢的 extremely rude and showing a lack of respect
mural ['mjʊərəl]	n. 壁画 a large painting done on a wall
scrutiny ['skru:tənɪ]	n. 仔细检查 careful and thorough examination
emulate ['emjʊleɪt]	v. 效法 to try to do sth as well as sb else because you admire them
residue ['rezɪdju:]	n. 残渣 a small amount of sth that remains at the end of a process
perturb [pə'tɜ:b]	v. 使烦恼 to make sb worried or anxious
aerosol ['eərəsɒl]	n. 悬浮颗粒 a suspension of fine solid or liquid particles in gas
flank [flæŋk]	n. 侧面 the side of sth such as a building or mountain
plume [plu:m]	n. 烟柱；v. 自夸 a cloud of sth that rises and curves upwards in the air；to indulge (oneself) in pride with an obvious or vain display of self-satisfaction
epitome [ɪ'pɪtəmɪ]	n. 缩影 a summary of a written work
arduous ['ɑ:djuəs]	adj. 费力的 involving a lot of effort and energy，especially over a period of time
inadvertently [ˌɪnəd'vɜ:təntlɪ]	adv. 不经意地 by accident；without intending to
predominant [prɪ'dɒmɪnənt]	adj. 占据优势地位的 having superior strength，influence，or authority
console [kən'səʊl]	v. 抚慰 to give comfort or sympathy to sb who is unhappy or disappointed

新 SAT 阅读真题对应词汇

Word List 5 Khan1

moody ['muːdɪ]	adj. 易怒的 likely to become unhappy or angry for no particular reason
sloppy ['slɒpɪ]	adj. 马虎的 not done carefully or thoroughly
veracity [və'ræsətɪ]	n. 诚实 devotion to the truth
dazzle ['dæzl]	v. 使目眩 to shine brilliantly
diabolical [ˌdaɪə'bɒlɪkl]	adj. 恶毒的 extremely bad or annoying
little short of	几乎是
countenance ['kaʊntənəns]	v. 赞同 to support sth or agree to sth happening
credulous ['kredjələs]	adj. 易受骗的 ready to believe things and therefore easy to deceive
reel off	v. 流利地说 to tell or recite readily and usually at length
glib [glɪb]	adj. 油嘴滑舌的 speaking easily but without thinking carefully – used to show disapproval
matrimony ['mætrɪmənɪ]	n. 婚姻 marriage
feud [fjuːd]	n. 宿怨 to have an angry and bitter argument with sb over a long period of time
agog [ə'gɒg]	adj. 激动的，渴望的 excited and very interested to find out sth

ecstasy ['ekstəsɪ]	n. 狂喜 a feeling or state of very great happiness
jolly ['dʒɒlɪ]	adj. 快乐的 happy and cheerful
bluff [blʌf]	v. 虚张声势 to deter or frighten by pretense or a mere show of strength
disrobe [dɪs'rəʊb]	v. 使脱光 to strip of clothing or covering
clandestine [klæn'destɪn]	adj. 秘密的 done secretly or kept secret
brash [bræʃ]	adj. 轻率的 done in haste without regard for consequences ; RASH
quintessential [ˌkwɪntɪ'senʃl]	adj. 精髓的 perfect as an example of a type of person or thing
dwarf [dwɔ:f]	v. 使显得矮小 to make something seem small or unimportant
plummet ['plʌmɪt]	v. 垂直落下 to fall perpendicularly
slog [slɒg]	v. 苦干 to work hard and steadily at sth , especially sth that takes a long time and is boring or difficult
nightmarish ['naɪtˌmeərɪʃ]	adj. 噩梦似的 a very frightening dream
allometric [æ'lɒmetrɪk]	adj. 异速生长的 relative growth of a part in relation to an entire organism or to a standard , also : the measure and study of such growth
in lieu of	代替 intead of
tack [tæk]	v.（用平头钉）钉 to fasten or affix with tacks
verify ['verɪfaɪ]	v. 证实 to check that sth is true or accurate
substrate ['sʌbstreɪt]	n. 底层；底物 an underlying layer ; a substance acted upon (as by an enzyme)

extrapolate [ɪkˈstræpəleɪt]	v. 外推 to infer (values of a variable in an unobserved interval) from values within an already observed interval
pivotal [ˈpɪvətl]	adj. 关键的 extremely important and affecting how something develops
retrospection [ˌretrəˈspekʃn]	n. 回顾 thinking about past events or situations
couple [ˈkʌpl]	v. 连接 to fasten together
spontaneous [spɒnˈteɪniəs]	adj. 自发的 happening in a natural way without being planned or thought about
postural [ˈpɒstʃərəl]	adj. 姿势的 connected with the way you hold your body when sitting or standing
temporal [ˈtempərəl]	adj. 世间的 related to practical instead of religious affairs
locus [ˈləʊkəs]	n. 场所 the place where something is situated or occurs
anterior [ænˈtɪəriə (r)]	adj. 前部的 at or near the front
misanthrope [ˈmɪsənθrəʊp]	n. 不愿与人来往者 a person who hates or distrusts humankind
pelt [pelt]	v. 连续投掷 to strike with a succession of blows or missiles
ambush [ˈæmbʊʃ]	v. 伏击 to make a surprise attack on sb/sth from a hidden position
stash [stæʃ]	v. 隐藏起来 to store sth in a safe or secret place
crafty [ˈkrɑːftɪ]	adj. 狡猾的 clever at getting what you want，especially by indirect or dishonest methods
escapade [ˌeskəˈpeɪd]	n. 恶作剧 a usually adventurous action that runs counter to approved or conventional conduct

episodic [ˌepɪˈsɒdɪk]	adj. 片段式的 containing or consisting of many separate and different events
semantic [sɪˈmæntɪk]	adj. 句式的 connected with the meaning of words and sentences
swat [swɒt]	n./v. 重击 to hit sth, especially an insect, using your hand or a flat object
antagonize [ænˈtægənaɪz]	v. 敌对 to act in opposition to
indispensable [ˌɪndɪˈspensəbl]	adj. 不可缺少的 essential; too important to be without
unfeigned [ʌnˈfeɪnd]	adj. 真实的 genuine
affection [əˈfekʃn]	n. 喜爱 a feeling of liking or love and caring
appropriate [əˈprəupriət]	v. 拨款; 合适的 to take or give sth, especially money, for a particular purpose; suitable, acceptable or correct for the particular circumstances
furnish [ˈfɜːnɪʃ]	v. 提供 to supply or provide sb/sth with sth
spur [spɜː(r)]	v. 激励 to make sth happen faster or sooner
preoccupation [priˌɒkjuˈpeɪʃn]	n. 全神贯注 a mood created by thinking or worrying about sth and ignoring everything else
merge [mɜːdʒ]	v. 合并 to cause to combine, unite, or coalesce
drastic [ˈdræstɪk]	adj. 激烈的 acting rapidly or violently
prerequisite [ˌpriːˈrekwəzɪt]	n. 前提条件 something that is necessary to an end or to the carrying out of a function

新 SAT 阅读真题对应词汇

Word List 6 Khan2

ballroom ['bɔːlruːm]	n. 舞厅 a very large room used for dancing on formal occasions
protegee [pˈrəʊteʒeɪ]	n. 女门徒 a young woman who receives help or training from an older experienced person
asunder [əˈsʌndə (r)]	adv. 成碎片 into pieces
exertion [ɪgˈzɜːʃn]	n. 运用 the use of power, influence etc. to make something happen
irksome [ˈɜːksəm]	adj. 令人厌烦的 annoying or irritating
serenity [səˈrenəti]	n. 平静 a feeling of being calm or peaceful
taxon [ˈtæksɒn]	n. 分类单元 a taxonomic category or group, such as a phylum, order, family, genus, or species
infectious [ɪnˈfekʃəs]	adj. 有传染性的 spreading or capable of spreading rapidly to others
compelling [kəmˈpelɪŋ]	adj. 令人注目的 that makes you pay attention to it because it is so interesting and exciting
paradoxical [ˌpærəˈdɒksɪkl]	adj. 自相矛盾的 consisting of two parts that seem to mean the opposite of each other
vulnerable [ˈvʌlnərəbl]	adj. 易受伤害的 weak and easily hurt physically or emotionally
sentinel [ˈsentɪnl]	n. 哨兵 soldier whose job is to guard sth

cutaneous [kjuˈteɪnɪəs]	adj. 皮肤的 of，relating to，or affecting the skin
vascularize [ˈvæskjələˌraɪz]	v. 血管化 to make or become vascular
montane [ˈmɒnteɪn]	adj. 山区的 of，growing in，or inhabiting mountain areas
acclimation [ˌækləˈmeɪʃn]	n. 环境适应 physiological adjustment by an organism to environmental change
regime [reɪˈʒiːm]	n. 政体 a form of government
accentuate [əkˈsentʃueɪt]	v. 强调 to emphasize sth or make it more noticeable
liken [ˈlaɪkən]	v. 比作 to compare one person or thing to another and say they are similar
increment [ˈɪŋkrəmənt]	n. 增加 an increase in a number or an amount
manifest [ˈmænɪfest]	v. 证明 to show something such as a feeling or ability，so that it is easy to notice
tumour [ˈtjuːmə (r)]	n. 肿瘤 a mass of diseased cells in your body that have divided and increased too quickly
confess [kənˈfes]	v. 承认（罪） to admit，especially formally or to the police，that you have done sth wrong or illegal
constitution [ˌkɒnstɪˈtjuːʃn]	n. 宪法；体质 the system of laws and basic principles that a state，a country or an organization is governed by；the physical makeup of the individual especially with respect to the health，strength，and appearance of the body
despotic [dɪˈspɒtɪk]	adj. 专制的 using power in a cruel and unreasonable way：TYRANNICAL
confound [kənˈfaʊnd]	v. 使困惑 to confuse and surprise sb

salutary ['sæljətrɪ]	adj. 有益的 producing a beneficial effect
unanimity [ˌjuːnə'nɪmətɪ]	n. 一致同意 complete agreement among all the members of a group
procure [prə'kjʊə (r)]	v.（努力）获得 to obtain sth, especially with difficulty
integrity [ɪn'tegrətɪ]	n. 诚实 the quality of being honest and having strong moral principles
posterity [pɒ'sterətɪ]	n. 子孙 all the people who will live in the future
infallible [ɪn'fæləbl]	adj. 绝无错误的 never wrong

新 SAT 阅读真题对应词汇

Word List 7 Khan3

mansion ['mænʃn]	n. 大厦 a large impressive house
sumptuous ['sʌmptʃuəs]	adj. 华丽的 very expensive and looking very impressive
prompt [prɒmpt]	adj. 迅速的；v. 促使 done without delay ; to cause sth to happen
parade [pə'reɪd]	n. 游行 a public celebration of a special day or event, usually with bands in the streets and decorated vehicles
itinerant [aɪ'tɪnərənt]	adj. 巡回的 travelling from place to place, especially to find work
tranquil ['træŋkwɪl]	adj. 平静的 quiet and peaceful
predecessor ['pri:dɪsesə (r)]	n. 前辈 a person who did a job before sb else
provocative [prə'vɒkətɪv]	adj. 挑衅的 intended to start arguments between people or to make people angry or upset
corroborate [kə'rɒbəreɪt]	v. 证实 to support with evidence or authority
gist [dʒɪst]	n. 要旨 the main or general meaning of a piece of writing, a speech or a conversation
robust [rəʊ'bʌst]	adj. 强健的 strong and healthy
fabric ['fæbrɪk]	n. 构造 the basic structure of a society, an organization, etc.
swirl [swɜ:l]	v. 打旋 to move around quickly with a circular movement

warp [wɔːp]	v. 弯曲 to turn or twist
obscure [əbˈskjʊə (r)]	v. 使难理解 difficult to understand
accretion [əˈkriːʃn]	n. 增加 increase by external addition or accumulation
vicinity [vəˈsɪnətɪ]	n. 接近 the quality or state of being near
precedent [ˈpresɪdənt]	n. 先例 an earlier occurrence of something similar
profound [prəˈfaʊnd]	adj. 深奥的 having intellectual depth and insight
mighty [ˈmaɪtɪ]	adj. 强大的 very strong and powerful
superintendent [ˌsuːpərɪnˈtendənt]	n. 监管者 person who has a lot of authority and manages and controls an activity, a place, a group of workers, etc.
enterprise [ˈentəpraɪz]	n. 事业 a project or undertaking that is especially difficult, complicated, or risky
renown [rɪˈnaʊn]	n. 声望 fame and respect because of sth you have done that people admire
pledge [pledʒ]	v. 保证 to formally promise to give or do sth
triumphant [traɪˈʌmfənt]	adj. 胜利的 very successful in a way that causes great satisfaction
shuffle [ˈʃʌfl]	v. 拖着脚走 to walk slowly without lifting your feet completely off the ground
topple [ˈtɒpl]	v. 使倒塌 to become unsteady and fall down
symptom [ˈsɪmptəm]	n. 症状 a sign that sth exists, especially sth bad
susceptible [səˈseptəbl]	adj. 易受 … 影响的 very likely to be influenced, harmed or affected by sb/sth
prioritize [praɪˈɒrətaɪz]	v. 优先对待 to treat sth as being more important than other things

新 SAT 阅读真题对应词汇

Word List 8 Khan4

wharf [wɔːf]	n. 码头 a structure that is built out into the water so that boats can stop next to it
vent [vent]	n. 通风孔；（感情）发泄口 give (full) vent to sth (formal) to express a feeling, especially anger, strongly
skirmish [ˈskɜːmɪʃ]	n. 小口角 a brisk preliminary verbal conflict
pervade [pəˈveɪd]	v. 遍布 to spread through and be noticeable in every part of sth
expedition [ˌekspəˈdɪʃn]	n. 探险 a journey or excursion undertaken for a specific purpose
tumble [ˈtʌmbl]	v. 翻倒 to fall suddenly and helplessly
rapturous [ˈræptʃərəs]	adj. 狂喜的 expressing extreme pleasure or enthusiasm for sb/sth
surefire [ˈʃʊəˌfaɪə]	adj. 一定成功的 certain to get successful or expected results
unravel [ʌnˈrævl]	v. 阐明 to resolve the intricacy, complexity, or obscurity of
cascade [kæˈskeɪd]	n. 一连串事情接连发生 a large number of things falling or coming quickly at the same time
invigorate [ɪnˈvɪɡəreɪt]	v. 鼓舞 to make sb feel healthy and full of energy
membrane [ˈmembreɪn]	n. 薄膜 a thin soft pliable sheet or layer especially of animal or plant origin
apoptosis [ˌæpəˈtəʊsɪs]	n.（细胞）凋亡 cell death

surge [sɜ:dʒ]	n./v. 激增 a sudden increase in the amount or number of sth ; a large amount of sth
metabolism [mə'tæbəlɪzəm]	n. 新陈代谢 the chemical processes that take place in your body that change food and drink into energy
uptick ['ʌptɪk]	n. 增加 an increase, especially a small or incremental one
beef up	v. 增加 to improve something or make it more interesting, more important etc.
modulate ['mɒdjuleɪt]	v. 调节 to adjust to or keep in proper measure or proportion
homologue ['hɒməlɒg]	n. 相当或相同事物 having the same relative position, value, or structure
stave off	v. 延迟 to keep someone or something from reaching you or affecting you for a period of time
alleviate [ə'li:vieɪt]	v. 减轻 to make sth less severe
inflammation [ˌɪnflə'meɪʃn]	n. 燃烧；发炎 the act of inflaming ; swelling and pain in part of your body, which is often red and feels hot
prime [praɪm]	adj. 首要的；v. 做准备 main ; most important ; basic ; to prepare sb for a situation so that they know what to do, especially by giving them special information
microbial [maɪ'krəʊbɪəl]	adj. 微生物的 a minute life form ; a microorganism, especially a bacterium that causes disease
menace ['menəs]	n./v. 威胁 to make a show of intention to harm
inflict [ɪn'flɪkt]	v. 使遭受（不开心） to make sb/sth suffer sth unpleasant
accomplice [ə'kʌmplɪs]	n. 同谋 one associated with another especially in wrongdoing
deter [dɪ'tɜ: (r)]	v. 阻止 to make sb decide not to do sth or continue doing sth, especially by making them understand the difficulties and unpleasant results of their actions

drench [drentʃ]	v. 使湿透 to make sb/sth completely wet
graft [grɑːft]	v. 嫁接 to take a piece of skin, bone, etc. from one part of the body and attach it to a damaged part
consolidated government	n. 中央集权政府
sovereignty [ˈsɒvrəntɪ]	n. 君主制；独立自主 royal rank, authority, or power; complete freedom and power to govern
coercive [kəʊˈɜːsɪv]	adj. 强迫的 using force or the threat of force
degenerate [dɪˈdʒenəreɪt]	v. 堕落 to become worse
confederacy [kənˈfedərəsɪ]	n. 邦联（松散联盟） a group of people, states, or political parties that are united
hitherto [ˌhɪðəˈtuː]	adv. 迄今 until now
splendour [ˈsplendə (r)]	n. 壮丽 grand and impressive beauty
misery [ˈmɪzərɪ]	n. 悲惨 something that causes great suffering of mind or body
tyranny [ˈtɪrənɪ]	n. 暴政 oppressive power
languish [ˈlæŋgwɪʃ]	v. 使憔悴 to be or become feeble, weak, or enervated
supreme [suːˈpriːm]	adj. 至高的 highest in rank or position
overarching [ˌəʊvərˈɑːtʃɪŋ]	adj. 首要的 important, because it includes or influences many things
intersect [ˌɪntəˈsekt]	v. 交叉 to meet or cross each other
consonant [ˈkɒnsənənt]	n. 辅音；adj. 一致的 a speech sound made by completely or partly stopping the flow of air being breathed out through the mouth; being in agreement or harmony

outperform [ˌaʊtpəˈfɔːm]	v. 胜过 to achieve better results than sb/sth
visuospatial [vɪzjʊəʊˈspeɪʃəl]	adj. 视觉空间的 of, relating to, or being thought processes that involve visual and spatial awareness

新 SAT 阅读真题对应词汇

Word List 9 Khan5

entreat [ɪnˈtriːt]	v. 恳求 to ask someone, in a very emotional way, to do something for you
endeavor [ɪnˈdevə]	n./v. 努力 to strive to achieve or reach
trample [ˈtræmpl]	v. 践踏 to put your feet down on someone or something in a heavy way that causes injury or damage
lull [lʌl]	n. 中间休息 a quiet period between times of activity
prevail [prɪˈveɪl]	v. 流行；劝说；战胜 to be or continue in use or fashion；to use persuasion successfully；to gain ascendancy through strength or superiority；TRIUMPH
imperious [ɪmˈpɪəriəs]	adj. 傲慢的 expecting people to obey you and treating them as if they are not as important as you
plaintive [ˈpleɪntɪv]	adj. 哀伤的 sounding sad, especially in a weak complaining way
resignation [ˌrezɪgˈneɪʃn]	n. 无能为力而放弃；辞职 patient willingness to accept a difficult or unpleasant situation that you cannot change；the act of giving up your job or position；the occasion when you do this
dainty [ˈdeɪntɪ]	adj. 优雅的 small and attractive in a delicate way
demure [dɪˈmjʊə (r)]	adj. 端庄的 quiet, serious, and well-behaved, used especially about women in the past
tremor [ˈtremə (r)]	n. 颤抖 a slight shaking movement in a part of your body caused, for example, by cold or fear

solitude [ˈsɒlɪtjuːd]	n. 独居 the quality or state of being alone or remote from society
lash [læʃ]	v. 鞭打 to hit a person or an animal with a whip, rope, stick, etc.
lofty [ˈlɒftɪ]	adj. 傲慢的 having a haughty overbearing manner
convulsive [kənˈvʌlsɪv]	adj. 抽搐的 a sudden shaking movement of the body that cannot be controlled
sidle [ˈsaɪdl]	v. 悄悄移动 to move slowly in a particular direction, usually because you are nervous or do not want to be noticed
genome [ˈdʒiːnəʊm]	n. 基因组 the complete set of GENES in a cell or living thing
consortium [kənˈsɔːtɪəm]	n. 协会 an agreement, combination, or group (as of companies) formed to undertake an enterprise beyond the resources of any member
nucleotide [ˈnjuːklɪətaɪd]	n. 核苷酸 any of several compounds that consist of a ribose or deoxyribose sugar joined to a purine or pyrimidine base and to a phosphate group and that are the basic structural units of nucleic acids (as RNA and DNA)
ethnicity [eθˈnɪsətɪ]	n. 种族特点 the fact of belonging to a particular race
decipher [dɪˈsaɪfə (r)]	v. 解密 to understand something mysterious or confusing
predisposition [ˌpriːdɪspəˈzɪʃn]	n. 倾向 the state of being predisposed; tendency, inclination, or susceptibility
piddling [ˈpɪdlɪŋ]	adj. 不重要的 small and unimportant
dizzy [ˈdɪzɪ]	adj. 眩晕的 mentally confused
sturdy [ˈstɜːdɪ]	adj. 强健的 strong and not easily damaged
rupture [ˈrʌptʃə (r)]	v. 破裂 to burst or break apart sth inside the body

hoard [hɔːd]	n./v. 贮藏 to collect and keep large amounts of food, money, etc., especially secretly
intact [ɪnˈtækt]	adj. 原封不动的 complete and not damaged
scatter [ˈskætə (r)]	v. 使分散 to cause to separate widely
harbor [ˈhɑːbə]	n./v. 庇护 to give shelter or refuge to
shrewd [ʃruːd]	adj. 精明的 showing good judgement and likely to be right
configuration [kənˌfɪɡəˈreɪʃn]	n. 结构 relative arrangement of parts or elements
prosperity [prɒˈsperətɪ]	n. 繁荣 the state of being successful, especially financially
protrude [prəˈtruːd]	v. 使突出 to stick out from a place or a surface
innate [ɪˈneɪt]	adj. 与生俱来的 that you have when you are born
compartment [kəmˈpɑːtmənt]	n. 隔间 a separate division or section
deliberate [dɪˈlɪbərət]	adj. 深思熟虑的 to think very carefully about sth, usually before making a decision
elucidate [iˈluːsɪdeɪt]	v. 阐明 to make sth clearer by explaining it more fully
perceptual [pəˈseptʃuəl]	adj. 知觉的 relating to the ability to notice or understand things by seeing or hearing

新 SAT 阅读真题对应词汇

Word List 10 Khan6

incantation [ˌɪnkænˈteɪʃn]	n. 咒语 special words that are spoken or sung to have a magic effect
aristocrat [ˈærɪstəkræt]	n. 贵族 someone who belongs to the highest social class
bureaucracy [bjʊəˈrɒkrəsɪ]	n. 官僚机构 the system of official rules and ways of doing things that a government or an organization has, especially when these seem to be too complicated
mutter [ˈmʌtə (r)]	v. 喃喃低语 to utter sounds or words indistinctly or with a low voice and with the lips partly closed
ruffle [ˈrʌfl]	v. 弄皱 to disturb the smooth surface of sth, so that it is not even
ruffle through	v. 快速翻阅
relentless [rɪˈlentləs]	adj. 不断的，未减轻的 not stopping or getting less strong
condense [kənˈdens]	v. 浓缩 to make denser or more compact
myriad [ˈmɪriəd]	adj. 大量的 an extremely large number of sth
telltale [ˈtelteɪl]	adj. 泄露内情的 signs etc. that clearly show something has happened or exists, often something that is a secret
elusive [iˈluːsɪv]	adj. 难捉摸的 difficult to find, define, or achieve
devoid [dɪˈvɔɪd]	adj. 缺乏的 completely lacking in sth

propagation [ˌprɒpəˈɡeɪʃn]	n. 增殖；传播 increase (as of a kind of organism) in numbers ; to spread an idea, belief etc. to many people
inert [ɪˈnɜːt]	adj. 惰性的 without power to move or act
verge on	v. 接近 to be on the verge or border
strife [straɪf]	n. 争吵 fighting or disagreement between people or groups
contention [kənˈtenʃn]	n. 争论 angry disagreement between people
dabble [ˈdæbl]	v. 浅赏 to work or involve oneself superficially or intermittently especially in a secondary activity or interest
entangle [ɪnˈtæŋɡl]	v. 卷入 to involve in a perplexing or troublesome situation
recurrence [rɪˈkʌrəns]	n. 再现 to come up again for consideration
cement [sɪˈment]	v. 巩固 to make a relationship, an agreement, etc. stronger
disseminate [dɪˈsemɪneɪt]	v. 传播 to spread information, knowledge, etc. so that it reaches many people
utilitarian [ˌjuːtɪlɪˈteəriən]	adj. 实用主义的 designed to be useful and practical rather than attractive
interdependency [ɪnˈtədɪpendənsɪ]	n. 相互依赖 reciprocally

新 SAT 阅读真题对应词汇

Word List 11 Khan7

inauspicious [ˌɪnɔːˈspɪʃəs]	adj. 不吉利的 showing signs that the future will not be good or successful
punctilious [pʌŋkˈtɪliəs]	adj. 一丝不苟的 very careful to behave correctly or to carry out your duties exactly as you should
ponderous [ˈpɒndərəs]	adj. 笨拙的 unwieldy or clumsy because of weight and size
eminent [ˈemɪnənt]	adj. 杰出的 famous and respected，especially in a particular profession
lieutenant [lefˈtenənt]	n. 副总督 an officer or official with the rank just below colonel，general，governor etc.
alight [əˈlaɪt]	v. 下车（马） to get out of a bus，a train or other vehicle
sheriff [ˈʃerɪf]	n. 郡治安官 an important official of a shire or county charged primarily with judicial duties
perusal [pəˈruːzl]	n. 细读 to read something，especially in a careful way
broach [brəʊtʃ]	v. 钻孔开瓶 to shape or enlarge (a hole) with a tool
tramp [træmp]	n. 沉重的脚步声 the sound of sb's heavy steps
choleric [ˈkɒlərɪk]	adj. 易怒的 easily made angry；bad-tempered
subside [səbˈsaɪd]	v. 逐渐平静 to become calmer or quieter
surreptitious [ˌsʌrəpˈtɪʃəs]	adj. 暗中的 done secretly or quickly，in the hope that other people will not notice

fling [flɪŋ]	v. 猛冲 to move yourself or part of your body suddenly and with a lot of force
wig [wɪg]	n. 假发 synthetic hair
contraption [kən'træpʃn]	n. 精巧的设计 a machine or piece of equipment, especially one that looks strange or complicated
crackle ['krækl]	v. 发噼啪声 to make small sharp sudden repeated noises
primeval [praɪ'miːvl]	adj. 初期的 belonging to the earliest time in the existence of the universe or the Earth
combo ['kɒmbəʊ]	n. 联合体 a combination of people or things
brew [bruː]	n. 混合；v. 酿造 a mixture of different ideas, circumstances, events, etc.; to mix with hot water and become ready to drink
wobbly ['wɒbli]	adj. 不稳定的 moving in an unsteady way from side to side
chock-full [ˌtʃɒk 'fʊl]	adj. 塞满的 completely full
tilt [tɪlt]	v. 倾斜 to cause to have an inclination
primordial [praɪ'mɔːdiəl]	adj. 原始的 existing at or from the beginning of the world
swaddle ['swɒdl]	v. 包住 to wrap a baby very tightly in cloth
laterality [ˌlætə'rælɪtɪ]	n. 一侧性 preference in using one side of the body over the other
cerebral ['serəbrəl]	adj. 大脑的 relating to the brain
synchronize ['sɪŋkrənaɪz]	v. 同时发生 to happen at the same time or to move at the same speed as sth
peripheral [pə'rɪfərəl]	adj. 周边的 connected with the outer edge of a particular area

downright ['daʊnraɪt]	adj. 完全的 completely or extremely
despise [dɪ'spaɪz]	v. 轻视 to dislike and have no respect for sb/sth
encomium [en'kəʊmiəm]	n. 赞美 warm, glowing praise
imbecility [ˌɪmbə'sɪlətɪ]	n. 低能 someone who is very stupid or behaves very stupidly
adduce [ə'dju:s]	v. 引证 to offer as example, reason, or proof in discussion or analysis
licentious [laɪ'senʃəs]	adj. 淫荡的 behaving in a way that is considered sexually immoral
abridgement [ə'brɪdʒmənt]	n. 删节 an abridged book, play etc. has been made shorter but keeps its basic structure and meaning
encroachment [ɪn'krəʊtʃmənt]	n. 侵占 to gradually take more of someone's time, possessions, rights etc. than you should
candid ['kændɪd]	adj. 无偏见的，公正的 free from bias, prejudice, or malice
turbulence ['tɜ:bjələns]	n. 骚乱 great commotion or agitation
commotion [kə'məʊʃn]	n. 骚动 sudden noisy confusion or excitement
peculiar [pɪ'kju:liə (r)]	adj. 独特的，不同的 different from the usual or normal
conglomeration [kənˌglɒmə'reɪʃn]	n. 混合物 a group of different things gathered together
transient ['trænziənt]	adj. 短暂的 continuing for only a short time
affiliation [əˌfɪli'eɪʃn]	n. 交际关系 one group or organization's official connection with another
deviate ['di:vieɪt]	v. 偏离 to be different from sth

新 SAT 阅读真题对应词汇

Word List 12 Khan8

portly ['pɔːtlɪ]	adj. 肥胖的 rather fat
pompous ['pɒmpəs]	adj. 傲慢的 showing that you think you are more important than other people，especially by using long and formal words
drab [dræb]	adj. 乏味的 dull and boring
fray [freɪ]	v. 磨损 to wear (as an edge of cloth) by or as if by rubbing
chagrin ['ʃægrɪn]	n. 失望懊恼 a feeling of being disappointed or annoyed
famine ['fæmɪn]	n. 饥荒 an extreme scarcity of food
avert [ə'vɜːt]	v. 避免 to prevent something bad or harmful from happening
calamitous [kə'læmɪtəs]	adj. 灾难的 causing great harm or damage
chronic ['krɒnɪk]	adj. 慢性的 lasting for a long time
intervene [ˌɪntə'viːn]	v. 阻碍；介入 to come in or between by way of hindrance or modification；to become involved in a situation in order to improve or help it
dissipate ['dɪsɪpeɪt]	v. 驱散 to cause to spread thin or scatter and gradually vanish
succor ['sʌkə]	v. 援助 to help someone
surplus ['sɜːpləs]	adj. 过剩的 more than is needed or used

mischievous ['mɪstʃɪvəs]	adj. 恶作剧的 enjoying playing tricks and annoying people
complexion [kəm'plekʃn]	n. 面部肤色 the natural colour and condition of the skin on a person's face
solicitude [sə'lɪsɪtjuːd]	n. 关心 the state of being concerned and anxious
opulence ['ɒpjələns]	n. 富裕 wealth ; affluence
villain ['vɪlən]	n. 恶棍 a wicked person

新 SAT 阅读真题对应词汇

Word List 13 Khan9

coax [kəʊks]	v. 哄骗 to persuade someone to do something that they do not want to do by talking to them in a kind, gentle, and patient way
vagary ['veɪgərɪ]	n. 反复无常 an erratic, unpredictable, or extravagant manifestation, action, or notion
trivial ['trɪvɪəl]	adj. 微不足道的 not important or serious
dejected [dɪ'dʒektɪd]	adj. 沮丧的 unhappy and disappointed
ajar [ə'dʒɑː(r)]	adj. 微开的 slightly open
behest [bɪ'hest]	n. 命令 an authoritative order；COMMAND
impetuous [ɪm'petʃuəs]	adj. 冲动的 marked by impulsive vehemence or passion
rapt [ræpt]	adj. 全神贯注的 so interested in one particular thing that you are not aware of anything else
cloak [kləʊk]	n. 斗篷; v. 掩盖 something likened to an outer garment；to cover or hide sth
tarry ['tærɪ]	v. 逗留 to stay in a place, especially when you ought to leave
flutter ['flʌtə(r)]	v.（小鹿乱撞）跳动 to move about or behave in an agitated aimless manner
expostulate [ɪk'spɒstʃuleɪt]	v. 抗议 to argue, disagree or protest about sth
brimful ['brɪmfʊl]	adj. 盈满的 completely full of sth

vehement ['vi:əmənt]	adj. 激烈的 showing very strong feelings, especially anger
disdain [dɪs'deɪn]	v. 蔑视 to look on with scorn
ridicule ['rɪdɪkju:l]	v. 嘲笑 to make fun of
mien [mi:n]	n. 风采 a person's appearance or manner that shows how they are feeling
strain [streɪn]	n. 气质；种类；v. 努力 particular tendency in the character of a person or group, or a quality in their manner；a particular type of plant or animal, or of a disease caused by bacteria, etc.；to make an effort to do sth, using all your mental or physical strength
embryo ['embriəʊ]	n. 胚胎 an animal or human before it is born, when it is beginning to develop and grow
progeny ['prɒdʒənɪ]	n. 后裔 a person's children
progenitor [prəʊ'dʒenɪtə (r)]	n. 祖先 an ancestor in the direct line
hallmark ['hɔ:lmɑ:k]	n. 标志 a feature or quality that is typical of sb/sth
discrete [dɪ'skri:t]	adj. 不连续的 constituting a separate entity
quiescence [kwɪ'esns]	n. 静止 marked by inactivity or repose : tranquilly at rest
churn out	v. 快速生产；搅动 to produce sth quickly and in large amounts；to stir or agitate violently
avian ['eɪviən]	adj. 鸟类的 of, relating to, or characteristic of birds
flagrant ['fleɪgrənt]	adj. 恶名昭著的 conspicuously bad, offensive, or reprehensible
outrageous [aʊt'reɪdʒəs]	adj. 暴虐的 very shocking and unacceptable

imposition [ˌɪmpəˈzɪʃn]	n. 强行征收（税） the introduction of something such as a rule, punishment, tax etc.
cordial [ˈkɔːdiəl]	adj. 热忱的 pleasant and friendly
intercourse [ˈɪntəkɔːs]	n. 交流 exchange especially of thoughts or feelings
wretched [ˈretʃɪd]	adj. 不幸的 deeply afflicted, dejected, or distressed in body or mind
subjoin [ˈsʌbˈdʒɔɪn]	v. 附加 append
inveteracy [ɪnˈvetərəsɪ]	n. 根深蒂固 the quality or state of being obstinate or persistent : TENACITY
demographer [dɪˈmɒgrəfə (r)]	n. 人口统计学家 the statistical study of human populations especially with reference to size and density, distribution, and vital statistics

新 SAT 阅读真题对应词汇

Word List 14 Khan10

grandeur ['grændʒə (r)]	n. 伟大 the quality of being great and impressive in appearance
covet ['kʌvət]	v. 贪图 to want sth very much，especially sth that belongs to sb else
sublime [sə'blaɪm]	adj. 崇高的 of very high quality and causing great admiration
jumble ['dʒʌmbl]	n./v. 混杂 to mix things together in a confused or untidy way
savage ['sævɪdʒ]	adj. 野蛮的 fierce and violent；causing great harm
snag [snæg]	n. 小困难 a problem or difficulty，especially one that is small，hidden or unexpected
butt [bʌt]	v. 用头猛撞 to hit or push sb/sth hard with your head
spar over	v. 争论 to argue with sb，usually in a friendly way
laborious [lə'bɔːriəs]	adj. 费力的 taking a lot of time and effort
clamber ['klæmbə (r)]	v. 攀登 to climb or move with difficulty or a lot of effort，using your hands and feet
shear [ʃɪə (r)]	v. 剪羊毛 to cut the wool off a sheep
sagacity [sə'gæsəti]	n. 睿智 good judgment and understanding
credential [krə'denʃl]	n. 凭证 warranting credit or confidence—used chiefly in the phrase credential letters

covert ['kʌvət]	adj. 隐秘的 not openly shown, engaged in, or avowed : VEILED
tease out	v. 戏弄 to laugh at sb and make jokes about them either in a friendly way or in order to annoy or embarrass them
intercept [ˌɪntəˈsept]	v. 拦截 to stop sb/sth that is going from one place to another from arriving
legitimate [lɪˈdʒɪtɪmət]	adj. 合法的 to give legal status or authorization to
implement ['ɪmplɪment]	v. 使生效 to make sth that has been officially decided start to happen or be used
scanty ['skæntɪ]	adj. 贫乏的 limited or less than sufficient in degree, quantity, or extent
righteous ['raɪtʃəs]	adj. 正直的 morally right and good
grove [grəʊv]	n. 小树林 a small group of trees
lumber ['lʌmbə (r)]	n. 木材 rough pieces of wood, or trees cut down for wood
strikingly ['straɪkɪŋlɪ]	adv. 显著地 attracting attention or notice through unusual or conspicuous qualities
plead [pliːd]	v. 辩护；恳求 to argue a case or cause in a court of law ; to ask sb for sth in a very strong and serious way
lament [ləˈment]	v. 哀悼 to feel or express great sadness or disappointment about sb/sth
indignation [ˌɪndɪgˈneɪʃn]	n. 愤怒 a feeling of anger and surprise caused by sth that you think is unfair or unreasonable
apathy ['æpəθɪ]	n. 冷漠 the feeling of not being interested in or enthusiastic about anything
aboriginal [ˌæbəˈrɪdʒənl]	adj. 土著的 being the first or earliest known of its kind present in a region

新 SAT 阅读真题对应词汇

Word List 15 Khan11

impugn [ɪmˈpjuːn]	v. 怀疑 to express doubts about whether sth is right, honest, etc.
autograph [ˈɔːtəgrɑːf]	n. 亲笔签名 a famous person's signature
sceptic [ˈskeptɪk]	n. 怀疑 chiefly British variant of skeptic, skeptical, skepticism
ruminate [ˈruːmɪneɪt]	v. 反复思考 to think deeply about sth
figment [ˈfɪgmənt]	n. 虚构的事 something made up or contrived
condescension [ˌkɒndɪˈsenʃn]	n. 居高临下 voluntary descent from one's rank or dignity in relations with an inferior
reminiscence [ˌremɪˈnɪsns]	n. 回忆 the act of remembering things that happened in the past
speculation [ˌspekjuˈleɪʃn]	n. 思考 contemplation or consideration of a subject ; meditation
marsupial [mɑːˈsuːpiəl]	n. 有袋类（袋鼠） any Australian animal that carries its young in a pocket of skin
murky [ˈmɜːkɪ]	adj. 不清晰的 not clear ; dark or dirty with mud or another substance
idiosyncratic [ˌɪdɪəsɪŋˈkrætɪk]	adj. 有特性的 unusual or strange, and not shared by other people
mangy [ˈmeɪndʒɪ]	adj. 破旧的 having many worn or bare spots
wither [ˈwɪðə (r)]	v. 枯萎 to become less or weaker, especially before disappearing completely

betoken [bɪ'təʊkən]	v. 预示 to be a sign of sth
thrust [θrʌst]	v. 猛推 to push or drive with force : SHOVE
tuck [tʌk]	v. 塞进 to pull up into a fold
coquettish [kɒ'ketɪʃ]	adj. 卖弄风情的 frequently tries to attract the attention of men without having sincere feelings for them
rumble ['rʌmbl]	v. 隆隆响；低沉地说话 to make a long deep sound or series of sounds ; to speak in a low rolling tone
shove [ʃʌv]	v. 猛推 to push sb/sth in a rough way
embankment [ɪm'bæŋkmənt]	n. 筑堤 a sloping wall of earth or stone beside a road, railroad, or river
growl [graʊl]	v. 咆哮 to utter with a growl : utter angrily
querulous ['kwerələs]	adj. 易怒的 habitually complaining
taut [tɔːt]	adj. 拉紧的 stretched tightly
batter ['bætə (r)]	v. 磨损 to wear or damage by hard usage or blows
tarnish ['tɑːnɪʃ]	v. 使失去光泽 to dull or destroy the luster of by or as if by air, dust, or dirt : SOIL, STAIN
glisten ['glɪsn]	v. 闪光 to shine
apprehension [ˌæprɪ'henʃn]	n. 恐惧；理解 worry or fear that sth unpleasant may happen ; the ability to apprehend or understand ; understanding
embroil [ɪm'brɔɪl]	v. 使卷入 to involve in conflict or difficulties

invidious [ɪnˈvɪdɪəs]	adj. 招致不满的 unpleasant and unfair
imputation [ɪnˈvɪdɪəs]	n. 归罪 to say, often unfairly, that someone is responsible for something bad or has bad intentions
conjecture [kənˈdʒektʃə (r)]	n./v. 猜测 a conclusion deduced by surmise or guesswork
swarm [swɔːm]	n. 蜂群 a large group of insects, especially bees, moving together in the same direction
riddle [ˈrɪdl]	n. 谜 a mystifying, misleading, or puzzling question posed as a problem to be solved or guessed : CONUNDRUM, ENIGMA
folkloristic [fəʊkˈlɔːrɪstɪk]	adj. 民间传说的 traditional customs, tales, sayings, dances, or art forms
retrieve [rɪˈtriːv]	v. 找回 to get back again : REGAIN
prerogative [prɪˈrɒgətɪv]	n. 特权 an exclusive or special right, power, or privilege
pedagogic [ˌpedəˈgɒdʒɪk]	adj. 教学法的 concerning teaching methods

新 SAT 阅读真题对应词汇

Word List 16 Khan12

jut [dʒʌt]	v. 突出 to extend out, up, or forward : PROJECT
squat [skwɒt]	adj. 矮胖的 short and wide or fat, in a way that is not attractive
unfurl [ˌʌnˈfɜːl]	v. 展开 to open
bustle [ˈbʌsl]	v. 奔忙 to move around in a busy way or to hurry sb in a particular direction
strap [stræp]	v. 用皮带捆扎 to wrap strips of material around a wound or an injured part of the body
muffle [ˈmʌfl]	v. 用皮带捆扎 to fasten or secure with a strap
scurry [ˈskʌrɪ]	v. 急跑 to move fast with small quick steps
jerk [dʒɜːk]	v. 猛拉 to give a quick suddenly arrested push, pull
gangway [ˈgæŋweɪ]	n. 过道 a passage between rows of seats in a theatre, an aircraft, etc.
stern [stɜːn]	adj. 严厉的 serious and often disapproving ; expecting sb to obey you
blare [bleə (r)]	v. 发出响而刺耳的声音 to make a loud unpleasant noise
thump [θʌmp]	v. 重击 to hit sb/sth hard, especially with your closed hand
desultory [ˈdesəltrɪ]	adj. 漫无目的的 going from one thing to another, without a definite plan and without enthusiasm

surmise [sə'maɪz]	n./v. 猜测 a thought or idea based on scanty evidence : CONJECTURE
stroll [strəʊl]	n./v. 漫步 to walk somewhere in a slow relaxed way
elude [i'lu:d]	v. 规避 to manage to avoid or escape from sb/sth，especially in a clever way
linger ['lɪŋgə (r)]	v. 逗留 to continue to exist for longer than expected
conspicuous [kən'spɪkjuəs]	adj. 显著的 easy to see or notice；likely to attract attention
conservatory [kən'sɜ:vətrɪ]	n. 音乐学校；温室 a school of music or dramatic art；a greenhouse for growing or displaying plants
imprudence [ɪm'pru:dns]	n. 轻率 not sensible or wise
tremulous ['tremjələs]	adj. 战栗的 shaking slightly because you are nervous；causing you to shake slightly
eloquence ['eləkwəns]	n. 雄辩 able to express your ideas and opinions well，especially in a way that influences people
pulpit ['pʊlpɪt]	n. 讲道坛 the place where a priest stands to talk to people in a church
lisp [lɪsp]	v. 口齿不清地说 to speak falteringly，childishly，or with a lisp
wreak [ri:k]	v. 引起（损失） to cause very great harm or damage
compendium [kəm'pendiəm]	n. 概略 a brief summary of a larger work or of a field of knowledge : ABSTRACT
monarchy ['mɒnəkɪ]	n. 独裁 undivided rule or absolute sovereignty by a single person
alienate ['eɪliəneɪt]	v. 剥夺（权利） to convey or transfer (as property or a right) usually by a specific act rather than the due course of law

sine qua non	n. 要素 something that is essential before you can achieve sth else
hostage ['hɒstɪdʒ]	n. 人质 a person taken by force to secure the taker's demands
tread [tred]	v. 践踏 to step or walk on or over
benevolence [bə'nevələns]	n. 仁慈 disposition to do good
stalemate ['steɪlmeɪt]	v. 使陷入僵局 a situation in a dispute or competition in which neither side is able to win or make any progress
divine [dɪ'vaɪn]	adj. 神圣的；v. 猜测 of, relating to, or proceeding directly from God or a god ; to find out sth by guessing
cloture ['kləʊtʃə]	n. 讨论终结 the closing or limitation of debate in a legislative body especially by calling for a vote
sentiment ['sentɪmənt]	n. 感情，观点 a feeling or an opinion, especially one based on emotions
agony ['ægənɪ]	n. 剧痛 intense pain of mind or body : ANGUISH, TORTURE
anew [ə'njuː]	adv. 重新 again, often in a new or different way
insofar [ˌɪnsəʊ'fɑː]	adv. 在 … 的范围 to such extent or degree
cavalier [ˌkævə'lɪə (r)]	adj. 傲慢的，散漫的 not caring about other people's feelings or about the seriousness of a situation
abdicate ['æbdɪkeɪt]	v. 退位 to give up the position of being king or queen
allegation [ˌælə'geɪʃn]	n. 断言 a public statement that is made without giving proof, accusing sb of doing sth that is wrong or illegal
lodging ['lɒdʒɪŋ]	n. 临时住宿 temporary accommodation

reckless ['rekləs]	adj. 鲁莽的 marked by lack of proper caution : careless of consequences
suffice [sə'faɪs]	v. 足够 to be enough for sb/sth
turmoil ['tɜ:mɔɪl]	n. 骚动 a state of great anxiety, confusion and uncertainty
whim [wɪm]	n. 反复无常 a capricious or eccentric and often sudden idea or turn of the mind : FANCY
slack [slæk]	adj. 松弛的 not stretched tight
exiguity [ˌeksɪ'gju:ɪtɪ]	n. 微少 scanty or meager

新 SAT 阅读真题对应词汇

Word List 17 PSAT1

vex [veks]	v. 使烦恼 to annoy or worry sb
indulgent [ɪnˈdʌldʒənt]	adj. 放纵的 tending to allow sb to have or do whatever they want
unexceptionable [ˌʌnɪkˈsepʃənəbl]	adj. 无懈可击的 not giving any reason for criticism
amiable [ˈeɪmiəbl]	adj. 和蔼可亲的 pleasant；friendly and easy to like
orchestrate [ˈɔːkɪstreɪt]	v. 把 … 协调起来 to organize a complicated plan or event very carefully or secretly
countervail [ˈkaʊntəveɪl]	v. 抵销 having an equal but opposite effect
chunky [ˈtʃʌŋkɪ]	adj. 矮矮胖胖的 thick and heavy
gluttony [ˈglʌtənɪ]	n. 贪食 the habit of eating and drinking too much
obesity [əʊˈbiːsətɪ]	n. 肥胖 when someone is very fat in a way that is unhealthy
tranquilize [ˈtræŋkwɪlaɪz]	v. 使平静 to make tranquil or calm : PACIFY
artery [ˈɑːtərɪ]	n. 动脉 any of the tubes that carry blood from the heart to the rest of the body
deplore [dɪˈplɔː (r)]	v. 哀叹 to feel or express grief for
hearth [hɑːθ]	n. 灶台 a brick，stone，or concrete area in front of a fireplace

disparaging [dɪˈspærɪdʒɪŋ]	adj. 蔑视的 to lower in rank or reputation : DEGRADE
stunning [ˈstʌnɪŋ]	adj. 惊人的 causing astonishment or disbelief
soar [sɔː (r)]	v. 高涨 to rise quickly and smoothly up into the air
vanish [ˈvænɪʃ]	v. 消失 to disappear suddenly and/or in a way that you cannot explain
woe [wəʊ]	n. 悲痛 a condition of deep suffering from misfortune, affliction, or grief
rampant [ˈræmpənt]	adj. 猖獗的 existing or spreading everywhere in a way that cannot be controlled
backdrop [ˈbækdrɒp]	n. 背景 a painted cloth hung across the rear of a stage
flamboyant [flæmˈbɔɪənt]	adj. 引人注目的，华丽的 different, confident and exciting in a way that attracts attention
resuscitate [rɪˈsʌsɪteɪt]	v. 复兴 to make sb start breathing again or become conscious again after they have almost died
resurrect [ˌrezəˈrekt]	v. 使复活 to bring back into use sth, such as a belief, a practice, etc., that had disappeared or been forgotten
conjure [ˈkʌndʒə (r)]	v. 恳求；变戏法 to charge or entreat earnestly or solemnly ; to do clever tricks such as making things seem to appear or disappear as if by magic
deprivation [ˌdeprɪˈveɪʃn]	n. 剥夺 the fact of not having sth that you need, like enough food, money or a home
morale [məˈrɑːl]	n. 士气 the amount of confidence and enthusiasm, etc. that a person or a group has at a particular time
retain [rɪˈteɪn]	v. 保留 to keep sth ; to continue to have sth
champion [ˈtʃæmpiən]	v. 支持 to fight for or speak in support of a group of people or a belief

drowsiness ['draʊzɪnəs]	n. 困 ready to fall asleep
soothe [su:ð]	v. 使平静 to bring comfort, solace, or reassurance to
effusive [ɪ'fju:sɪv]	adj. 感情横溢的 showing much or too much emotion
detrimental [ˌdetrɪ'mentl]	adj. 有害的 harmful
mortality [mɔː'tæləti]	n. 死亡率 the number of deaths in a particular situation or period of time
repercussion [ˌri:pə'kʌʃn]	n. 反响 an indirect and usually bad result of an action or event that may happen some time afterwards
wholesome ['həʊlsəm]	adj. 有益健康的 good for your health
hive [haɪv]	n. 蜂巢 a container for housing honeybees
wax [wæks]	v. 增大 to increase in size, numbers, strength, prosperity, or intensity
wane [weɪn]	v. 变小 to become gradually weaker or less important
germination [ˌdʒɜ:mɪ'neɪʃn]	n. 萌芽 to cause to sprout or develop
replenish [rɪ'plenɪʃ]	v. 补充 to make sth full again by replacing what has been used
recede [rɪ'si:d]	v. 后退 to move back or away : WITHDRAW
efficacy ['efɪkəsɪ]	有效 the power to produce an effect
culinary ['kʌlɪnərɪ]	adj. 烹饪的 connected with cooking or food
enlist [ɪn'lɪst]	v. 征募 to join or to make sb join the armed forces

transcribe [træn'skraɪb]	v. 抄写 to make a written copy of
archive ['ɑːkaɪv]	n. 档案 a collection of historical documents or records of a government, a family, a place or an organization
contestant [kən'testənt]	n. 竞争者 a person who takes part in a contest

新 SAT 阅读真题对应词汇

Word List 18 PSAT2

lap [læp]	n. 一圈 one journey from the beginning to the end of a track used for running, etc.
soggy ['sɒgɪ]	adj. 潮湿的 wet and soft, usually in a way that is unpleasant
claw [klɔ:]	v. 用爪子抓 to rake, seize, dig, or progress with or as if with claws
oblivious [ə'blɪvɪəs]	adj. 易忘的 lacking remembrance, memory, or mindful attention
swerve [swɜ:v]	v. 使突然转向 to change direction suddenly, especially in order to avoid hitting sb/sth
drain [dreɪn]	v. 流干 to make sth empty or dry by removing all the liquid from it
vindicate ['vɪndɪkeɪt]	v. 证实 to prove that sth is true or that you were right to do sth, specially when other people thought differently
underlying [ˌʌndə'laɪɪŋ]	adj. 潜在的 lying beneath or below
authoritarian [ɔ:ˌθɒrɪ'teərɪən]	n. 独裁主义者 controlling everything and forcing people to obey strict rules and laws
gear [gɪə (r)]	v. 使适合 to adjust so as to match, blend with, or satisfy something
dissent [dɪ'sent]	n./v. 异议 difference of opinion
beget [bɪ'get]	v. 招致 to cause something to happen or be created

holdout ['həʊldaʊt]	n. 拒不退让者 a holdout is someone who refuses to agree or act with other people in a particular situation and by doing so stops the situation from progressing or being resolved
rebound [rɪ'baʊnd]	v. 反弹 to bounce back after hitting sth
resurgence [rɪ'sɜ:dʒəns]	n. 复苏 a rising again into life, activity, or prominence : RENASCENCE
holistic [həʊ'lɪstɪk]	adj. 全盘的 considering a whole thing or being to be more than a collection of parts
segregation [ˌsegrɪ'geɪʃn]	n. 种族隔离 the act or policy of separating people of different races, religions or sexes and treating them differently
conscientious [ˌkɒnʃi'enʃəs]	adj. 有责任心的 taking care to do things carefully and correctly
whit [wɪt]	n. 些微 a very small amount
constable ['kʌnstəbl]	n. 巡警 a police officer of the lowest rank
esteem [ɪ'sti:m]	v. 尊敬 great respect and admiration
disgrace [dɪs'greɪs]	v. 使蒙受耻辱 to behave badly in a way that makes you or other people feel ashamed
outlaw ['aʊtlɔ:]	v. 宣告非法 to make sth no longer legal
square with	v. 协调一致 exactly adjusted : precisely constructed or aligned
uplift ['ʌplɪft]	v. 使情绪高涨 to make sb feel happier or more hopeful
degrade [dɪ'greɪd]	v. 使降级；降低 ... 的地位 to lower in grade, rank, or status : DEMOTE ; to show or treat sb in a way that makes them seem not worth any respect or not worth taking seriously

ordinance ['ɔ:dɪnəns]	n. 法令 an order or a rule made by a government or sb in a position of authority
evade [ɪ'veɪd]	v. 躲避 to escape from sb/sth or avoid meeting sb
comply [kəm'plaɪ]	v. 遵守 to obey a rule, an order, etc.
anarchy ['ænəkɪ]	n. 无政府状态 a situation in a country, an organization, etc. in which there is no government, order or control

新 SAT 阅读真题对应词汇

Word List 19 PSAT 20151014

protagonist [prəˈtægənɪst]	n. 主角 the main character in a play, film/movie or book
sacred [ˈseɪkrɪd]	adj. 神圣的 holy
scour [ˈskauə (r)]	v. 搜索 to search a place or thing thoroughly in order to find sb/sth
seditious [sɪˈdɪʃəs]	adj. 煽动性的 encouraging people to oppose the government or not obey the law
exile [ˈeksaɪl]	v. 流放 to banish or expel from one's own country or home
uproar [ˈʌprɔː (r)]	n. 喧嚣 a state of commotion, excitement, or violent disturbance
defy [dɪˈfaɪ]	v. 藐视 to refuse to obey or show respect for sb in authority, a law, a rule, etc.
in thrall to	受奴役于 controlled or strongly influenced by sb/sth
quail [kweɪl]	v. 胆怯 to be very afraid, often so afraid that your body shakes slightly
privy [ˈprɪvi]	adj. 私下的 allowed to know about sth secret
purge [pɜːdʒ]	v. 免罪 to clear of guilt
cadence [ˈkeɪdns]	n. 抑扬顿挫 the rise and fall of the voice in speaking
verse [vɜːs]	n. 诗 a line of metrical writing

forbode [fɔː'bəʊd]	v. 预示（不好的） to have an inward conviction of (as coming ill or misfortune)
bounty ['baʊntɪ]	n. 慷慨 generous actions ; sth provided in large quantities
convivial [kən'vɪvɪəl]	adj. 欢乐的 cheerful and friendly in atmosphere or character
provenance ['prɒvənəns]	n. 起源 the place that sth originally came from
endorse [ɪn'dɔːs]	v. 支持 to say publicly that you support a person, statement or course of action
tout [taʊt]	v. 兜售 to try to persuade people that sb/sth is important or valuable by praising them/it
palpable ['pælpəbl]	adj. 可触知的 that is easily noticed by the mind or the senses
ambience ['æmbɪəns]	n. 气氛 a feeling or mood associated with a particular place, person, or thing : ATMOSPHERE
scrumptious ['skrʌmpʃəs]	adj. 极为美味的 DELIGHTFUL, EXCELLENT especially : DELICIOUS
paradigm ['pærədaɪm]	n. 范例 a typical example or pattern of sth
aptitude ['æptɪtjuːd]	n. 资质 natural ability or skill at doing sth
divergent [daɪ'vɜːdʒənt]	adj. 分歧的 things that are divergent are different from each other
docile ['dəʊsaɪl]	adj. 温顺的 quiet and easy to control
reconcile ['rekənsaɪl]	v. 使和解 to restore to friendship or harmony
stymie ['staɪmɪ]	v. 妨碍 to prevent sb from doing sth

noted ['nəʊtɪd]	adj. 著名的 well known because of a special skill or feature
altar ['ɔːltə (r)]	n. 圣坛 a holy table in a church or TEMPLE
devout [dɪ'vaʊt]	adj. 虔诚的 devoted to religion or to religious duties or exercises
obdurate ['ɒbdjərət]	adj. 顽固的 refusing to change your mind or your actions in any way
stolid ['stɒlɪd]	adj. 麻木的 not showing much emotion or interest
swell [swel]	v. 膨胀 to become bigger or rounder
jubilee ['dʒuːbɪliː]	n. 纪念日 a special anniversary of an event
servitude ['sɜːvɪtjuːd]	n. 奴役 the condition of being a slave or being forced to obey another person
disparity [dɪ'spærəti]	n. 不同 a difference
bequeath [bɪ'kwiːð]	v. 遗留 to give or leave by will
fetter ['fetə (r)]	v. 束缚；n. 脚镣 to restrain from motion, action, or progress ; chains that are put around a prisoner's feet
anthem ['ænθəm]	n. 圣歌 a formal or religious song
mockery ['mɒkəri]	n. 嘲弄 insulting or contemptuous action or speech : DERISION
sacrilegious [ˌsækrə'lɪdʒəs]	adj. 亵渎神灵的 not showing respect for a holy place, object, or idea
cunning ['kʌnɪŋ]	adj. 狡猾的 able to get what you want in a clever way, especially by tricking or deceiving sb
wail [weɪl]	v. 哀号 to express sorrow audibly : LAMENT

chime in with	v. 与 ... 一致 harmonize with
reproach [rɪˈprəʊtʃ]	v. 斥责 blame or criticism for sth you have done
revere [rɪˈvɪə (r)]	v. 尊敬 to feel great respect or admiration for sb/sth
courtesy [ˈkɜːtəsɪ]	n. 礼貌 polite behaviour that shows respect for other people
aggregation [ˌægrɪˈgeɪʃn]	n. 聚集 the collecting of units or parts into a mass or whole

新 SAT 阅读真题对应词汇

Word List 20 PSAT 20151018

matriarch [ˈmeɪtriɑːk]	n. 母系制度 a woman who is the head of a family or social group
totter [ˈtɒtə (r)]	n./v. 蹒跚 to tremble or rock as if about to fall : SWAY
pinched [pɪntʃt]	adj. 痛的 to cause physical or mental pain to
subterranean [ˌsʌbtəˈreɪniən]	adj. 地下的 under the ground
inventive [ɪnˈventɪv]	adj. 善于创造的 able to think of new and interesting ideas
grim [grɪm]	adj. 冷酷的 looking or sounding very serious
mop [mɒp]	v. 擦去 to clean or clear away by mopping
mow [məʊ]	v. 割草 to cut grass
mop and mow	v. 扮鬼脸
squeak [skwiːk]	v. 吱吱叫 to utter or make a short shrill cry or noise
spice [spaɪs]	v. 使添趣味 to add interest or excitement to sth
flicker [ˈflɪkə (r)]	v. 闪烁 to move irregularly or unsteadily : FLUTTER
fraudulent [ˈfrɔːdjələnt]	adj. 欺诈的 intended to deceive sb, usually in order to make money illegally
deceptive [dɪˈseptɪv]	adj. 欺诈的 likely to make you believe sth that is not true

pernicious [pəˈnɪʃəs]	adj.有害的 having a very harmful effect on sb/sth, especially in a way that is gradual and not easily noticed
evangelize [ɪˈvændʒəlaɪz]	v.传福音 to try to persuade people to become Christians
oligarchy [ˈɒlɪgɑːkɪ]	n.寡头政治 a form of government in which only a small group of people hold all the power
unassailable [ˌʌnəˈseɪləbl]	adj.无懈可击的 that cannot be destroyed, defeated or questioned
cargo [ˈkɑːgəʊ]	n.货物 the goods carried in a ship or plane
climacteric [klaɪˈmæktərɪk]	adj.重要时期的 a major turning point or critical stage
trigger [ˈtrɪgə (r)]	v.引发 to initiate, actuate, or set off by a trigger
capricious [kəˈprɪʃəs]	adj.反复无常的 changing suddenly and quickly
encapsulate [ɪnˈkæpsjuleɪt]	v.压缩 to express the most important parts of sth in a few words, a small space or a single object
entrap [ɪnˈtræp]	v.骗入 to trick someone into doing something wrong
emancipate [ɪˈmænsɪpeɪt]	v.解放 to free sb, especially from legal, political or social restrictions
laurel [ˈlɒrəl]	n.桂冠 honour and praise given to sb because of sth that they have achieved
militate [ˈmɪlɪteɪt]	v.产生影响 to have weight or effect
rectitude [ˈrektɪtjuːd]	n.正直 moral integrity : RIGHTEOUSNESS
subtlety [ˈsʌtltoi]	n.微妙 the small but important details or aspects of sth

militarism ['mɪlɪtərɪzəm]	n. 军国主义 the belief that a country should have great military strength in order to be powerful
compulsion [kəm'pʌlʃn]	n. 强迫 strong pressure that makes sb do sth that they do not want to do
complacency [kəm'pleɪsnsɪ]	n. 自满 self-satisfaction especially when accompanied by unawareness of actual dangers or deficiencies
misnomer [ˌmɪs'nəʊmə (r)]	n. 误称 a name or a word that is not appropriate or accurate
masticate ['mæstɪkeɪt]	v. 咀嚼 to chew food
crest [krest]	n. 顶部 the top part of a hill or wave
exuberant [ɪg'zjuːbərənt]	adj. 兴奋的 full of energy, excitement and happiness
appendage [ə'pendɪdʒ]	n. 附加物 a smaller or less important part of sth larger
rooster ['ruːstə (r)]	n. 趾高气扬的男子 a cocky or vain man
garish ['geərɪʃ]	adj. 过分装饰的 very brightly coloured in an unpleasant way
strut [strʌt]	v. 趾高气扬地走 to walk with a pompous and affected air
intimidating [ɪn'tɪmɪdeɪtɪŋ]	adj. 令人生畏的 frightening in a way which makes a person feel less confident
prudish ['pruːdɪʃ]	adj. 过分拘谨的 very easily shocked by things connected with sex
quarry ['kwɒrɪ]	v. 从采石场采得 to dig or take from or as if from a quarry
crate [kreɪt]	v. 将 ... 装入大板条箱 to pack in a crate
bellow ['beləʊ]	v. 怒吼 to shout in a loud deep voice, especially because you are angry

exhale [eks'heɪl]	v. 呼出 to breathe out
chamber ['tʃeɪmbə (r)]	n. 房间 an enclosed space under the ground

新 SAT 阅读真题对应词汇

Word List 21 PSAT 20161015

abscond [əbˈskɒnd]	v. 潜逃 to escape from a place that you are not allowed to leave without permission
banister [ˈbænɪstə (r)]	n. 栏杆 a handrail with its supporting posts
attest [əˈtest]	v. 证明 to show or prove that sth is true
bother [ˈbɒðə (r)]	v. 费力 to spend time and/or energy doing sth
aloof [əˈluːf]	adj. 冷淡的 not friendly or interested in other people
fungibility [ˈfʌndʒɪbɪlɪtɪ]	n. 可互换 INTERCHANGEABLE
token [ˈtəʊkən]	n. 标记；代用币 an outward sign or expression ; a piece of paper that you pay for and that sb can exchange for sth in a shop/store
swap [swɒp]	n./v. 交换 to give in trade : BARTER
tally [ˈtæli]	v. 记录 to record on
unilateral [ˌjuːnɪˈlætrəl]	adj. 单方面的 done or undertaken by one person or party
intrinsic [ɪnˈtrɪnsɪk]	adj. 本质的 belonging to or part of the real nature of sth/sb
erode [ɪˈrəʊd]	v. 腐蚀 to gradually destroy sth or make it weaker over a period of time
reap [riːp]	v. 收获 reap a / the harvest

kinship ['kɪnʃɪp]	n. 血缘关系 the fact of being related in a family
unscrew [ˌʌn'skru:]	v. 旋松 to loosen or withdraw by turning
nudge [nʌdʒ]	v. 轻推 to push sb gently, especially with your elbow, in order to get their attention
maneuver [mə'nu:və]	n. 策略；操控 an adroit and clever management of affairs often using trickery and deception
juggle ['dʒʌgl]	v. 耍弄 to perform the tricks by a juggler
mound [maʊnd]	n. 土墩 a large pile of earth or stones；a small hill
subdue [səb'dju:]	v. 使服从 to bring sb/sth under control, especially by using force
unbridled [ʌn'braɪdld]	adj. 放肆的 not controlled and therefore extreme
beckon ['bekən]	v. 向 … 招手示意 to give sb a signal using your finger or hand, especially to tell them to move nearer or to follow you
enduring [ɪn'djʊərɪŋ]	adj. 持久的 lasting for a long time
condemn [kən'dem]	v. 责备 to express very strong disapproval of sb/sth, usually for moral reasons
weary ['wɪərɪ]	adj. 疲倦的 very tired
trudge [trʌdʒ]	v. 沉重地走 to walk slowly or with heavy steps
on par with	与 … 势均力敌
seizure ['si:ʒə (r)]	n. （疾病）发作 a sudden attack of an illness, especially one that affects the brain
fluorescent [ˌflɔ:'resnt]	adj. 荧光的 producing bright light by using some forms of RADIATION

anesthetize [ə'nesθətaɪz]	v. 麻醉 to give someone an anaesthetic so that they do not feel pain
tantalize ['tæntəlaɪz]	v. 逗弄 to tease or torment by or as if by presenting something desirable to the view but continually keeping it out of reach
cogitation [ˌkɒdʒɪ'teɪʃn]	n. 沉思 the act of cogitating : MEDITATION
rigorous ['rɪgərəs]	adj. 严格的 strict or severe
allergic [ə'lɜːdʒɪk]	adj. 过敏的 having a strong dislike of sth/sb

新 SAT 阅读真题对应词汇

Word List 22 PSAT 20161019

curt [kɜ:t]	adj. 敷衍了事的 using few words in a way that shows you are impatient or angry
stale [steɪl]	adj. 不新鲜的 no longer fresh and therefore unpleasant to eat
apprentice [əˈprentɪs]	n. 学徒 an inexperienced person : NOVICE
scorn [skɔ:n]	v. 轻蔑 open dislike and disrespect or derision often mixed with indignation
debutante [ˈdebjutɑ:nt]	n. 初入社会之少女 a young, rich or UPPER-CLASS woman who is going to fashionable social events for the first time
torment [ˈtɔ:ment]	v. 使痛苦 to make sb suffer very much
swallow [ˈswɒləʊ]	v. 吞咽 to make food, drink, etc. go down your throat into your stomach
arrogant [ˈærəgənt]	adj. 傲慢的 behaving in a proud, unpleasant way, showing little thought for other people
grumble [ˈgrʌmbl]	v. 抱怨 to complain about sb/sth in a bad-tempered way
coddle [ˈkɒdl]	v. 溺爱 to treat sb with too much care and attention
furious [ˈfjʊəriəs]	adj. 狂怒的 very angry
waive [weɪv]	v. 免除 to choose not to demand sth in a particular case, even though you have a legal or official right to do so

sag [sæg]	n./v. 下跌 to become weaker or fewer
intuition [ˌɪntjuˈɪʃn]	n. 直觉 immediate apprehension or cognition
ingenuity [ˌɪndʒəˈnjuːəti]	n. 创造力 the ability to invent things or solve problems in clever new ways
dwindle [ˈdwɪndl]	v. 减少 to become gradually less or smaller
paramount [ˈpærəmaʊnt]	adj. 最重要的 more important than anything else
perpetual [pəˈpetʃuəl]	adj. 永久的 continuing for a long period of time without interruption
muddle [ˈmʌdl]	v. 困惑 to mix confusedly
hone [həʊn]	v. 磨炼 to develop and improve sth, especially a skill, over a period of time
staple [ˈsteɪpl]	n. 主要部分，主食 forming a basic, large or important part of sth; a basic type of food that is used a lot
eavesdrop [ˈiːvzdrɒp]	v. 窃听 to listen secretly to what is said in private
cutting-edge [ˈkʌtɪŋˈedʒ]	n. 前沿 the foremost part or place : VANGUARD
patch [pætʃ]	n. 小块土地 a small area of sth, especially one which is different from the area around it
euphoria [juːˈfɔːriə]	n. 陶醉 a feeling of well-being or elation
botch [bɒtʃ]	v. 笨拙地修补 to repair or mend clumsily
sprinkle [ˈsprɪŋkl]	v. 洒 to scatter a liquid in fine drops
congregation [ˌkɒŋgrɪˈgeɪʃn]	n. 集合 an assembly of persons : GATHERING

filament ['fɪləmənt]	n. 细丝 a single thread or a thin flexible threadlike object, process, or appendage
gallant ['gælənt]	adj.（对女士）殷勤的 giving polite attention to women
haphazard [hæp'hæzəd]	adj. 偶然的 marked by lack of plan, order, or direction
enormous [ɪ'nɔ:məs]	adj. 巨大的 marked by extraordinarily great size, number, or degree
allegorical [ˌælə'gɒrɪkl]	adj. 比喻的 a story, painting etc. in which the events and characters represent ideas or teach a moral lesson
blemish ['blemɪʃ]	n. 瑕疵 a noticeable imperfection
squirm [skwɜ:m]	v. 蠕动 to twist about like a worm : FIDGET
manipulation [məˌnɪpjʊ'leɪʃ(ə)n]	n. 操纵 behavior that influences someone or controls something in a clever or dishonest way
obedience [ə'bi:dɪəns]	n. 顺从 when someone does what they are told to do, or what a law, rule etc. says they must do
perfunctory [pə'fʌŋktərɪ]	adj. 敷衍的 done as a duty or habit, without real interest, attention or feeling
dispel [dɪ'spel]	v. 驱散 to make sth, especially a feeling or belief, go away or disappear

新 SAT 阅读真题对应词汇

Word List 23 20160305NA

arrant ['ærənt]	adj. 完全的，极恶的 being notoriously without moderation : EXTREME
harry ['hæri]	v. 使苦恼 to annoy or upset sb by continuously asking them questions or for sth
an armload of	一堆
layout ['leɪaʊt]	n. 设计 the plan or design or arrangement of something laid out
cook up	v. 编造 make up
exhume [eks'hju:m]	v. 发掘 to remove a dead body from the ground especially in order to examine how the person died
aspiration [ˌæspə'reɪʃn]	n. 渴望 a strong desire to have or do sth
saint [seɪnt]	n. 圣人 one officially recognized especially through canonization as preeminent for holiness
slay [sleɪ]	v. 杀害 to kill sb/sth
demoralize [dɪ'mɒrəlaɪz]	v. 使士气低落 to make sb lose confidence or hope
flee [fli:]	v. 逃避 to run away often from danger or evil
retaliation [rɪˌtæli'eɪʃn]	n. 报复 action that a person takes against sb who has harmed them in some way
stamina ['stæmɪnə]	n. 精力 the physical or mental strength that enables you to do sth difficult for long periods of time

tenacity [təˈnæsətɪ]	n. 坚韧 determined to do something and unwilling to stop trying even when the situation becomes difficult
cringe [krɪndʒ]	v. 畏缩 to shrink in fear or servility
confrontation [ˌkɒnfrʌnˈteɪʃn]	n. 对抗 a situation in which there is a lot of angry disagreement between two people or groups
injunction [ɪnˈdʒʌŋkʃn]	n. 命令 an official order given by a court of law which demands that sth must or must not be done
paternalism [pəˈtɜːnəlɪzəm]	n. 家长式的作风 the system in which a government or an employer protects the people who are governed or employed by providing them with what they need, but does not give them any responsibility or freedom of choice
exploitation [ˌeksplɔɪˈteɪʃn]	n. 剥削 a situation in which sb treats sb else in an unfair way, especially in order to make money from their work
unionism [ˈjuːnɪənɪzəm]	n. 工会主义 the principle or policy of forming or adhering to a union: as a capitalized : adherence to the policy of a firm federal union between the states of the United States especially during the Civil War period
plumpness [plʌmpnəs]	n. 丰满 slightly fat in a fairly pleasant way
scrawny [ˈskrɔːni]	adj. 骨瘦如柴的 very thin in a way that is not attractive
insulate [ˈɪnsjuleɪt]	v. 使绝缘 to protect sb/sth from unpleasant experiences or influences
subcutaneous [ˌsʌbkjuˈteɪniəs]	adj. 皮下的 under the skin
buffer [ˈbʌfə (r)]	v. 缓冲 to reduce the harmful effects of sth
nomination [ˌnɒmɪˈneɪʃn]	n. 任命 the act of suggesting or choosing sb as a candidate in an election, or for a job or an award

forensic [fə'rensɪk]	adj. 适合于法庭的 belonging to, used in, or suitable to courts of judicature or to public discussion and debate
arbitrary ['ɑ:bɪtrərɪ]	adj. 专制的，专横的 (formal) using power without restriction and without considering other people
mishap ['mɪshæp]	n. 不幸之事 an unfortunate accident
subduction [səb'dʌkʃən]	n. 下沉 the action or process in plate tectonics of the edge of one crustal plate descending below the edge of another
briny ['braɪnɪ]	adj. 盐水的 containing a lot of salt
submersible [səb'mɜ:səbl]	n. 潜水器 a submersible machine or vehicle can work under water
slab [slæb]	n. 平板 a thick plate or slice
igneous ['ɪgnɪəs]	adj. 火（山）成的 formed when MAGMA (= melted or liquid material lying below the earth's surface) becomes solid, especially after it has poured out of a VOLCANO
bolster ['bəʊlstə (r)]	v. 加强 to improve sth or make it stronger
timeworn ['taɪmwɔ:n]	adj. 陈旧的 worn or impaired by time
extract ['ekstrækt]	v. 提取，萃取 to remove or obtain a substance from sth, for example by using an industrial or a chemical process
aqueous ['eɪkwɪəs]	adj. 水的 containing water; like water
tournament ['tʊənəmənt]	n. 比赛 a sports competition
hinge [hɪndʒ]	v. 靠铰链链接 to attach sth with a hinge

fluted ['flu:tɪd]	adj. 有凹槽的 with a pattern of curves cut around the outside
matte [mæt]	n. 无光泽 lacking or deprived of luster or gloss
clad [klæd]	adj. 穿衣的 wearing a particular type of clothing
extraneous [ɪkˈstreɪnɪəs]	adj. 无关的 not directly connected with the particular situation you are in or the subject you are dealing with
beacon ['bi:kən]	n. 灯塔 a light that is placed somewhere to guide vehicles and warn them of danger
per capita	人均 equally to each individual
pertain [pəˈteɪn]	v. 与 ... 相关 to be connected with sth/sb

新 SAT 阅读真题对应词汇

Word List 24 20160414NA

successive [sək'sesɪv]	adj. 连续的 following immediately one after the other
vanity ['vænətɪ]	n. 虚荣心 too much pride in your own appearance, abilities or achievements
infatuation [ɪnˌfætʃu'eɪʃn]	n. 陶醉 very strong feelings of love or attraction for sb/sth, especially when these are unreasonable and do not last long
confide [kən'faɪd]	v. 吐露 to tell sb secrets and personal information that you do not want other people to know
conceited [kən'si:tɪd]	adj. 自负的 having too much pride in yourself and what you do
discretionary [dɪ'skreʃənərɪ]	adj. 自主支配的 based on someone's judgment of a particular situation rather than on a set of rules
stereotype ['steriətaɪp]	n. 陈词滥调 to repeat without variation : make hackneyed
chore [tʃɔ: (r)]	n. 家务杂事 an unpleasant or boring task
aggravate ['æɡrəveɪt]	v. 恶化 to make worse, more serious, or more severe
tribunal [traɪ'bju:nl]	n. 法庭 a type of court with the authority to deal with a particular problem or disagreement
palliation [ˌpælɪ'eɪʃən]	n. 缓和 to reduce the violence of
culprit ['kʌlprɪt]	n. 罪犯 a person who has done sth wrong or against the law

deterrent [dɪˈterənt]	n. 威慑力量 a thing that makes sb less likely to do sth
efficacious [ˌefɪˈkeɪʃəs]	adj. 有效的 having the power to produce a desired effect
insuperable [ɪnˈsuːpərəbl]	adj. 不可战胜的 that cannot be dealt with successfully
consign [kənˈsaɪn]	v. 将…置于某种境地 to put sb/sth in an unpleasant situation
mitigate [ˈmɪtɪgeɪt]	v. 缓和 to make sth less harmful, serious, etc.
mandate [ˈmændeɪt]	v. 授权 to give sb, especially a government or a committee, the authority to do sth
ameliorate [əˈmiːliəreɪt]	v. 改善 to make sth better
deficient [dɪˈfɪʃnt]	adj. 缺乏的 not having enough of sth, especially sth that is essential
augmentation [ˌɔːgmenˈteɪʃn]	n. 增加 to increase the value, amount, effectiveness etc. of something
inundate [ˈɪnʌndeɪt]	v. 淹没 to give or send sb so many things that they cannot deal with them all
deterioration [dɪˌtɪəriəˈreɪʃn]	n. 恶化 to become worse
proponent [prəˈpəʊnənt]	n. 支持者 a person who supports an idea or course of action
stewardship [ˈstjuːədʃɪp]	n. 管理工作 the act of taking care of or managing sth, for example, property, an organization, money or valuable objects
contusion [kənˈtjuːʒn]	n. 擦伤 an injury to part of the body that does not break the skin
traction [ˈtrækʃn]	n. 牵引 the act of drawing
ventilate [ˈventɪleɪt]	v. 使通风 to allow fresh air to enter and move around a room, building, etc.

loathe [ləʊð]	v. 厌恶 to dislike sb/sth very much
manual ['mænjuəl]	adj. 手动的 operated or controlled by hand rather than automatically or using electricity, etc.
resemble [rɪ'zembl]	v. 相似 to look like or be similar to another person or thing
lethal ['li:θl]	adj. 致命的 causing or able to cause death

新 SAT 阅读真题对应词汇

Word List 25 20160506AS

contaminate [kən'tæmɪneɪt]	v. 污染 to make something dirty, polluted, or poisonous by adding a chemical, waste, or infection
malice ['mælɪs]	n. 怨恨 a feeling of hatred for sb that causes a desire to harm them
unsightly [ʌn'saɪtli]	adj. 难看的 not pleasant to look at
odorous ['əʊdərəs]	adj. 有气味的 having a smell
depletion [dɪ'pliːʃn]	n. 消耗 to reduce the amount of something that is present or available
demur [dɪ'mɜː(r)]	v. 反对 refusal or disagreement
kudo ['kjuːdɒ]	n. 奖励 a praising remark ; an accolade or compliment
grizzle ['ɡrɪzl]	v. 变成灰色 to make grayish
aviator ['eɪvieɪtə(r)]	n. 飞行家 a person who flies an aircraft
smudge [smʌdʒ]	v. 弄脏 to make a dirty mark on a surface
ubiquitous [juː'bɪkwɪtəs]	adj. 普遍存在的 present everywhere
fixture ['fɪkstʃə(r)]	n. 设备 a piece of furniture
florid ['flɒrɪd]	adj. 华丽的 having too much decoration or detail

crux [krʌks]	n. 难题 the most important or difficult part of a problem or an issue
limp [lɪmp]	v. 跛行 to walk slowly or with difficulty because one leg is injured
flap [flæp]	v. 拍动 if a bird flaps its wings, or if its wings flap, they move quickly up and down
vestigial [veˈstɪdʒiəl]	adj. 退化的 a trace, mark, or visible sign left by something (as an ancient city or a condition or practice) vanished or lost
grin [grɪn]	v. 咧嘴笑 to smile widely
unrest [ʌnˈrest]	n. 动荡的局面 a political situation in which people protest or behave violently
deride [dɪˈraɪd]	v. 嘲笑 to laugh at contemptuously
adamant [ˈædəmənt]	adj. 坚定不移的 determined not to change your mind or to be persuaded about sth
liaison [liˈeɪzn]	n. 联系 a close bond or connection
bluster [ˈblʌstə (r)]	n./v. 咆哮 to talk or act with noisy swaggering threats
conflation [kənˈfleɪʃən]	n. 合并 to combine two or more things to form a single new thing
slant [slɑ:nt]	n. 倾斜 a sloping position
parity [ˈpærətɪ]	n. 平等 the state of being equal
paramedic [ˌpærəˈmedɪk]	n. 护理人员 a person who works in a health field in an auxiliary capacity to a physician
avenue [ˈævənjuː]	n. 方法 a choice or way of making progress towards sth
by virtue of	凭借 through the force of : by authority of

flare [fleə (r)]	v. 闪耀 to burn brightly, but usually for only a short time or not steadily
squashy ['skwɒʃɪ]	adj. 容易压坏的 soft and easy to crush or squeeze
defecate ['defəkeɪt]	v. 除去污物 to get rid of solid waste from your body through your bowels
floral ['flɔ:rəl]	adj. 花的 consisting of pictures of flowers ; decorated with pictures of flowers
scent [sent]	n. 气味 the pleasant smell that sth has
feces ['fi:si:z]	n. 粪便 solid waste material from the bowels
repel [rɪ'pel]	v. 击退 to successfully fight sb who is attacking you, your country, etc. and drive them away
ramp up	v. 提升 to bolster or strengthen
franchise ['fræntʃaɪz]	n. 特许权 formal permission given by a company to sb who wants to sell its goods or services in a particular area ; formal permission given by a government to sb who wants to operate a public service as a business
hurdle ['hɜ:dl]	v. 跳过 to jump over sth while you are running
infuse [ɪn'fju:z]	v. 注入 to cause to be permeated with something
paragon ['pærəgən]	n. 模范 a model of excellence or perfection
archetypal [ˌɑ:ki'taɪpl]	adj. 原型的 the original pattern or model of which all things of the same type are representations or copies : PROTOTYPE
mundane [mʌn'deɪn]	adj. 平凡的；世俗的 not interesting or exciting ; of, relating to, or characteristic of the world
squabble ['skwɒbl]	n./v. 争吵 a noisy altercation or quarrel usually over petty matters

ostracism ['ɒstrəsɪzəm]	n. 排斥 exclusion by general consent from common privileges or social acceptance
pressingly [p'resɪŋlɪ]	adv. 恳切地 urgently important : CRITICAL
grievance ['gri:vəns]	n. 抱怨 something that you think is unfair and that you complain or protest about
redress [rɪ'dres]	n./v. 纠正 to correct sth that is unfair or wrong
provision [prə'vɪʒn]	n. 供应（食物）；临时条款 the act of supplying sb with sth that they need or want ; a measure taken beforehand to deal with a need or contingency : PREPARATION
repeal [rɪ'pi:l]	v. 撤销 to rescind or annul by authoritative act
promulgation [ˌprɒml'geɪʃn]	n. 宣传 to spread an idea or belief to as many people as possible
abolitionism [ˌæbə'lɪʃnizəm]	n. 废奴主义 principles or measures fostering abolition especially of slavery
transgress [trænz'gres]	v. 违法 to violate a command or law : SIN
friction ['frɪkʃn]	n. 摩擦 the force that resists relative motion between two bodies in contact
perchance [pə'tʃɑ:ns]	adv. 偶然 perhaps
doldrums ['dɒldrəmz]	n. 忧郁 the state of feeling sad or depressed

新 SAT 阅读真题对应词汇

Word List 26 20160506NA

squirt [skwɜ:t]	v. 喷出 to come forth in a sudden rapid stream from a narrow opening : SPURT
boon [bu:n]	n. 恩惠 something useful that brings great benefits or makes your life easier
excavate ['ekskəveɪt]	v. 挖掘 to dig out and remove
prop [prɒp]	v. 支撑 to support by placing something under or against
legible ['ledʒəbl]	adj. 清晰的 clear enough to read
plenipotentiary [ˌplenɪpə'tenʃərɪ]	n. 全权大使 a person who has full powers to take action, make decisions, etc. on behalf of their government, especially in a foreign country
convoke [kən'vəʊk]	v. 召集 to gather together a group of people for a formal meeting
preside [prɪ'zaɪd]	v. 主持 to exercise guidance, direction, or control
pendent ['pendənt]	adj. 下垂的 hanging down ; dangling ; suspended
skim [skɪm]	v. 浏览 to read sth quickly in order to find a particular point or the main points
pretension [prɪ'tenʃn]	n. 主张；自负 a claim to be or to do sth ; an attempt to seem more important, more intelligent, or of a higher class than you really are
tug [tʌg]	v. 猛拉 to pull sth hard, often several times

crony ['krəʊnɪ]	n. 密友 a close friend especially of long standing : PAL
bloated ['bləʊtɪd]	adj. 膨胀的 being much larger than what is warranted
caption ['kæpʃn]	n. 字幕 words that are printed underneath a picture, CARTOON, etc. that explain or describe it
illiterate [ɪ'lɪtərət]	adj. 不识字的 not knowing how to read or write
prosecute ['prɒsɪkjuːt]	v. 起诉 to officially charge sb with a crime in a court of law
larceny ['lɑːsənɪ]	n. 盗窃罪 the crime of stealing sth from sb
unwittingly [ʌn'wɪtɪŋlɪ]	adv. 不知情地 not knowing : UNAWARE
pinnacle ['pɪnəkl]	n. 小尖塔 a small pointed stone ornament built on the roof of a building
hail [heɪl]	v. 欢迎 to greet or summon by calling
refined [rɪ'faɪnd]	adj. 优雅的 to free from what is coarse, vulgar, or uncouth
unassuming [ˌʌnə'sjuːmɪŋ]	adj. 谦逊的 not wanting to draw attention to yourself or to your abilities or status
banish ['bænɪʃ]	v. 流放 to order sb to leave a place
piety ['paɪəti]	n. 虔诚 the quality or state of being pious
wrest from	v. 剥夺 to take sth such as power or control from sb/sth with great effort
proprietor [prə'praɪətə (r)]	n. 所有者 the owner of a business, a hotel, etc.
enthrone [ɪn'θrəʊn]	v. 使登位 to make someone the new king, queen, or BISHOP in a formal ceremony

exacerbate [ɪɡˈzæsəbeɪt]	v. 恶化；激怒 to make more violent, bitter, or severe ; exasperate or irritate
subvert [səbˈvɜːt]	v. 颠覆 to try to destroy the power and influence of a government or the established system
presumption [prɪˈzʌmpʃn]	n. 傲慢；推断 behaviour that is too confident and shows a lack of respect for other people ; something that is thought to be true or probable
diverge [daɪˈvɜːdʒ]	v. 分叉 to separate and go in different directions
compost [ˈkɒmpɒst]	n. 混合物 a mixture of decayed plants, food, etc. that can be added to soil to help plants grow
deploy [dɪˈplɔɪ]	v. 使展开 to extend (a military unit) especially in width
sheer [ʃɪə (r)]	adj. 纯粹的 complete and not mixed with anything else
precipitous [prɪˈsɪpɪtəs]	adj. 陡峭的 very steep, high and often dangerous
viable [ˈvaɪəbl]	adj. 能养活的 capable of growing or developing
understaffed [ˌʌndəˈstɑːft]	adj. 人手不足的 not having enough people working and therefore not able to function well
ensue [ɪnˈsjuː]	v. 跟着发生 to happen after or as a result of another event
malfeasance [ˌmælˈfiːzəns]	n. 不法行为 wrongdoing or misconduct especially by a public official
tangible [ˈtændʒəbl]	adj. 摸得着的 capable of being perceived especially by the sense of touch : PALPABLE
steer [stɪə (r)]	v. 驾驶 to control the direction in which a boat, car, etc. moves
boost [buːst]	v. 促进 to make sth increase, or become better or more successful

spook [spu:k]	v. 惊吓 to frighten a person or an animal
posterior [pɒˈstɪəriə (r)]	adj. 后面的 the hinder parts of the body
mutable [ˈmjuːtəbl]	adj. 易变的 that can change ; likely to change
overdrive [ˈəʊvədraɪv]	v. 过度活跃 to become very active or excited, usually more than is necessary or healthy

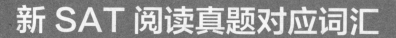

新 SAT 阅读真题对应词汇

Word List 27 20160604AS

long [lɒŋ]	v. 渴望 to want sth very much especially if it does not seem likely to happen soon
implore [ɪmˈplɔ: (r)]	v. 哀求 to ask sb to do sth in an anxious way because you want or need it very much
upshot [ˈʌpʃɒt]	n. 结局 the final result of a particular series of events
reprehensible [ˌreprɪˈhensəbl]	adj. 应该谴责的 morally wrong and deserving criticism
hiss [hɪs]	v. 发出嘶嘶声 to make a sound like a long 's'
to wit	也就是说 that is to say : NAMELY
regale [rɪˈgeɪl]	v. 款待 to entertain sumptuously : feast with delicacies
sentimental [ˌsentɪˈmentl]	adj. 多愁善感的 producing emotions such as pity, romantic love or sadness, which may be too strong or not appropriate
savant [ˈsævənt]	n. 博学者 a person with great knowledge and ability
apathetic [ˌæpəˈθetɪk]	adj. 缺乏兴趣的 showing no interest or enthusiasm
demeaning [dɪˈmiːnɪŋ]	adj. 贬低身份的 showing less respect for someone than they deserve, or making someone feel
elaborate [ɪˈlæbərət]	adj. 精心设计的 planned or carried out with great care

approbation [ˌæprəˈbeɪʃn]	n. 许可 approval or agreement
assail [əˈseɪl]	v. 攻击 to attack sb violently，either physically or with words
gross [grəʊs]	adj. 粗野的；总共的 very obvious and unacceptable；being the total amount of sth before anything is taken away
slander [ˈslɑːndə (r)]	v. 诽谤 a false spoken statement intended to damage the good opinion people have of sb；the legal offence of making this kind of statement
utter [ˈʌtə (r)]	v. 发声；adj. 完全的 to say something；used to emphasize how complete sth is
malignant [məˈlɪgnənt]	adj. 有恶意的 having or showing a strong desire to harm sb
destitute [ˈdestɪtjuːt]	adj. 困穷的 without money，food and the other things necessary for life
skepticism [ˈskeptɪsɪzəm]	n. 怀疑论 an attitude of doubt or a disposition to incredulity either in general or toward a particular object
plea [pliː]	n./v. 恳求 an urgent emotional request
culpability [ˌkʌlpəˈbɪlətɪ]	n. 有罪 GUILTY，CRIMINAL
extenuation [ɪksˈtenjʊˈeɪʃən]	n. 减轻 to lessen or to try to lessen the seriousness or extent of by making partial excuses：MITIGATE
dissident [ˈdɪsɪdənt]	adj. 意见不同的 disagreeing especially with an established religious or political system，organization，or belief
adhere [ədˈhɪə (r)]	v. 坚持 to stick firmly to sth
elicit [iˈlɪsɪt]	v. 引出 to draw forth or bring out
omnipotent [ɒmˈnɪpətənt]	adj. 无所不能的 having total power；able to do anything

winnow ['wɪnəʊ]	v. 精选 to separate desirable and undesirable elements
barge [bɑ:dʒ]	n. 驳船 a large boat with a flat bottom, used for carrying goods and people on canals and rivers
inhale [ɪn'heɪl]	v. 吸入 to draw in by breathing
trump [trʌmp]	v. 胜过 to get the better of : OVERRIDE
enormity [ɪ'nɔ:məti]	n. 巨大 the very great size, effect, etc. of sth ; the fact of sth being very serious
sift [sɪft]	v. 筛选 to separate sth, usually sth you do not want, from a group of things
atrocious [ə'trəʊʃəs]	adj. 残暴的 very bad or unpleasant
vicious ['vɪʃəs]	adj. 邪恶的 full of hatred and anger
eternal [ɪ't3:nl]	adj. 永恒的 without an end ; existing or continuing for ever
rote [rəʊt]	n. 死记硬背 the use of memory usually with little intelligence
engrain [ɪn'greɪn]	v. 使根深蒂固 to work indelibly into the natural texture or mental or moral constitution
gullible ['gʌləbl]	adj. 易受骗的 easily duped or cheated
calculate ['kælkjuleɪt]	v. 深思熟虑 to judge to be true or probable
distraction [dɪ'strækʃn]	n. 娱乐 an activity that amuses or entertains you
attendant [ə'tendənt]	n. 随从 a person who takes care of and lives or travels with an important person or a sick or DISABLED person

folly ['fɒli]	n. 愚蠢 a lack of good judgement
troupe [tru:p]	n. 剧团 a group of actors, singers, etc. who work together
acme ['ækmɪ]	n. 顶点 the highest point or stage
libel ['laɪbl]	n./v. 诽谤 to publish a written statement about sb that is not true
plague [pleɪg]	n. 折磨 a disastrous evil or affliction : CALAMITY
pamphlet ['pæmflət]	n. 小册子 a very thin book with a paper cover, containing information about a particular subject
upright ['ʌpraɪt]	adj. 正直的 behaving in a moral and honest way
vile [vaɪl]	adj. 卑鄙的 extremely unpleasant or bad
factious ['fækʃəs]	adj. 好搞派系的 of, relating to, produced by, or characterized by internal dissension
expedient [ɪk'spi:dɪənt]	n. 权宜之计 an action that is useful or necessary for a particular purpose, but not always fair or right
terrify ['terɪfaɪ]	v. 恐吓 to make sb feel extremely frightened
scepticism ['skeptɪsɪzəm]	n. 怀疑论 an attitude of doubting that claims or statements are true or that sth will happen
noxious ['nɒkʃəs]	adj. 有害的 poisonous or harmful
heretic ['herətɪk]	n. 异教徒 a dissenter from established religious dogma
stoke [stəʊk]	v. 添油加醋 to make people feel sth more strongly

abort [ə'bɔ:t]	v. 使流产；阻止 to end a pregnancy；to end or cause sth to end before it has been completed，especially because it is likely to fail
screw up	v. 搞砸 to cause to act or function in a crazy or confused way
tempting ['temptɪŋ]	adj. 吸引人的 having an appeal：ENTICING
savior ['seɪvjə]	n. 救世主 one that saves from danger or destruction
feasible ['fi:zəbl]	adj. 可行的 that is possible and likely to be achieved
trade off	n. 权衡 the act of balancing two things that you need or want but which are opposed to each other
wicked ['wɪkɪd]	adj. 邪恶的 morally very bad：EVIL
impending [ɪm'pendɪŋ]	adj. 逼近的 that is going to happen very soon
upend [ʌp'end]	v. 颠倒 to turn sb/sth upside down
vocalization [ˌvəʊkəlaɪ'zeɪʃn]	n. 发声 a word or sound that is produced by the voice
hominid ['hɒmɪnɪd]	n. 原始人 a primate of the family Hominidae，of which Homo sapiens is the only extant species

新 SAT 阅读真题对应词汇

Word List 28 20160604NA

epoch ['i:pɒk]	n. 新纪元 a period of time in history, especially one during which important events or changes happen
magnificent [mæg'nɪfɪsnt]	adj. 华丽的 extremely attractive and impressive ; deserving praise
prodigal ['prɒdɪgl]	adj. 浪费的 too willing to spend money or waste time, energy or materials
expenditure [ɪk'spendɪtʃə (r)]	n. 消费 the act of spending or using money
glitter ['glɪtə (r)]	v. 闪烁 to shine brightly with little flashes of light, like a diamond
gaudy ['gɔ:dɪ]	adj. 俗丽的 ostentatiously or tastelessly ornamented
manifestation [ˌmænɪfe'steɪʃn]	n. 证明 an event, action or thing that is a sign that sth exists or is happening
coruscate ['kɒrəskeɪt]	v. 闪烁 to give off or reflect light in bright beams or flashes : SPARKLE
imminent ['ɪmɪnənt]	adj. 即将来临的 likely to happen very soon
recoil [rɪ'kɔɪl]	v. 弹回 to shrink back physically or emotionally
ignoble [ɪg'nəʊbl]	adj. 名誉不佳的 not good or honest
betwixt [bɪ'twɪkst]	prep. 模棱两可 betwixt and between (old-fashioned) in a middle position
retribution [ˌretrɪ'bju:ʃn]	n. 报复 severe punishment for sth seriously wrong that sb has done

multitude ['mʌltɪtjuːd]	n. 群众 an extremely large number of things or people
abode [ə'bəʊd]	n. 住所 the place where sb lives
forlorn [fə'lɔːn]	adj. 凄凉的 appearing lonely and unhappy
embroider [ɪm'brɔɪdə (r)]	n. 刺绣 to decorate fabric with a pattern of stitches usually using coloured thread
tatter ['tætə]	v. 撕碎 to make or become ragged
deface [dɪ'feɪs]	v. 损伤外观 to damage the appearance of sth especially by drawing or writing on it
gibe [dʒaɪb]	v. 嘲笑 to deride or tease with taunting words
obscurity [əb'skjʊərətɪ]	n. 模糊 the quality of being difficult to understand
ostentation [ˌɒsten'teɪʃn]	n. 虚有其表 an exaggerated display of wealth, knowledge or skill that is made in order to impress people
penury ['penjərɪ]	n. 贫困 the state of being very poor
skulk [skʌlk]	v. 鬼鬼祟祟地活动 to hide or move around secretly, especially when you are planning sth bad
morbid ['mɔːbɪd]	adj. 病态的 having or expressing a strong interest in sad or unpleasant things, especially disease or death
avenger [ə'vendʒə (r)]	n. 复仇者 to do something to hurt or punish someone because they have harmed or offended you
harness ['hɑːnɪs]	v. 利用产生动力 to control and use the force or strength of sth to produce power or to achieve sth

salient [ˈseɪliənt]	adj. 突出的 most important or noticeable
astute [əˈstjuːt]	adj. 狡猾的 very clever and quick at seeing what to do in a particular situation, especially how to get an advantage
fringe [frɪndʒ]	v. 加饰边于 to form a border around sth
spurious [ˈspjʊəriəs]	adj. 伪造的 false, although seeming to be genuine
conspiracy [kənˈspɪrəsɪ]	n. 同谋 a secret plan by a group of people to do sth harmful or illegal
tactics [ˈtæktɪks]	n. 策略 the art or skill of employing available means to accomplish an end
distillation [ˌdɪstɪˈleɪʃn]	n. 蒸馏 the process of purifying a liquid by successive evaporation and condensation
tentative [ˈtentətɪv]	adj. 暂时的 not definite or certain because you may want to change it later
auspicious [ɔːˈspɪʃəs]	adj. 吉兆的 showing signs that sth is likely to be successful in the future
harass [ˈhærəs]	v. 使烦恼 to annoy or worry sb by putting pressure on them or saying or doing unpleasant things to them
gratify [ˈgrætɪfaɪ]	v. 使满足 to please or satisfy sb
grievous [ˈgriːvəs]	adj. 痛苦的 very serious and often causing great pain or suffering
burthen [bɜːrðən]	n. 负担 burden
impunity [ɪmˈpjuːnətɪ]	n. 免于惩罚 exemption or freedom from punishment, harm, or loss
gripping [ˈgrɪpɪŋ]	adj. 吸引人的 exciting or interesting in a way that keeps your attention

sprout [spraʊt]	v. 很快地成长 to appear ; to develop sth, especially in large numbers
handicap ['hændikæp]	n./v. 妨碍 to make sth more difficult for sb to do
domesticate [də'mestikeit]	v. 驯养 to make a wild animal used to living with or working for humans
resilient [rɪ'zɪliənt]	adj. 迅速恢复精力的 able to feel better quickly after sth unpleasant such as shock, injury, etc.
tillage ['tɪlɪdʒ]	n. 耕种 the process of preparing and using land for growing crops
wilt [wɪlt]	v. 枯萎 to become weak or tired or less confident
perpendicular [ˌpɜ:pən'dɪkjələ (r)]	adj. 垂直的 standing at right angles to the plane of the horizon : exactly upright

新 SAT 阅读真题对应词汇

Word List 29 20161001AS

belie [bɪˈlaɪ]	v. 与 ...不符 to give a false impression of sb/sth
placid [ˈplæsɪd]	adj. 平静的 not easily excited or irritate
wayward [ˈweɪwəd]	adj. 任性的 difficult to control
thwart [θwɔ:t]	v. 阻碍 to prevent sb from doing what they want to do
freak [fri:k]	n. 怪诞的人 a person who is considered to be unusual because of the way they behave，look or think
vice [vaɪs]	n. 恶行 criminal activities that involve sex or drugs
vivacious [vɪˈveɪʃəs]	adj. 活泼的 having a lively，attractive personality
gay [geɪ]	adj. 欢乐的 happy and full of fun
prattle [ˈprætl]	v. 闲聊 to talk a lot about unimportant things
idolatrous [aɪˈdɒlətrəs]	adj. 崇拜偶像的 the practice of worshipping idols
cant [kænt]	n. 伪善的言辞 statements，especially about moral or religious issues，that are not sincere and that you cannot trust
humbug [ˈhʌmbʌg]	n. 欺骗 dishonest language or behaviour that is intended to deceive people

exultant [ɪgˈzʌltənt]	adj. 非常高兴的 filled with or expressing great joy or triumph : JUBILANT
heave [hi:v]	v. 举起 to lift, pull or throw sb/sth very heavy with one great effort
revolt [rɪˈvəult]	n./v. 叛乱 to take violent action against the people in power
ferment [fəˈment]	v. 煽动 to be in a state of agitation or intense activity
ferocity [fəˈrɒsətɪ]	n. 残暴 violence ; fierce or aggressive behaviour
connexion [kəˈnekʃən]	n. 连接 connection
fallacious [fəˈleɪʃəs]	adj. 谬误的 wrong ; based on a false idea
engross [ɪnˈgrəus]	v. 使全神贯注 to take or engage the whole attention of : occupy completely
brute [bru:t]	adj. 野蛮的 unrelievedly harsh
jesuitically [dʒeˌzjuɪˈtɪkəlɪ]	adv. 与耶稣有关地
asylum [əˈsaɪləm]	n. 庇护所 an inviolable place of refuge and protection giving shelter to criminals and debtors : SANCTUARY
oxymoron [ˌɒksɪˈmɔːrɒn]	n. 矛盾修饰法 a combination of contradictory or incongruous words
flashback [ˈflæʃbæk]	n. 倒叙 a part of a film/movie, play, etc. that shows a scene that happened earlier in time than the main story
stall [stɔ:l]	v. 停止 to stop sth from happening until a later date ; to stop making progress
encompass [ɪnˈkʌmpəs]	v. 包围 to surround or cover sth completely
sweeping [ˈswi:pɪŋ]	adj. 广泛的 having an important effect on a large part of sth

sliver [ˈslɪvə (r)]	n. 薄片 a small or thin piece of sth that is cut or broken off from a larger piece
nuance [ˈnjuːɑːns]	n. 细微差别 a very slight difference in meaning, sound, colour or sb's feelings that is not usually very obvious
waft [wɒft]	v. 飘荡 to move, or make sth move, gently through the air
stitch [stɪtʃ]	v. 编织，缝补 to sew sth ; to use a needle and thread to mend, join, or decorate pieces of fabric
tinker [ˈtɪŋkə (r)]	v. 修补 to make small changes to sth in order to repair or improve it, especially in a way that may not be helpful

新 SAT 阅读真题对应词汇

Word List 30 20161001NA

toddle ['tɒdl]	v.东倒西歪地走 when a young child who has just learnt to walk toddles, it walks with short, unsteady steps
pluck [plʌk]	v.拔 to take hold of sth and remove it by pulling it
hush [hʌʃ]	n/v.（使）安静 to be quiet; to stop talking or crying
enfeeble [ɪn'fi:bl]	v.使衰弱 to make sb/sth weak
stupefy ['stju:pɪfaɪ]	v.使惊呆 to make stupid, groggy, or insensible
articulate [ɑ:'tɪkjuleɪt]	v.清楚地讲话 to express or explain your thoughts or feelings clearly in words
imperative [ɪm'perətɪv]	adj.势在必行的；命令式的 very important and needing immediate attention or action; expressive of a command, entreaty, or exhortation
restorative [rɪ'stɔ:rətɪv]	adj.恢复健康的 making you feel strong and healthy again
antithetical [ˌæntɪ'θetɪkl]	adj.对立的 being in direct and unequivocal opposition
sluggish ['slʌgɪʃ]	adj.懒惰的 moving or reacting more slowly than normal
stagnate [stæg'neɪt]	v.使停止 to stop developing or making progress
decouple [di:'kʌpl]	v.断开联系 to end the connection or relationship between two things
sync [sɪŋk]	v.同时发生 moving or working at exactly the same time and speed as sb/sth else

oscillate ['ɒsɪleɪt]	v.摇摆 to keep moving from one position to another and back again
ripple ['rɪpl]	n.涟漪 a small wave on the surface of a liquid, especially water in a lake, etc.
exhilarate [ɪg'zɪləreɪt]	v.使高兴 to make sb feel very happy and excited
conceive [kən'si:v]	v.构思 to form an idea, a plan, etc. in your mind
medley ['medlɪ]	n.混杂 a mixture of people or things of different kinds
faculty ['fækltɪ]	n.能力 any of the physical or mental abilities that a person is born with
amicable ['æmɪkəbl]	adj.友善的 done or achieved in a polite or friendly way and without quarrelling
entrench [ɪn'trentʃ]	v.根深蒂固 to establish sth very firmly so that it is very difficult to change
heft [heft]	n.重量，重要性 weight；heaviness；bulk；IMPORTANCE, INFLUENCE
quantum ['kwɒntəm]	n.量子 a very small quantity of ELECTROMAGNETIC energy
toehold ['təʊhəʊld]	n.立足之地 a position in a place or an activity which you hope will lead to more power or success
overwrought [ˌəʊvə'rɔ:t]	adj.过度紧张的 very worried and upset；excited in a nervous way
relegate ['relɪgeɪt]	v.贬谪 to give sb a lower or less important position, rank, etc. than before
vernacular [və'nækjələ (r)]	n.方言；adj.地方的 the language spoken in a particular area or by a particular group, especially one that is not the official or written language
contextualization [kən'tekstʃuəlaɪzeɪʃn]	n.根据上下文 to place (as a word or activity) in a context
enact [ɪ'nækt]	v.制定 to pass a law

catalyst ['kætəlɪst]	n. 催化剂 a substance that makes a chemical reaction happen faster without being changed itself
spawn [spɔ:n]	v. 产生 to cause sth to develop or be produced
birthright ['bɜ:θraɪt]	n. 生来就有的权利 a right, privilege, or possession to which a person is entitled by birth
cohort ['kəʊhɔ:t]	n. 一群 a group of people who share a common feature or aspect of behaviour
hoax [həʊks]	n./v. 欺骗 to trick sb by making them believe sth that is not true, especially sth unpleasant
swamp [swɒmp]	v. 淹没；使应接不暇 to fill with or as if with water : INUNDATE, SUBMERGE ; to make sb have more of sth than they can deal with
hysteria [hɪ'stɪəriə]	n. 歇斯底里症 a state of extreme excitement, fear or anger in which a person, or a group of people, loses control of their emotions and starts to cry, laugh, etc.
ulterior [ʌl'tɪəriə (r)]	adj. 隐藏的 that sb keeps hidden and does not admit

新 SAT 阅读真题对应词汇

Word List 31 20161105AS

surf [sɜ:f]	n. 海浪；v. 冲浪 large waves in the sea or ocean；to take part in the sport of riding on waves on a SURFBOARD
rein [reɪn]	n./v. 控制 to control sb/sth more strictly
bait [beɪt]	n./v. 诱饵 food put on a hook to catch fish or in nets，traps，etc. to catch animals or birds
pamper ['pæmpə (r)]	v. 使放纵 to take care of sb very well and make them feel as comfortable as possible
plaintiff ['pleɪntɪf]	n. 原告 a person who brings a legal action — compare DEFENDANT
defendant [dɪ'fendənt]	n. 被告 a person required to make answer in a legal action or suit— compare PLAINTIFF
discrepancy [dɪs'krepənsɪ]	n. 差异 a difference between two or more things that should be the same
exotica [ɪg'zɒtɪkə]	n. 异国风情 unusual and exciting things，especially from other countries
asperity [æ'sperətɪ]	n. 严酷；粗糙 the fact of being harsh or severe；roughness of surface
jagged ['dʒægɪd]	adj. 锯齿状的 with rough，pointed，often sharp edges
bump [bʌmp]	n. 肿块 a swelling on the body，often caused by a blow
repudiate [rɪ'pju:dieɪt]	v. 否认 to refuse to have anything to do with：DISOWN

delineate [dɪˈlɪnieɪt]	v. 描绘 to describe, draw or explain sth in detail
dough-baked	adj. 愚昧的 half-witted, stupid
harangue [həˈræŋ]	n./v. 热烈的演说 to speak loudly and angrily in a way that criticizes sb/sth or tries to persuade people to do sth
imbibe [ɪmˈbaɪb]	v. 吸入 to drink sth, especially alcohol
rage [reɪdʒ]	n. 狂怒 feeling of violent anger that is difficult to control
inculcate [ˈɪnkʌlkeɪt]	v. 反复灌输 to teach and impress by frequent repetitions or admonitions
groan [grəʊn]	n./v. 呻吟 to make a long deep sound because you are annoyed, upset or in pain, or with pleasure
brethren [ˈbreðrən]	n. 弟兄们 used to talk to people in church or to talk about the members of a male religious group
fanatical [fəˈnætɪkl]	adj. 狂热的 very enthusiastic about a sport or activity
xenophobia [ˌzenəˈfəʊbiə]	n. 仇外 a strong feeling of dislike or fear of people from other countries
mesic [ˈmiːsɪk]	adj. 湿地的 characterized by, relating to, or requiring a moderate amount of moisture
protocol [ˈprəʊtəkɒl]	n. 草案 an original draft, minute, or record of a document or transaction
clear-cut	adj. 清晰的 definite and easy to see or identify
mutate [mjuːˈteɪt]	v. 变化 to change into a new form
tuck away	v. 收藏 if someone or something is tucked away, they are hidden or difficult to find

instigate ['ɪnstɪgeɪt]	v. 煽动 to make sth start or happen，usually sth official
accrue [ə'kru:]	v. 增加 to increase over a period of time
exhaustive [ɪg'zɔ:stɪv]	adj. 详尽的 very thorough；looking at every detail

新 SAT 阅读真题对应词汇

Word List 32 20161105NA

suffocate ['sʌfəkeɪt]	v. 使窒息 to die because there is no air to breathe ; to kill sb by not letting them breathe air
rattle down	v. 喋喋不休地说 to make a series of short loud sounds when hitting against sth hard ; to make sth do this
stupor ['stju:pə (r)]	n. 麻木 a state of extreme apathy or torpor resulting often from stress or shock : DAZE
drugged [drʌgd]	adj. 麻木的 to lull or stupefy as if with a drug
bugle with	v. 吹号 to give forth a deep , prolonged sound similar to the bay of a hound
raft [rɑ:ft]	n. 筏 a small boat made of rubber or plastic that is filled with air
tackle ['tækl]	v. 处理 to make a determined effort to deal with a difficult problem or situation
compromise ['kɒmprəmaɪz]	n. 折衷 an agreement made between two people or groups in which each side gives up some of the things they want so that both sides are happy at the end
probity ['prəʊbətɪ]	n. 诚实 the quality of being completely honest
slaveholder ['sleɪv‚həʊldə]	n. 奴隶主 an owner of slaves
commonwealth ['kɒmənwelθ]	n. 共和国 used in the official names of , and to refer to , some states of the US (Kentucky , Massachusetts , Pennsylvania and Virginia)

sprint [sprɪnt]	v. 奋力短跑 to run a short distance very fast
ungainly [ʌnˈɡeɪnlɪ]	adj. 难看的 moving in a way that is not graceful
infrastructure [ˈɪnfrəstrʌktʃə (r)]	n. 基建 the basic systems and services that are necessary for a country or an organization, for example buildings, transport, water and power supplies and administrative systems
stricture [ˈstrɪktʃə (r)]	n. 苛评 a severe criticism, especially of sb's behaviour
recalcitrant [rɪˈkælsɪtrənt]	adj. 反抗的 unwilling to obey rules or follow instructions ; difficult to control
institute [ˈɪnstɪtjuːt]	v. 创立 to establish in a position or office
hold up	v. 持续 to continue in the same condition without failing or losing effectiveness or force
reciprocal [rɪˈsɪprəkl]	adj. 相互的 involving two people or groups who agree to help each other or behave in the same way to each other
confer [kənˈfɜː (r)]	v. 授予 to give sb an award, a university degree or a particular honour or right

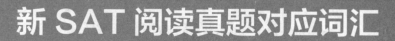

Word List 33 20161203AS

solicitor [sə'lɪsɪtə (r)]	n. 律师 a lawyer who prepares legal documents
vulgarity [vʌl'gærətɪ]	n. 粗俗 the fact of being rude or not having good taste
take up	v. 开始从事 to begin to occupy
sunder ['sʌndə (r)]	n./v. 分开 to split or break sth/sb apart, especially by force
addict ['ædɪkt]	v. 使沉溺 to devote or surrender (oneself) to something habitually or obsessively
venality [viː'nælətɪ]	n. 贪赃枉法 willing to use power and influence in a dishonest way in return for money
overrule [ˌəʊvə'ruːl]	v. 驳回 to change a decision or reject an idea from a position of greater power
providence ['prɒvɪdəns]	n. 上帝 God
entertain [ˌentə'teɪn]	v. 有 to keep, hold, or maintain in the mind
heat [hiːt]	n. 狂热 strong feelings, especially of anger or excitement
fawn [fɔːn]	v. 奉承 to try to please sb by praising them or paying them too much attention
pull off	v. 成功完成 to carry out despite difficulties : accomplish successfully against odds
tandem ['tændəm]	n. 双轮马车 a 2-seated carriage drawn by horses harnessed one before the other

astray [ə'streɪ]	adv. 迷途地；被偷地 to become lost；to be stolen
work off	v. 清理 to dispose of or get rid of by work or activity
quorum ['kwɔːrəm]	n. 法定最低人数 the smallest number of people who must be at a meeting before it can begin or decisions can be made
count on	v. 指望 to look forward to as certain : ANTICIPATE
apiece [ə'piːs]	adv. 每个 for each one : INDIVIDUALLY
cue [kjuː]	v. 暗示 to give sb a signal so they know when to start doing sth
sniff out	v. 发现 to discover or find something by its smell
cons-old	adj. 万古的
ragged ['rægɪd]	adj. 破烂的 old and torn
ruddy ['rʌdi]	adj. 红润的 looking red and healthy
run-of-the-mill	adj. 普通的 ordinary，with no special or interesting features
translucent [træns'luːsnt]	adj. 半透明的 allowing light to pass through but not transparent

Word List 34 20161203NA

devotee [ˌdevəˈtiː]	n. 仰慕者 a person who admires and is very enthusiastic about sb/sth
obituary [əˈbɪtʃuərɪ]	n. 讣告 a notice of a person's death usually with a short biographical account
brittle [ˈbrɪtl]	adj. 易碎的 hard but easily broken
hunch over	v. 被 ... 感动 move by
holler [ˈhɒlə (r)]	v. 叫喊 to cry out (as to attract attention or in pain) : SHOUT
snip away	v. 剪断 to cut sth with scissors using short quick strokes
flip through	v. 浏览
supercilious [ˌsuːpəˈsɪlɪəs]	adj. 自大的 coolly and patronizingly haughty
clumsy [ˈklʌmzɪ]	adj. 笨拙的 difficult to move or use easily
asterisk [ˈæstərɪsk]	n. 星号 the character *
inextricable [ˌɪnɪkˈstrɪkəbl]	adj. 无法分开的 incapable of being disentangled or untied
parochial [pəˈrəʊkɪəl]	adj. 狭小的 confined or restricted as if within the borders of a parish : limited in range or scope (as to a narrow area or region) : PROVINCIAL, NARROW
elliptical [ɪˈlɪptɪkl]	adj. 椭圆的 of，relating to，or shaped like an ellipse

dichotomy [daɪˈkɒtəmɪ]	n. 二分法 a division into two especially mutually exclusive or contradictory groups or entities
starkly [staːk lɪ]	adv. 完全地 to an absolute or complete degree : WHOLLY
mediocrity [ˌmiːdiˈɒkrətɪ]	n. 平庸之才 the quality of being average or not very good
idle [ˈaɪdl]	adj. 闲散的 without work ; unemployed
expatriate [ˌeksˈpætrɪət]	v. 逐出国外 expel from a country
ratify [ˈrætɪfaɪ]	v. 批准 to approve and sanction formally : CONFIRM
condescending [ˌkɒndɪˈsendɪŋ]	adj. 高傲的，屈尊的 behaving as though you are more important and more intelligent than other people
extol [ɪkˈstəʊl]	v. 颂扬 to praise sb/sth very much
outbreak [ˈaʊtbreɪk]	n. 暴发 the sudden start of sth unpleasant，especially violence or a disease
expel [ɪkˈspel]	v. 逐出 to force to leave
trove [trəʊv]	n. 收藏的东西 a valuable collection : TREASURE
ceramic [səˈræmɪk]	adj. 陶器的 a pot or other object made of clay that has been made permanently hard by heat
lavish [ˈlævɪʃ]	adj. 浪费的；v. 慷慨给予 large in amount，or impressive，and usually costing a lot of money ; giving or doing sth generously
cemetery [ˈsemətrɪ]	n. 墓地 an area of land used for burying dead people，especially one that is not beside a church
exquisite [ɪkˈskwɪzɪt]	adj. 精致的 extremely beautiful or carefully made

counterfeit ['kaʊntəfɪt]	v.伪造 to make an exact copy of sth in order to trick people into thinking that it is the real thing
fertilizer ['fɜːtəlaɪzə (r)]	n.肥料 a substance added to soil to make plants grow more successfully
adhesive [əd'hiːsɪv]	adj.黏的 that can stick to sth
ditch [dɪtʃ]	n.沟渠 a long narrow excavation dug in the earth
runoff ['rʌnˌɔːf]	n.决赛；径流 a final race, contest, or election to decide an earlier one that has not resulted in a decision in favor of any one competitor ; a flow of water or chemicals from one place to another
curb [kɜːb]	v.抑制 to control or limit sth, especially sth bad
oversight ['əʊvəsaɪt]	n.失察；监督 the fact of making a mistake because you forget to do sth or you do not notice sth ; the state of being in charge of sb/sth

新 SAT 阅读真题对应词汇

Word List 35 20170121NA

scatterbrained ['skætəbreɪnd]	adj. 注意力不集中的 not thinking in an organized way and often forgetting or losing things
miser ['maɪzə (r)]	n. 守财奴 a person who loves money and hates spending it
sanctuary ['sæŋktʃuərɪ]	n. 避难所 safety and protection, especially for people who are being chased or attacked
pittance ['pɪtns]	n. 施舍少量的钱 a small portion, amount, or allowance
clout [klaʊt]	n. 权势 power and influence
null [nʌl]	adj. 无效的 having no legal or binding force : INVALID
sway [sweɪ]	v. 影响, 控制 to exert a guiding or controlling influence on
squelch [skweltʃ]	v. 镇压 to stop sth from growing, increasing or developing
boast [bəʊst]	v. 自夸 to talk with too much pride about sth that you have or can do
tweak [twi:k]	v. 轻微调整 to make slight changes to a machine, system, etc. to improve it
razor ['reɪzə (r)]	n. 剃刀 an instrument that is used for shaving
elasticity [ˌi:læ'stɪsətɪ]	n. 弹性 capability of a strained body to recover its size and shape after deformation : SPRINGINESS
restrain [rɪ'streɪn]	v. 抑制 to stop sb/sth from doing sth, especially by using physical force

senate ['senət]	n. 参议员 an assembly or council usually possessing high deliberative and legislative functions
convulsion [kən'vʌlʃn]	n. 动乱 a violent disturbance
annexation [ˌænek'seɪʃn]	n. 合并 to join together materially : UNITE
abate [ə'beɪt]	v. 减轻 to become less strong ; to make sth less strong
crawl [krɔ:l]	v. 爬行 to move forward on your hands and knees, with your body close to the ground
dawdle ['dɔ:dl]	v. 磨蹭 to take a long time to do sth or go somewhere
meander [mi'ændə (r)]	v. 漫步 to walk slowly and change direction often, especially without a particular aim
rig up	v. 装配 to make a piece of equipment, furniture etc. quickly from objects that you find around you
melodramatic [ˌmelədrə'mætɪk]	adj. 耸人听闻的 full of exciting and extreme emotions or events ; behaving or reacting to sth in an exaggerated way
scrap [skræp]	n. 碎片 fragments of discarded or leftover food
annihilate [ə'naɪəleɪt]	v. 消灭 to destroy sb/sth completely
oust [aʊst]	v. 取代，驱逐 to force sb out of a job or position of power, especially in order to take their place
discard [dɪs'kɑ:d]	v. 抛弃 to get rid of sth that you no longer want or need
squander ['skwɒndə (r)]	v. 挥霍 to waste money, time, etc. in a stupid or careless way
drape with	v. 垂挂 to hang clothes, materials, etc. loosely on sb/sth

snare [sneə (r)]	v. 谋得 to win or attain by artful or skillful maneuvers
scrupulous ['skru:pjələs]	adj. 小心谨慎的 careful about paying attention to every detail
mumble ['mʌmbl]	v. 含糊地说 to speak or say sth in a quiet voice in a way that is not clear
parabolic [ˌpærə'bɒlɪk]	adj. 抛物线的 a curve in the shape of the imaginary line an object makes when it is thrown high in the air and comes down a little distance away

新 SAT 阅读真题对应词汇

Word List 36 20170311NA

a stew of	大量的 a large number of
shrine [ʃraɪn]	n.圣坛 a place where people come to worship because it is connected with a holy person or event
demon [ˈdiːmən]	n.魔鬼 an evil spirit
varnish [ˈvɑːnɪʃ]	v.涂油漆于；粉饰 to put varnish on the surface of sth；to cover or conceal (as something unpleasant) with something that gives an attractive appearance
funfair [ˈfʌnfeə (r)]	n.游乐场 a noisy outdoor event where you can ride on machines，play games to win prizes etc.
skull [skʌl]	n.头盖骨 the bone structure that forms the head and surrounds and protects the brain
cryptographic [ˈkrɪptəʊˈɡræfɪk]	adj.密码学的 the art of writing or solving CODES
mayhem [ˈmeɪhem]	n.混乱 a very confused situation: CHAOS
affliction [əˈflɪkʃn]	n.痛苦 pain and suffering or sth that causes it
wince [wɪns]	v.畏缩 to shrink back involuntarily
affectionate [əˈfekʃənət]	adj.充满深情的 showing caring feelings and love for sb
studious [ˈstjuːdiəs]	adj.爱好学习的；热心的 spending a lot of time studying or reading；giving a lot of attention and care to what you are doing or learning

verbiage ['vɜːbɪɪdʒ]	n.冗长 written or spoken language that is long, boring, and unnecessary
stinking ['stɪŋkɪŋ]	adj.发恶臭的 having a very strong, unpleasant smell
retention [rɪ'tenʃn]	n.保留 the action of keeping sth rather than losing it or stopping it
rudiment ['ruːdɪmənt]	n.雏形 a basic principle or element or a fundamental skill
lurk [lɜːk]	v.潜伏 to wait in a place of concealment especially for an evil purpose
synonym ['sɪnənɪm]	n.同义字 a word or expression that has the same or nearly the same meaning as another in the same language
enchant [ɪn'tʃɑːnt]	v.使迷惑 to influence by or as if by charms and incantation : BEWITCH
superlative [suː'pɜːlətɪv]	adj.最高的 surpassing all others : SUPREME
colossal [kə'lɒsl]	adj.巨大的 extremely large
tapper off	v.逐渐下降 to decrease gradually
align [ə'laɪn]	v.排列 to bring into line or alignment
roam [rəʊm]	v.漫步 to walk or travel around an area without any definite aim or direction
correspond [ˌkɒrə'spɒnd]	v.协调 to be the same as or match sth
abstain [əb'steɪn]	v.自制 to refrain deliberately and often with an effort of self-denial from an action or practice
dominion [də'mɪnɪən]	n.控制权 authority to rule ; control
overstep [ˌəʊvə'step]	v.逾越 to go beyond what is normal or allowed

blunder ['blʌndə (r)]	n. 大错 a stupid or careless mistake
end [end]	n. 目标 an aim or a purpose
vague [veɪg]	adj. 含糊的 not clear in a person's mind
quixotic [kwɪk'sɒtɪk]	adj. 狂想的 having or involving imaginative ideas or plans that are usually not practical
ordain [ɔː'deɪn]	v. 任命 to make sb a priest or minister of a Church
satire ['sætaɪə (r)]	n. 讽刺 a literary work holding up human vices and follies to ridicule or scorn
antidote ['æntidəʊt]	n. 矫正方法 something that relieves, prevents, or counteracts
supersede [ˌsuːpə'siːd]	v. 取代 to take the place, room, or position of
shabby ['ʃæbi]	adj. 破烂的 in poor condition because they have been used a lot
educe [ɪ'djuːs]	v. 引出 to bring out
coronation [ˌkɒrə'neɪʃn]	n. 加冕礼 a ceremony at which a CROWN is formally placed on the head of a new king or queen
vantage ['vɑːntɪdʒ]	n. 优势 a position giving a strategic advantage, commanding perspective, or comprehensive view
angelic [æn'dʒelɪk]	adj. 天使的 good, kind or beautiful ; like an angel
meridian [mə'rɪdiən]	n. 正午 the hour of noon : MIDDAY
corollary [kə'rɒləri]	n. 结果 a situation, an argument or a fact that is the natural and direct result of another one

whittle ['wɪtl]	v. 削弱 to reduce the size or number of sth
at stake	在危急关头 at issue : in jeopardy

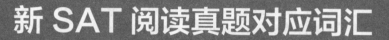

新 SAT 阅读真题对应词汇

Word List 37 20170506AS

shed [ʃed]	n. 小屋 a small simple building, usually built of wood or metal, used for keeping things in
sporadic [spəˈrædɪk]	adj. 零星的 happening only occasionally or at intervals that are not regular
shudder [ˈʃʌdə (r)]	v. 颤抖 to shake because you are cold or frightened, or because of a strong feeling
ponder [ˈpɒndə (r)]	v. 仔细考虑 to think about sth carefully for a period of time
fuss [fʌs]	v. 大惊小怪 unnecessary excitement, worry or activity
anteroom [ˈæntiruːm]	n. 接待室 an outer room that leads to another room and that is often used as a waiting room
obeisance [əʊˈbeɪsəns]	n. 敬礼 respect for sb/sth or willingness to obey sb
secular [ˈsekjələ (r)]	adj. 现世的（非精神的） not connected with spiritual or religious matters
paucity [ˈpɔːsətɪ]	n. 缺乏 a small amount of sth; less than enough of sth
inflate [ɪnˈfleɪt]	v. 使膨胀 to make sth appear to be more important or impressive than it really is
upheaval [ʌpˈhiːvl]	n. 巨变 a big change that causes a lot of confusion, worry and problems
rampage [ˈræmpeɪdʒ]	n./v. 横冲直撞 to move through a place in a group, usually breaking things and causing damage

refugee [ˌrefjuˈdʒiː]	n. 难民 a person who flees to a foreign country or power to escape danger or persecution
vaporize [ˈveɪpəraɪz]	v. 蒸发 to turn into gas
pin [pɪn]	v. 弄清楚 to explain or understand sth exactly
veneration [ˌvenəˈreɪʃn]	n. 尊敬 respect or awe inspired by the dignity, wisdom, dedication, or talent of a person
actuate [ˈæktʃueɪt]	v. 启动 to move to action
insurrection [ˌɪnsəˈrekʃn]	n. 暴动 a situation in which a large group of people try to take political control of their own country with violence
whither [ˈwɪðə (r)]	adv. 到哪里 where ; to which
misgiving [ˌmɪsˈgɪvɪŋ]	n. 担忧 to suggest doubt or fear to
stiffen [ˈstɪfn]	v. 变坚强；使僵硬 to make an attitude or idea stronger or more powerful ; to become stronger ; to make yourself or part of your body firm, straight and still, especially because you are angry or frightened
pummel [ˈpʌml]	v. 用拳头连续打 to keep hitting sb/sth hard, especially with your FISTS
impede [ɪmˈpiːd]	v. 阻碍 to delay or stop the progress of sth
empirical [ɪmˈpɪrɪkl]	adj. 以实验为依据的 based on experiments or experience rather than ideas or THEORIES
impervious [ɪmˈpɜːviəs]	adj. 透不过的 not allowing entrance or passage : IMPENETRABLE

新 SAT 阅读真题对应词汇

Word List 38 20170506NA

pal [pæl]	n. 朋友 a friend
primly [prɪmlɪ]	adv. 拘谨地 always behaving in a careful and formal way, and easily shocked by anything that is rude
profuse [prəˈfjuːs]	adj. 浪费的 produced in large amounts
downcast [ˈdaʊnkɑːst]	adj. 气馁的 sad or depressed
throb [θrɒb]	v. 震动 to beat or vibrate rhythmically
thrifty [ˈθrɪfti]	adj. 节俭的 careful about spending money and not wasting things
mercenary [ˈmɜːsənərɪ]	adj. 唯利是图的 only interested in making or getting money
censure [ˈsenʃə (r)]	v. 谴责 to criticize sb severely
sordid [ˈsɔːdɪd]	adj. 肮脏的 immoral or dishonest
liberal [ˈlɪbərəl]	adj. 开明的 willing to understand and respect other people's behaviour, opinions, etc.
execrate [ˈeksɪkreɪt]	v. 憎恨 to detest utterly
majesty [ˈmædʒəstɪ]	n. 权威 sovereign power, authority, or dignity
evince [ɪˈvɪns]	v. 表明 to show clearly that you have a feeling or quality

wherefore ['weəfɔ: (r)]	conj. 为何 for what reason or purpose : WHY
desolate ['desələt]	adj. 荒凉的 empty and without people，making you feel sad or frightened
initiate [ɪ'nɪʃieɪt]	v. 发动 to make sth begin
iota [aɪ'əʊtə]	n. 一点点 an extremely small amount
felicity [fə'lɪsətɪ]	n. 幸福 great happiness
eclipse [ɪ'klɪps]	v. 使黯然失色 to make sb/sth seem dull or unimportant by comparison
betray [bɪ'treɪ]	v. 泄漏 to show that something is true or exists，especially when it is not easily noticed
barrel ['bærəl]	v. 高速行进 to move very fast in a particular direction，especially in a way that you cannot control
lockstep ['lɒkstep]	n. 同步 in perfect or rigid often mindless conformity or unison
vice versa	adv. 反之亦然 used to say that the opposite of what you have just said is also true
communal [kə'mju:nl]	adj. 公有的 shared by，or for the use of，a number of people，especially people who live together
patrilocal [ˌpætrɪ'ləʊkəl]	adj. 居住在男方的 relating to residence with a husband's kin group or clan
hereditary [hə'redɪtrɪ]	adj. 遗传的 genetically transmitted or transmittable from parent to offspring
rancher ['rɑ:ntʃə (r)]	n. 农场主 a person who owns，manages or works on a ranch
overlap [ˌəʊvə'læp]	v. 重叠 to extend over or past and cover a part of
overtake [ˌəʊvə'teɪk]	v. 压倒；突然来袭 if sth unpleasant overtakes a person，it unexpectedly starts to happen and to affect them；to become greater in number，amount or importance than sth else

新 SAT 阅读真题对应词汇

Word List 39 20170603NA

leave off	v. 停止 STOP, CEASE
wear off	v. 逐渐减弱 if pain or the effect of something wears off, it gradually stops
slam [slæm]	v. 猛击 to put, push or throw sth into a particular place or position with a lot of force
fist [fɪst]	n. 拳头 a hand when it is tightly closed with the fingers bent into the PALM
baritone ['bærɪtəʊn]	n. 男中音 male singing voice of medium compass between bass and tenor
antic ['æntɪk]	n. 滑稽的动作 an attention-drawing often wildly playful or funny act or action : CAPER
groundbreaking ['graʊndbreɪkɪŋ]	adj. 创新的 making new discoveries ; using new methods
maze [meɪz]	n. 迷宫 a system of paths separated by walls or HEDGES built in a park or garden, that is designed so that it is difficult to find your way through
blindfold ['blaɪndfəʊld]	v. 遮眼 to cover sb's eyes
override [ˌəʊvə'raɪd]	v. 推翻 to use your authority to reject sb's decision, order, etc.
glare [gleə (r)]	n. 刺眼的强光; v. 怒视 a very bright, unpleasant light ; to look at sb/sth in an angry way
ardent ['ɑ:dnt]	adj. 热心的 very enthusiastic and showing strong feelings about sth/sb

sap [sæp]	v. 使大伤元气；n. 树液 to make sth/sb weaker ; to destroy sth gradually ; the liquid in a plant or tree that carries food to all its parts
blight [blaɪt]	v. 使枯萎 to spoil or damage sth, especially by causing a lot of problems
pique [piːk]	v. 使生气 to make sb annoyed or upset
deduce [dɪ'djuːs]	v. 演绎出 to form an opinion about sth based on the information or evidence that is available
assembly [ə'semblɪ]	n. 议会 a group of people who have been elected to meet together regularly and make decisions or laws for a particular region or country
fickle ['fɪkl]	adj. 变幻无常的 changing often and suddenly
remiss [rɪ'mɪs]	adj. 怠慢的 not giving sth enough care and attention
caravan ['kærəvæn]	n. 有篷顶的大车 a road vehicle without an engine that is pulled by a car, designed for people to live and sleep in, especially when they are on holiday/vacation
laden ['leɪdn]	adj. 装满的 heavily loaded with sth
unresponsive [ˌʌnrɪ'spɒnsɪv]	adj. 反应迟钝的 not reacting to sb/sth ; not giving the response that you would expect or hope for
constituent [kən'stɪtjuənt]	n. 选民 a person who lives, and can vote in a constituency
gut [gʌt]	n. 毅力；肠 the courage and determination that it takes to do sth difficult or unpleasant ; the tube in the body through which food passes when it leaves the stomach
vaccine ['væksiːn]	n. 疫苗 a substance that is put into the blood and that protects the body from a disease

signature ['sɪɡnətʃə (r)]	n.（基因）表达 something (as a tune, style, or logo) that serves to set apart or identify
obliterate [ə'blɪtəreɪt]	v. 删除 to remove all signs of sth, either by destroying or covering it completely
adjuvant ['ædʒʊvənt]	n. 助理员 serving to aid or contribute : AUXILIARY

新 SAT 阅读真题对应词汇

Word List 40 20170826NA

gesticulate [dʒeˈstɪkjuleɪt]	v. 做手势 to make movements with your hands and arms when you are talking, usually because you want to emphasize what you are saying or because you are excited
sheepish [ˈʃiːpɪʃ]	adj. 懦弱的 resembling a sheep in meekness, stupidity, or timidity
ordeal [ɔːˈdiːl]	n. 折磨 a difficult or unpleasant experience
formidable [ˈfɔːmɪdəbl]	adj. 可怕的 causing fear, dread, or apprehension
choke [tʃəʊk]	v. 使窒息 to make sb stop breathing by squeezing their throat
fright [fraɪt]	n./v. 惊骇 a feeling of fear
raucous [ˈrɔːkəs]	adj. 喧闹的 sounding loud and harsh
company [ˈkʌmpənɪ]	n. 人群 a group of people who work or perform together
grit [grɪt]	n. 坚韧 the courage and determination that makes it possible for sb to continue doing sth difficult or unpleasant
bit [bɪt]	n. 抑制 something that curbs or restrains
composure [kəmˈpəʊʒə (r)]	n. 镇静 a calmness or repose especially of mind, bearing, or appearance : SELF-POSSESSION
jeopardize [ˈdʒepərdaɪz]	v. 使陷危地 to risk harming or destroying sth/sb

subsist [səb'sɪst]	v. 活下去 to manage to stay alive, especially with limited food or money
militia [mə'lɪʃə]	n. 民兵 a group of people who are not professional soldiers but who have had military training and can act as an army
want [wɒnt]	n. 缺乏；需要 lack；to need sth
depress [dɪ'pres]	v. 使沮丧 to make sb sad and without enthusiasm or hope
depredation [ˌdeprə'deɪʃn]	n. 破坏 acts that cause harm or damage
despoil [dɪ'spɔɪl]	v. 掠夺 to strip of belongings, possessions, or value : PILLAGE
freeholder ['fri:həʊldə (r)]	n. 不动产的终身保有者 a person who owns the freehold of a building or piece of land
contend [kən'tend]	v. 竞争 to strive or vie in contest or rivalry or against difficulties : STRUGGLE
indebted [ɪn'detɪd]	adj. 感激的 grateful to sb for helping you
chalk up	v. 说闲话 to accept a failure or disappointment calmly and regard it as an experience that you can learn something from
cheek [tʃi:k]	n. 脸颊 either side of the face
polymath ['pɒlimæθ]	n. 博学者 a person who knows a lot about many different subjects
posit ['pɒzɪt]	v. 假设 to assume or affirm the existence of : POSTULATE
refrain [rɪ'freɪn]	v. 抑制 to stop yourself from doing sth, especially sth that you want to do
pass up	v. 拒绝 to let go by without accepting or taking advantage of
reciprocate [rɪ'sɪprəkeɪt]	v. 交换 to give and take mutually

preclude [prɪˈkluːd]	v. 阻止 to prevent something or make something impossible
fracture [ˈfræktʃə (r)]	v. 使断裂 to break or crack
shatter [ˈʃætə (r)]	v. 打碎 to suddenly break into small pieces
zoom [zuːm]	v. 快速移动 to move or go somewhere very fast
ledge [ledʒ]	n. 壁架 a narrow flat piece of rock that sticks out from a cliff
hurl [hɜːl]	v. 用力投掷 to throw sth/sb violently in a particular direction
breakneck [ˈbreɪknek]	adj. 非常危险的 very fast and dangerous
lubrication [ˌluːbrɪˈkeɪʃn]	n. 润滑 to make smooth or slippery
granular [ˈɡrænjələ (r)]	adj. 粒状的 consisting of small GRANULES
slosh [slɒʃ]	v. 在泥中荡 to walk noisily in water or mud

新 SAT 阅读真题对应词汇

Word List 41 20171007AS

stipple ['stɪpl]	v. 点彩 to paint or draw sth using small dots or marks
straggler ['stræglə (r)]	n. 流浪者 to wander from the direct course or way
adrift [ə'drɪft]	adj. 漂浮着 floating on the water without being tied to anything or controlled by anyone
careen [kə'ri:n]	v. 倾侧 to move forward very quickly especially in a way that is dangerous or uncontrolled
hunker ['hʌŋkə (r)]	v. 蹲下 to sit close to the ground on your heels with your knees bent up in front of you
tickle ['tɪkl]	v. 呵痒 to move your fingers on a sensitive part of sb's body in a way that makes them laugh
clamber ['klæmbə (r)]	v. 爬上 to climb or move with difficulty or a lot of effort, using your hands and feet
punch [pʌntʃ]	v. 用力按 to press buttons or keys on a computer, telephone, etc. in order to operate it
droop [dru:p]	v. 使下垂 to bend, hang or move downwards, especially because of being weak or tired
bristle ['brɪsl]	v. 使怒发冲冠 to suddenly become very annoyed or offended at what sb says or does
pendulous ['pendjələs]	adj. 下垂的 hanging down loosely and swinging from side to side

masquerade [ˌmæskəˈreɪd]	v. 伪装 to pretend to be sth that you are not
witchy [wɪtʃɪ]	adj. 巫婆的 a woman who is believed to have magic powers, especially to do evil things
writhe [raɪð]	v. 蠕动 to twist or move your body without stopping, often because you are in great pain
jockey [ˈdʒɒkɪ]	v. 耍花招 to deal shrewdly or fraudulently with
reprimand [ˈreprɪmɑːnd]	v. 谴责 to reprove sharply or censure formally usually from a position of authority
smash [smæʃ]	v. 打碎 to break sth
deflationary [ˌdiːˈfleɪʃənrɪ]	adj. 通货紧缩的 causing prices and the level of economic activity to become lower or stop increasing
gigantic [dʒaɪˈɡæntɪk]	adj. 巨大的 extremely large
rout [raʊt]	n. 溃败 a situation in which sb is defeated easily and completely in a battle or competition
unscathed [ʌnˈskeɪðd]	adj. 未受伤的 not hurt
casualty [ˈkæʒʊəltɪ]	n. 伤亡 an accident, especially one involving serious injury or loss of life
undergird [ˈʌndəˈɡɜːd]	v. 加强 to form the basis or foundation of : STRENGTHEN, SUPPORT
vaunt [vɔːnt]	n./v. 自吹自擂 to call attention to pridefully and often boastfully
outlay [ˈaʊtleɪ]	n./v. 花费 the act of expending
hegemonic [ˌheɡɪˈmɒnɪk]	adj. 支配的 preponderant influence or authority over others : DOMINATION

prestige [pre'sti:ʒ]	n. 声望 standing or estimation in the eyes of people
gummy ['gʌmɪ]	adj. 胶粘的 sticky or covered in gum
eternity [ɪ'tɜ:nətɪ]	n. 不朽 time without end
preeminently [p'ri:maɪnəntlɪ]	adv. 卓越地 having paramount rank, dignity, or importance
bondage ['bɒndɪdʒ]	n. 奴役 the state of being a slave or prisoner
unshackle ['ʌn'ʃækl]	v. 使获自由 to free from shackles
knit [nɪt]	v. 编织 to tie together
abyssal [ə'bɪsl]	adj. 深渊的 of or relating to the bottom waters of the ocean depths

新 SAT 阅读真题对应词汇

Word List 42 20171007NA

haggle ['hægl]	v. 争论 to argue with sb in order to reach an agreement, especially about the price of sth
squint [skwɪnt]	v. 眯着眼看 to look at sth with your eyes partly shut in order to keep out bright light or to see better
exclaim [ɪk'skleɪm]	v. 呼喊 to say sth suddenly and loudly
delicacy ['delɪkəsɪ]	n. 脆弱 the quality of being, or appearing to be, easy to damage or break
attune [ə'tjuːn]	v. 使协调 to bring into harmony : TUNE
transactive memory	n. 交互记忆
virtual ['vɜːtʃuəl]	adj. 虚拟的 almost or very nearly the thing described, so that any slight difference is not important
validate ['vælɪdeɪt]	v. 使生效 to make legally valid : RATIFY
erase [ɪ'reɪz]	v. 抹去 to remove sth completely
pinpoint ['pɪnpɔɪnt]	v. 准确地确定 to find and show the exact position of sb/sth or the exact time that sth happened
unstinting [ʌn'stɪntɪŋ]	adj. 慷慨的；无限制的 given or giving generously ; not restricting or holding back
rapacious [rə'peɪʃəs]	adj. 贪婪的 wanting more money or goods than you need or have a right to

tributary ['trɪbjətrɪ]	n. 支流；进贡品 a river or stream that flows into a larger river or a lake ; paying tribute to another to acknowledge submission, to obtain protection, or to purchase peace : SUBJECT
descendant [dɪ'sendənt]	n. 后代 proceeding from an ancestor or source
transplant [træns'plɑ:nt]	v. 移植 to take an organ, skin, etc. from one person, animal, part of the body, etc. and put it into or onto another
thrive [θraɪv]	v. 繁荣 to become, and continue to be, successful, strong, healthy, etc.
toil [tɔɪl]	n. 苦差事 hard unpleasant work that makes you very tired
dignity ['dɪgnətɪ]	n. 尊严 a sense of your own importance and value
reckon ['rekən]	v. 认为 to think sth or have an opinion about sth
sinew ['sɪnju:]	n. 肌肉 a strong band of tissue in the body that joins a muscle to a bone
caprice [kə'pri:s]	n. 反复无常 a sudden change in attitude or behaviour for no obvious reason
dictate [dɪk'teɪt]	v. 命令 to tell sb what to do, especially in an annoying way
suppress [sə'pres]	v. 镇压 to put down by authority or force : SUBDUE
yoke [jəʊk]	n. 奴役 harsh treatment or sth that restricts your freedom and makes your life very difficult to bear
taskmaster ['tɑ:skmɑ:stə (r)]	n. 监工 a person who gives other people work to do, often work that is difficult
bayonet ['beɪənət]	n. 刺刀 a long, sharp knife that is fastened onto the end of a RIFLE and used as a weapon in battle
slumber ['slʌmbə (r)]	n./v. 沉睡 sleep

overthrow [ˌəʊvəˈθrəʊ]	n./v. 打倒 to remove a leader or a government from a position of power by force
remonstrance [rɪˈmɒnstrəns]	n. 抗议 a protest or complaint
headlong [ˈhedlɒŋ]	adj. 轻率的 without thinking carefully before doing sth

新 SAT 阅读真题对应词汇

Word List 43 20171104NA

erudition [ˌeruˈdɪʃn]	n. 博学 great academic knowledge
indifference [ɪnˈdɪfrəns]	n. 冷漠 a lack of interest, feeling or reaction towards sb/sth
adorable [əˈdɔːrəbl]	adj. 可爱的 very attractive and easy to feel love for
benignant [bɪˈnɪgnənt]	adj. 仁慈的 serenely mild and kindly : BENIGN
self-absorbed [ˈselfəbˈsɔːbd]	adj. 自我陶醉的 only concerned about or interested in yourself
afflict [əˈflɪkt]	v. 使痛苦 to affect sb/sth in an unpleasant or harmful way
downtrodden [ˈdaʊntrɒdn]	adj. 受压迫的 suffering oppression
alimony [ˈælɪmənɪ]	n. 赡养费 an allowance made to one spouse by the other for support pending or after legal separation or divorce
nebulous [ˈnebjələs]	adj. 朦胧的 not developed or clear enough to describe: VAGUE
scarcity [ˈskeəsətɪ]	n. 缺乏 a situation in which there is not enough of something
privilege [ˈprɪvəlɪdʒ]	n. 特权 a special right or advantage that a particular person or group of people has
culminate [ˈkʌlmɪneɪt]	v. 在最后到达顶点 to end with a particular result, or at a particular point
partition [pɑːˈtɪʃn]	n./v. 区分 to divide sth into two parts

concatenate [kɒnˈkætɪneɪt]	v. 使连锁 to link together in a series or chain
captive [ˈkæptɪv]	adj. 被俘的；被迷住的 kept as a prisoner or in an enclosed space ; unable to escape ; not free to leave a particular place or to choose what you want do
codify [ˈkəʊdɪfaɪ]	v. 编成法典 to arrange laws , rules , etc. into a system
forestall [fɔːˈstɔːl]	v. 预先阻止 to prevent sth from happening or sb from doing sth by doing sth first
pre-ordained [ˌpriːɔːˈdeɪnd]	adj. 预先注定的 foreordain or determine beforehand
inflection [ɪnˈflekʃn]	n. 变音 a change in how high or low your voice is as you are speaking
emoji	n. 表情符号
veritable [ˈverɪtəbl]	adj. 真实的 being truly so called ; real or genuine
invasive [ɪnˈveɪsɪv]	adj. 侵入性的；攻击性的；扩散性的 invasive medical treatment involves putting something into the body or cutting into the body ; spreading very quickly and difficult to stop
indigenous [ɪnˈdɪdʒənəs]	adj. 本地的 belonging to a particular place rather than coming to it from somewhere else
abuse [əˈbjuːs]	v. 滥用 to make bad use of sth, or to use so much of sth that it harms your health
bane [beɪn]	n. 祸害 something that causes trouble and makes people unhappy
contortion [kənˈtɔːʃn]	n. 扭曲 the state of the face or body being twisted out of its natural shape
omniscient [ɒmˈnɪsiənt]	adj. 无所不知的 knowing everything

新 SAT 阅读真题对应词汇

Word List 44 20171202AS

megalith [ˈmeɡəlɪθ]	n. 巨石 a very large stone
escort [ˈeskɔːt]	v. 护送 to go with sb to protect or guard them or to show them the way
constellation [ˌkɒnstəˈleɪʃn]	n. 星座 a group of stars that forms a shape in the sky and has a name
firmament [ˈfɜːməmənt]	n. 天空 the sky
collar [ˈkɒlə (r)]	v. 拦住某人谈话 to stop sb in order to talk to them
astrology [əˈstrɒlədʒɪ]	n. 占星术 the study of the positions and movements of the stars and how they might influence people and events
crumb [krʌm]	n. 少量 a small fragment especially of something baked
blanch [blɑːntʃ]	v. 漂白 to take the color out of
rod [rɒd]	n. 竿 a long straight piece of wood，metal or glass
palsy [ˈpɔːlzɪ]	n. 麻痹 a condition marked by uncontrollable tremor of the body or a part
tedious [ˈtiːdiəs]	adj. 冗长乏味的 lasting or taking too long and not interesting
derivative [dɪˈrɪvətɪv]	adj. 非原创的 copied from sth else；not having new or original ideas
moult [məʊlt]	v. 脱毛 to lose feathers or hair before new feathers or hair grow

pupate [pjuːˈpeɪt]	v. 成蛹 to develop into a pupa
hinge on	v. 取决于 depend on
milieu [miːˈljɜː]	n. 周围环境 the social environment that you live or work in
writ [rɪt]	v. 写（过去式） old-fashioned past participle of write
superfluous [suːˈpɜːfluəs]	adj. 多余的 more than you need or want
cast aside	v. 废除 to remove or get rid of someone or something because you no longer want or need them
cone [kəʊn]	n. 圆锥体 a solid or hollow object with a round flat base and sides that slope up to a point
tamper [ˈtæmpə (r)]	v. 篡改 to make changes to sth without permission, especially in order to damage it
automata [ɔː ˈtɒmətə]	n. 自动机器 a mechanism that is relatively self-operating especially : ROBOT
forage [ˈfɒrɪdʒ]	v. 搜寻食物 to search for food
nascent [ˈnæsnt]	adj. 新生的 beginning to exist ; not yet fully developed
tart [tɑːt]	adj. 尖酸的 quick and unkind
emeritus [iˈmerɪtəs]	adj. 名誉退休的 used with a title to show that a person, usually a university teacher, keeps the title as an honour, although he or she has stopped working
outreach [ˈaʊtriːtʃ]	n. 扩大服务范围 the activity of an organization that provides a service or advice to people in the community, especially those who cannot or are unlikely to come to an office, a hospital, etc. for help
trajectory [trəˈdʒektərɪ]	n. 轨道 the curved path of sth that has been fired, hit or thrown into the air

新 SAT 阅读真题对应词汇

Word List 45 20171202NA

commend [kəˈmend]	v. 表扬 to praise sb/sth
overture [ˈəʊvətʃʊə (r)]	n. 示好 a suggestion or an action by which sb tries to make friends, start a business relationship, have discussions, etc. with sb else
scruple [ˈskruːpl]	n./v. 犹豫 a feeling that prevents you from doing sth that you think may be morally wrong
address [əˈdres]	n./v. 演说 to make a formal speech to a group of people
chuse [tʃuːz]	v. 选择 choose
likewise [ˈlaɪkwaɪz]	adv. 同样地 the same; in a similar way
quaint [kweɪnt]	adj. 奇怪的 unusual or different in character or appearance : ODD
itinerary [aɪˈtɪnərərɪ]	n. 既定的旅行路线 the route of a journey or tour or the proposed outline of one
facility [fəˈsɪlətɪ]	n. 能力 ease in performance : APTITUDE
impair [ɪmˈpeə (r)]	v. 损害 to damage sth or make sth worse
frown [fraʊn]	v. 不赞成 to give evidence of displeasure or disapproval by or as if by facial expression
observe [əbˈzɜːv]	v. 遵守（法律） to obey rules, laws, etc.

roster ['rɒstə (r)]	n. 花名册 a roll or list of personnel
cross [krɒs]	v. 反对（某人或计划、意愿） to oppose sb or speak against them or their plans or wishes
seesaw ['si:sɔ:]	v. 反复摇动 to move backward and forward or up and down
phenotype ['fi:nətaɪp]	n. 生物表现特征 the observable properties of an organism that are produced by the interaction of the genotype and the environment
trait [treɪt]	n. 特征 a particular quality in your personality
vertebrate ['vɜ:tɪbrət]	n. 脊椎 having a spinal column
delinquent [dɪ'lɪŋkwənt]	n. 流氓 showing a tendency to commit crimes
neurotic [njuə'rɒtɪk]	adj. 神经质的 not behaving in a reasonable, calm way, because you are worried about sth
protest ['prəutest]	v. 抗议 to say or do sth to show that you disagree with or disapprove of sth, especially publicly
void [vɔɪd]	adj. 空的 a large empty space
compound ['kɒmpaund]	v. 使恶化；n. 混合物 to make sth bad become even worse by causing further harm；a thing consisting of two or more separate things combined together
agglomerate [ə'glɒməreɪt]	v. 使凝聚 to gather into a ball, mass, or cluster
vacancy ['veɪkənsɪ]	n.（职位）空缺 a job that is available for sb to do
diffuse [dɪ'fju:s]	v. 扩散 to spread sth or become spread widely in all directions
mechanism ['mekənɪzəm]	n. 机理 a method or a system for achieving sth

alloy [ˈælɔɪ]	n. 合金 the degree of mixture with base metals : FINENESS
fission [ˈfɪʃn]	n. 分裂 a splitting or breaking up into parts
fusion [ˈfjuːʒn]	n. 熔合 the process or result of joining two or more things together to form one

新 SAT 阅读真题对应词汇

Word List 46 20180310AS

creep [kri:p]	v. 爬行 to move or develop very slowly
hem [hem]	v. 给 ... 缝边 to make a hem on sth
rafter ['rɑ:ftə (r)]	n. 椽 one of the sloping pieces of wood that support a roof
panic ['pænɪk]	n. 恐慌 a sudden feeling of great fear that cannot be controlled and prevents you from thinking clearly
thoroughfare ['θʌrəfeə (r)]	n. 大道 a public road or street used by traffic, especially a main road in a city or town
exhaust [ɪg'zɔ:st]	n. 废气；v. 耗尽 waste gases that come out of a vehicle, an engine or a machine ; to consume entirely
rev [rev]	v. 加速 when you rev an engine or it revs, it runs quickly
headline ['hedlaɪn]	n. 大标题 words set at the head of a passage or page to introduce or categorize
stool [stu:l]	n. 凳子 a seat usually without back or arms supported by three or four legs or by a central pedestal
satchel ['sætʃəl]	n. 小背包 a small bag often with a shoulder strap
contort [kən'tɔ:t]	v. 扭曲 to become twisted or make sth twisted out of its natural or normal shape
upset [ʌp'set]	v. 推翻；adj. 不高兴的 to force out of the usual upright, level, or proper position : OVERTURN ; to make sb/yourself feel unhappy, anxious or annoyed

stoop [stu:p]	v. 弯腰 to bend your body forwards and downwards
doggedly ['dɒgɪdlɪ]	adv. 顽固地 marked by stubborn determination
extirpate ['ekstəpeɪt]	v. 毁灭 to destroy or get rid of sth that is bad or not wanted
rapine ['ræpɪn]	n. 抢夺 the process of taking someone else's property using force
clemency ['klemənsɪ]	n. 仁慈 kindness shown to sb when they are being punished
internecine [ˌɪntə'ni:saɪn]	adj. 两败俱伤的 internecine fighting or struggles happen between members of the same group or nation
payoff ['peɪɔ:f]	n. 收益 the benefit you get from doing something
parasitize ['pærəsɪtaɪz]	v. 寄生于 to infest or live on or with as a parasite
imposter [ɪm'pɑstɚ]	n. 冒名顶替 one that assumes false identity or title for the purpose of deception
fledged [fledʒd]	adj. 成熟的 to rear until ready for flight or independent activity
fecundity [fɪ'kʌndətɪ]	n. 多产 fruitful in offspring or vegetation : PROLIFIC
peg [peg]	n. 桩；v. 钉住 a small usually cylindrical pointed or tapered piece (as of wood) used to pin down or fasten things or to fit into or close holes；to fasten sth with pegs
flesh out	v. 充实 to add more details to something in order to make it clear，more interesting
the saying goes	俗话说
plumbing ['plʌmɪŋ]	n. 垂直 exactly vertical or true
rift [rɪft]	n. 裂缝 a large crack or opening in the ground，rocks or clouds

rip apart	v. 撕裂 to tear something or be torn quickly and violently
rim [rɪm]	n. 边 the edge of sth that is circular
spew [spju:]	v. 喷出 to flow out quickly, or to make sth flow out quickly, in large amounts
convective [kən'vektɪv]	v. 对流的 to circulate (as air) by convection

Word List 47 20180310NA

border ['bɔ:də (r)]	v. 近似 to come very close to being sth, especially a strong or unpleasant emotion or quality
crush [krʌʃ]	v. 压碎；压垮 to break sth into small pieces or into a powder by pressing hard ; to destroy sb's confidence or happiness
heartbreaking ['hɑ:tbreɪkɪŋ]	adj. 令人心碎的 causing intense sorrow or distress
nostalgia [nɒ'stældʒə]	n. 怀旧 a feeling of sadness mixed with pleasure and affection when you think of happy times in the past
aisle [aɪl]	n. 过道 a passage between rows of seats in a church, theatre, train, etc.
wear off	v. 逐渐减弱 if pain or the effect of something wears off, it gradually stops
lighthearted ['laɪt'hɑ:tɪd]	adj. 轻松愉快的 happy and not worried about anything
aficionado [ə,fɪʃə'nɑ:dəʊ]	n. 狂热爱好者 a person who likes a particular sport, activity or subject very much and knows a lot about it
inhibition [,ɪnhɪ'bɪʃn]	n. 抑制 the act of restricting or preventing a process or an action
blindfold ['blaɪndfəʊld]	v. 遮眼，蒙骗 to prevent from seeing and especially from comprehending
traverse [trə'vɜ:s]	v. 穿过 to cross an area of land or water
stripe [straɪp]	n. 条纹 a long narrow line of colour, that is a different colour from the areas next to it

camouflage ['kæməflɑ:ʒ]	n. 伪装 behavior or artifice designed to deceive or hide
thermoregulation [θɜ:məʊˌregjʊˈleɪʃn]	n. 体温调节 the maintenance of a particular temperature of the living body
equatorial [ˌekwəˈtɔ:riəl]	adj. 赤道的 near the equator
breeze [bri:z]	n. 微风 a light wind
dispassionate [dɪsˈpæʃənət]	adj. 客观的 not influenced by emotion
acuteness [əˈkju:tnəs]	n. 敏锐 marked by keen discernment or intellectual perception especially of subtle distinctions : PENETRATING
shrewdness [ʃru:dnəs]	n. 敏锐 good at judging what people or situations are really like
bountiful ['baʊntɪfl]	adj. 丰富的 available in large quantities: ABUNDANT
desert ['dezət]	v. 抛弃 to stop using，buying or supporting sth
overreach [ˌəʊvəˈri:tʃ]	v. 贪功致败 to defeat (oneself) by seeking to do or gain too much
antibody ['æntibɒdɪ]	n. 抗体 a substance that the body produces in the blood to fight disease
immune [ɪˈmju:n]	adj. 免疫的 not affected by sth

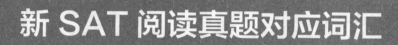

新 SAT 阅读真题对应词汇

Word List 48 20180505AS

foppish ['fɔpɪʃ]	adj. 浮夸的 devoted to or vain about his appearance or dress
seductive [sɪ'dʌktɪv]	adj. 引人注意的 attractive in a way that makes you want to have or do sth
withal [wɪ'ðɔ:l]	adv. 此外 in addtion
enshroud [ɪn'ʃraʊd]	v. 掩盖 to cover or surround sth completely so that it cannot be seen or understood
irremediably [ˌɪrɪ'mi:dɪəblɪ]	adv. 无可救药地 INCURABLE
dauber ['dɔ:bə]	n. 涂鸦者 an unskilled painter
implacable [ɪm'plækəbl]	adj. 执拗的 that cannot be changed
cache [kæʃ]	n. 存储 a hidden store of things such as weapons
eerie ['ɪərɪ]	adj. 怪诞的 strange, mysterious and frightening
lure [lʊə (r)]	n. 诱饵 the attractive qualities of sth
sauce [sɔ:s]	n. 调味汁 a thick liquid that is eaten with food to add flavour to it
volatile ['vɒlətaɪl]	adj. 易挥发的 readily vaporizable at a relatively low temperature
infest [ɪn'fest]	v. 侵扰 to exist in large numbers in a particular place, often causing damage or disease

indifferent [ɪnˈdɪfrənt]	adj. 漠不关心的 having or showing no interest in sb/sth
proclamation [ˌprɒkləˈmeɪʃn]	n. 宣言 an official statement about sth important that is made to the public；the act of making an official statement
delusion [dɪˈluːʒn]	n. 错觉 a false belief or opinion about yourself or your situation
reduce [rɪˈdjuːs]	v. 导致 to force to capitulate b : FORCE，COMPEL
phraseology [ˌfreɪziˈɒlədʒɪ]	n. 措辞 a manner of organizing words and phrases into longer elements : STYLE
enfranchisement [ɪnˈfræntʃɪzmənt]	n. 授予选举权 to give a group of people the right to vote
chastisement [ˈtʃæstɪzmənt]	n. 斥责 to censure severely : CASTIGATE
statute [ˈstætʃuːt]	n. 法律 a law
orator [ˈɒrətə (r)]	n. 演说家 a person who makes formal speeches in public or is good at public speaking
patrician [pəˈtrɪʃn]	n. 贵族 typical of the highest social class
testify [ˈtestɪfaɪ]	v. 作证 to make a statement based on personal knowledge or belief
industrious [ɪnˈdʌstriəs]	adj. 勤勉的 working hard；busy
covenant [ˈkʌvənənt]	n. 契约 a usually formal，solemn，and binding agreement : COMPACT
superscription [ˈsjuːpəˈskɪpʃən]	n. 题词 something written or engraved on the surface of，outside，or above something else : INSCRIPTION
deprive [dɪˈpraɪv]	v. 剥夺 to prevent sb from having or doing sth，especially sth important

新 SAT 阅读真题对应词汇

Word List 49 20180505NA

merriment ['merimənt]	n. 欢喜 happy talk, laughter and enjoyment
knick-knack ['nɪk næk]	n. 小装饰品 a small object used as a decoration
tapestry ['tæpəstrɪ]	n. 挂毯 heavy handwoven reversible textile used for hangings, curtains, and upholstery and characterized by complicated pictorial designs
stable ['steɪbl]	n. 马棚 a building in which horses are kept
champ [tʃæmp]	v. 不耐烦 to be unable to wait for something patiently
sleek [sli:k]	adj. 光滑的 smooth and shiny
gorgeous ['gɔːdʒəs]	adj. 华丽的 very beautiful and attractive
lounge [laʊndʒ]	v. 休闲 to stand, sit or lie in a lazy way
groom [gru:m]	n. 马夫 a person whose job is to feed and take care of horses
boudoir ['buːdwɑː(r)]	n. 化妆室 a woman's dressing room, bedroom, or private sitting room
bower ['baʊə(r)]	n. 闺房 a lady's private apartment in a medieval hall or castle
pang [pæŋ]	n. 剧痛 a brief piercing spasm of pain
gild [gɪld]	v. 镀金 to make sth look bright, as if covered with gold

bon-mot	n. 警句 a funny and clever remark
livery ['lɪvərɪ]	n. 制服 a special old-fashioned type of uniform that some people wear for their job, usually a job that involves serving people
matinee ['mætɪneɪ]	n. 白天音乐会 a musical or dramatic performance or social or public event held in the daytime and especially the afternoon
clinch [klɪntʃ]	v. 赢得 to succeed in achieving or winning sth
dame [deɪm]	n. 夫人 a title given to a woman as a special honour
woo [wu:]	v. 追求 to try to persuade a woman to love him and marry him
peer [pɪə (r)]	v. 盯着看 to look very carefully, especially because something is difficult to see
inscrutable [ɪn'skru:təbl]	adj. 难以理解的 not readily investigated, interpreted, or understood : MYSTERIOUS
feral ['ferəl]	adj. 野生的 living wild
tame [teɪm]	v. 驯化 reduced from a state of native wildness especially so as to be tractable and useful to humans : DOMESTICATED
nitty-gritty [ˌnɪti 'grɪtɪ]	n. 基本要素 the basic or most important details of an issue or a situation
slink [slɪŋk]	v. 溜走 to go or move stealthily or furtively
feline ['fi:laɪn]	n. 猫 a cat
morph [mɔ:f]	v. 改变 to change smoothly
jibe with	v. 相符
cede [si:d]	v. 放弃 to give sb control of sth or give them power, a right, etc., especially unwillingly

take issue	v. 不同意 DISAGREE
demarcation [ˌdiːmaːˈkeɪʃn]	n. 分界 a border or line that separates two things
avow [əˈvaʊ]	v. 承认 to say firmly and often publicly what your opinion is, what you think is true, etc.
quibble [ˈkwɪbl]	v. 说模棱两可的话 to evade the point of an argument by caviling about words
swindle [ˈswɪndl]	n./v. 诈骗 to cheat someone
indubitable [ɪnˈdjuːbɪtəbəl]	adj. 不容置疑的 too evident to be doubted : UNQUESTIONABLE
wickedness [ˈwɪkɪdnəs]	n. 邪恶 behaving badly in a way that is amusing
attorney [əˈtɜːnɪ]	n. 律师 a lawyer
transcendent [trænˈsendənt]	adj. 卓越的 going beyond the usual limits ; extremely great
functionary [ˈfʌŋkʃənərɪ]	n. 官员 a person with official duties
suffice it to say	无需多说
infrared [ˌɪnfrəˈred]	adj. 红外线的 having or using ELECTROMAGNETIC waves which are longer than those of red light in the SPECTRUM
exposure [ɪkˈspəʊʒə (r)]	n. 暴露 the act of showing sth that is usually hidden
pinprick [ˈpɪnprɪk]	n. 针孔 a very small hole in sth, especially one that has been made by a pin

新 SAT 阅读真题对应词汇

Word List 50 20180602NA

brilliancy ['brɪljənsɪ]	n. 出色 great skill or intelligence
encounter [ɪnˈkaʊntə (r)]	v. 不期而遇 a meeting, especially one that was not planned
withhold [wɪðˈhəʊld]	v. 抑制 to hold back from action : CHECK
affluence [ˈæfluəns]	n. 富足 an abundant flow or supply : PROFUSION
snatch [snætʃ]	v. 抢夺 to take sb/sth away from a person or place, especially by force ; to steal sth
wearing [ˈweərɪŋ]	adj. 疲倦的 that makes you feel very tired mentally or physically
ardour [ˈɑːdə]	n. 热情 very strong feelings of enthusiasm or love
bewitching [bɪˈwɪtʃɪŋ]	adj. 迷人的 so beautiful or interesting that you cannot think about anything else
headstrong [ˈhedstrɒŋ]	adj. 顽固的 a headstrong person is determined to do things their own way and refuses to listen to advice
deprecate [ˈdeprəkeɪt]	v. 不赞成 to feel and express strong disapproval of sth
consult [kənˈsʌlt]	v. 向 ... 请教，考虑，商议 to go to sb for information or advice ; to have regard to : CONSIDER ; to discuss sth with sb to get their permission for sth
part [pɑːt]	v. 使分开 to separate from or take leave of someone

relinquishment [rɪˈlɪŋkwɪʃmənt]	n. 放弃 GIVE UP
stamp out	v. 消灭 end or extinguish by forceful means
unspool [ʌnˈspuːl]	v. 展开 to execute or present artfully or gracefully
splice [splaɪs]	v. 接合 to join the ends of two pieces of rope by weaving them together
stumble [ˈstʌmbl]	n./v. 失误 to make a mistake or mistakes and stop while you are speaking, reading to sb or playing music
suture [ˈsuːtʃə (r)]	n./v. 缝合 a stitch or stitches made when sewing up a wound, especially after an operation
gracile [ˈgræsl]	adj. 细长的 SLENDER, SLIGHT
comeback [ˈkʌmbæk]	n. 恢复 if a person in public life makes a comeback, they start doing sth again which they had stopped doing, or they become popular again
herald [ˈherəld]	v. 宣布 to give notice of : ANNOUNCE
snout [snaʊt]	n. 鼻子 the long nose and area around the mouth of some types of animal, such as a pig
overrun [ˌəʊvəˈrʌn]	v. 蹂躏 to invade and occupy or ravage
observance [əbˈzɜːvəns]	n. 遵守 the practice of obeying a law
enjoin [ɪnˈdʒɔɪn]	v. 命令 to order or strongly advise sb to do sth
consent [kənˈsent]	n./v. 同意 to agree to sth or give your permission for sth
apprehend [ˌæprɪˈhend]	v. 理解；担忧 to become aware of ; to anticipate especially with anxiety, dread, or fear

armor [ˈɑːmə]	n. 盔甲 defensive covering for the body
dorsal [ˈdɔːsl]	adj. 后背的 on or connected with the back of a fish or an animal
regress [rɪˈgres]	v. 退回 to return to an earlier or less advanced form or way of behaving

新 SAT 阅读真题对应词汇

Word List 51 20181006AS

foul [faʊl]	v. 弄脏 to make sth dirty，usually with waste material
malevolent [məˈlevələnt]	adj. 有恶意的 having or showing a desire to harm other people
consolation [ˌkɒnsəˈleɪʃn]	n. 安慰 something that makes you feel less unhappy or disappointed
sear [sɪə (r)]	v. 烤焦 to burn the surface of sth in a way that is sudden and powerful
torrentially [təˈrenʃəlɪ]	adj. 奔流的 resembling a torrent in violence or rapidity of flow
ramble [ˈræmbl]	v. 漫步 to walk for pleasure，especially in the countryside
slap [slæp]	v. 拍打 to hit sb/sth with the flat part of your hand
volubility [vɒljʊˈbɪlɪtɪ]	n. 健谈 characterized by ready or rapid speech
babble [ˈbæbl]	v. 模糊不清地说话 to talk in a quick and excited way that is difficult to understand
bay [beɪ]	v. 吠叫 to make a long deep sound，especially while hunting
lame [leɪm]	adj. 跛足的 unable to walk well because of an injury to the leg or foot
goblin [ˈgɒblɪn]	n. 小妖精 a small ugly creature that likes to trick people or cause trouble
valor [ˈvælə]	n. 英勇 the quality of being very brave，especially in war
rostrum [ˈrɒstrəm]	n. 讲台 a small raised platform that a person stands on to make a speech，CONDUCT music，receive a prize，etc.

mammoth ['mæməθ]	adj. 巨大的 extremely large
torture ['tɔːtʃə (r)]	v. 折磨 to make sb feel extremely unhappy or anxious
induction [ɪn'dʌkʃn]	n. 入会，就职 the process of introducing sb to a new job, skill, organization, etc. ; a ceremony at which this takes place
panicky ['pænɪkɪ]	adj. 恐慌的 anxious about sth ; feeling or showing panic
quaver ['kweɪvə (r)]	n./v. 颤抖 a shaking sound in sb's voice
spillover	n. 溢出 the results or the effects of sth that have spread to other situations or places
compliance	n. 服从 the practice of obeying rules or requests made by people in authority
soak [səʊk]	v. 浸泡 to put sth in liquid for a time so that it becomes completely wet
boom [buːm]	n. 兴旺 a sudden increase in trade and economic activity ; a period of wealth and success
dip [dɪp]	v. 下沉 to go downwards or to a lower level
quirk [kwɜːk]	n. 怪 a little strange
canon ['kænən]	n. 正典 a generally accepted rule, standard or principle by which sth is judged
morphological [ˌmɔːfə'lɒdʒɪkl]	adj. 形态的 the form and structure of an organism or any of its parts
gradient ['greɪdɪənt]	n. 倾斜度 the degree to which the ground slopes
dusk [dʌsk]	n. 黄昏 the time of day when the light has almost gone, but it is not yet dark

新 SAT 阅读真题对应词汇

Word List 52 20181006NA

tap [tæp]	v.轻拍 to hit sb/sth quickly and lightly
swathe [sweɪð]	v.包裹 to wrap or cover sb/sth in sth
transit ['trænzɪt]	n.交通 a system of buses, trains, etc. that people use to travel around a particular city or area: TRANSPORTATION
grid [grɪd]	n.格子 a pattern of straight lines, usually crossing each other to form squares
clamp [klæmp]	v.夹住 to hold sth tightly, or fasten two things together
relay ['ri:leɪ]	v.转播 to receive and send on information, news, etc. to sb
poke [pəʊk]	n./v.戳 to quickly push your fingers or another object into sb/sth
insular ['ɪnsjələ (r)]	adj.狭隘的 only interested in your own country, ideas, etc. and not in those from outside
virile ['vɪraɪl]	adj.有男子气概的 a man who is virile is strong, active, and full of sexual energy
propagandist [ˌprɒpə'gændɪst]	n.宣传者 the spreading of ideas, information, or rumor for the purpose of helping or injuring an institution, a cause, or a person
keynote ['ki:nəʊt]	n.主旨 the central idea of a book, a speech, etc.
germinate ['dʒɜ:mɪneɪt]	v.使发芽 to begin to grow : SPROUT
skeptical ['skeptɪkəl]	adj.怀疑的 having doubts about something that other people think is true or right

新 SAT 阅读真题对应词汇

Word List 53 20181103NA

mosque [mɒsk]	n. 清真寺 a building in which Muslims worship
usher [ˈʌʃə (r)]	v. 引导 to take or show sb where they should go
tangle [ˈtæŋgl]	n./v. 缠绕 a twisted mass of threads，hair，etc. that cannot be easily separated
clap [klæp]	v. 拍手；啪地关上 to hit your open hands together
bark [bɑːk]	v. 吠；n. 树皮 when a dog barks，it makes a short loud sound；the outer covering of a tree
conditioned to	习惯于 accustomed to
splay [spleɪ]	v. 展开 to cause to spread outward
chin [tʃɪn]	n. 下巴 the part of the face below the mouth and above the neck
taper [ˈteɪpə (r)]	v. 逐渐变细 to become gradually narrower
tenure [ˈtenjə (r)]	n. 任期 the period of time when sb holds an important job，especially a political one
litigant [ˈlɪtɪgənt]	n. 诉讼当事人 a person who is making or defending a claim in a court of law
robe [rəʊb]	n. 长袍 a long loose outer piece of clothing，especially one worn as a sign of rank or office at a special ceremony
fealty [ˈfiːəltɪ]	n. 忠诚 a promise to be loyal to sb，especially a king or queen

ruling ['ru:lɪŋ]	n. 裁决 an official decision made by sb in a position of authority, especially a judge
infiltrate ['ɪnfɪltreɪt]	v. 渗透 to cause (as a liquid) to permeate something by penetrating its pores or interstices
hoary ['hɔ:rɪ]	adj. 灰白的 grey or white because a person is old
pitch [pɪtʃ]	v. 投掷 to throw sb/sth in a rough or forceful way
bat [bæt]	v. 用球棒打 to hit a ball with a bat, especially in a game of cricket or baseball
avidly ['ævɪdlɪ]	adv. 热望地 desirous to the point of greed : urgently eager : GREEDY
damn [dæm]	v. 诅咒 critical of sb/sth ; suggesting that sb is guilty
pup [pʌp]	n. 幼崽 a young animal of various SPECIES
fast [fɑ:st]	v. 禁食 to eat little or no food for a period of time, especially for religious reasons
bank [bæŋk]	v. 堆积 to form sth into piles
outfit ['aʊtfɪt]	v. 配备 to provide sb/sth with equipment or clothes for a special purpose
molt [məʊlt]	v. 换毛 to shed hair, feathers, shell, horns, or an outer layer periodically
rove [rəʊv]	v. 流浪 to travel from one place to another, often with no particular purpose
binge [bɪndʒ]	n. 狂饮 a short period of time when you do too much of a particular activity, especially eating or drinking alcohol
gear up	v. 准备 to get ready

soothsayer ['suːθseɪə (r)]	n. 算命者 a person who is believed to be able to tell what will happen in the future
tidbit ['tɪdbɪt]	n. 趣闻 a small piece of interesting news or information
tortoise ['tɔːtəs]	n. 迟缓的人 someone or something regarded as slow or laggard
slump [slʌmp]	n./v. 暴跌 to fall in price, value, number, etc., suddenly and by a large amount
nibble ['nɪbl]	v. 咬 to take small bites of sth, especially food
onslaught ['ɒnslɔːt]	n. 攻击 a strong or violent attack
ward off	v. 避开 to do something to try to protect yourself from something bad, such as illness, danger, or attack

新 SAT 阅读真题对应词汇

Word List 54 20181201AS

loquaciousness [ləˈkweɪʃəsnəs]	n. 话多 full of excessive talk : WORDY
overlay [ˌəʊvəˈleɪ]	v. 覆盖 to put sth on top of a surface so as to cover it completely
patchy [ˈpætʃɪ]	adj. 有补丁的 irregular or uneven in quality, texture, etc.
dally [ˈdælɪ]	v. 嬉戏 to act playfully
vie [vaɪ]	v. 争胜 to compete strongly with sb in order to obtain or achieve sth
ferret [ˈferɪt]	v. 搜寻 to discover information or to find sb/sth by searching thoroughly, asking a lot of questions, etc.
canvass [ˈkænvəs]	v. 兜揽生意 to go through (a district) or go to (persons) in order to solicit orders or political support or to determine opinions or sentiments
pilgrimage [ˈpɪlgrɪmɪdʒ]	n. 朝圣之旅 a journey to a holy place for religious reasons
transfix [trænsˈfɪks]	v. 刺穿 to pierce through with or as if with a pointed weapon : IMPALE
banter [ˈbæntə (r)]	n./v. 戏谑 friendly remarks and jokes
dull [dʌl]	adj. 钝的；无趣的 lacking in force, intensity, or sharpness ; not interesting or exciting
repertoire [ˈrepətwɑː (r)]	n. 全部剧目 all the plays, songs, pieces of music, etc. that a performer knows and can perform

lusty [ˈlʌstɪ]	adj. 健壮的 healthy and strong
commensurate [kəˈmenʃərət]	adj. 同量的 matching sth in size, importance, quality, etc.
collapse [kəˈlæps]	n./v. 倒塌 to fall down or fall in suddenly, often after breaking apart
tag [tæg]	n./v.（加）标签 a small piece of paper, fabric, plastic, etc. attached to sth to identify it or give information about it
strangle [ˈstræŋgl]	v. 压制 to prevent sth from growing or developing
bard [bɑːd]	n. 吟游诗人 a person who writes poems
pesky [ˈpeskɪ]	adj. 讨厌的 annoying
ingest [ɪnˈdʒest]	v. 摄取 to take food, drugs, etc. into your body, usually by swallowing
sterilize [ˈsterɪlaɪz]	v. 杀菌 to make something completely clean by killing any bacteria in it
enzyme [ˈenzaɪm]	n. 酶 a substance, usually produced by plants and animals, which helps a chemical change happen or happen more quickly, without being changed itself
profligate [ˈprɒflɪgət]	adj. 浪费的 using money, time, materials, etc. in a careless way
craft [krɑːft]	v. 精巧地制作 to make sth using special skills, especially with your hands
seniority [ˌsiːniˈɒrətɪ]	n. 前辈 the fact of being older or of a higher rank than others
glaringly [ˈgleərɪŋlɪ]	adv. 耀目地 obtrusively and often painfully obvious
bewilder [bɪˈwɪldə (r)]	v. 使迷惑 to confuse sb
steadfast [ˈstedfɑːst]	adj. 坚定的 not changing in your attitudes or aims

tempt [tempt]	v. 诱惑 to attract sb or make sb want to do or have sth，even if they know it is wrong
standstill ['stændstɪl]	n. 停滞 a situation in which all activity or movement has stopped
turf [tɜːf]	n. 草地 short grass and the surface layer of soil that is held together by its roots
burrow ['bʌrəʊ]	v. 掘洞穴 to make a hole or a tunnel in the ground by digging
nurture ['nɜːtʃə (r)]	v. 养育 to care for and protect sb/sth while they are growing and developing
fare [feə (r)]	v. 进展 to get along

新 SAT 阅读真题对应词汇

Word List 55 20181201NA

disembark [ˌdɪsɪmˈbɑːk]	v. 登陆 to leave a vehicle, especially a ship or an aircraft, at the end of a journey
gaze [geɪz]	v. 凝视 to look steadily at sb/sth for a long time
uncluttered [ˌʌnˈklʌtəd]	adj. 整洁的 not containing too many objects, details or unnecessary items
dock [dɒk]	v. 靠岸 if a ship docks or you dock a ship, it sails into a harbour and stays there
scrabble [ˈskræbl]	v. 乱抓，乱写 to scratch, claw, or grope about clumsily or frantically
peek [piːk]	v. 偷看 to look at sth quickly and secretly because you should not be looking at it
preoccupied [priˈɒkjupaɪd]	adj. 被迷住的 thinking and/or worrying continuously about sth so that you do not pay attention to other things
opponent [əˈpəʊnənt]	n. 对手 a person that you are playing or fighting against in a game, competition, argument, etc.
shill [ʃɪl]	n. 托，骗子 someone who pretends to be interested in something in order to persuade other people to buy it or do it
monger [ˈmʌŋgə]	n. 贩卖者，传播者 a person who attempts to stir up or spread something that is usually petty or discreditable
luddite [ˈlʌdaɪt]	n. 保守的人 a person who is opposed to new technology or working methods

fallout [ˈfɔːlaʊt]	n. 后果 the bad results of a situation or an action
curtail [kɜːˈteɪl]	v. 缩减 to reduce or limit something, especially something good
astral [ˈæstrəl]	adj. 星界的 of, relating to, or coming from the stars
rub [rʌb]	v. 摩擦 to press two surfaces against each other and move them backwards and forwards
prosaically [prəˈzeɪɪklɪ]	adv. 无想象力地 DULL, UNIMAGINATIVE
dub [dʌb]	v. 把 ... 叫作 to give sb/sth a particular name
syncopate [ˈsɪŋkəpeɪt]	v. 中间部分省略 omit a sound or letter in a word
partake [pɑːˈteɪk]	v. 参与 to take part in an activity
dredge [dredʒ]	v. 挖掘 to remove mud, stones, etc. from the bottom of a river, canal, etc. using a boat or special machine

历 史 词 汇

　　历史词汇（618 个）要么比较古老，要么是在法律或历史文献等特定文章里出现的特殊意思，在平时背诵单词的时候可能就没有注意到这个意思，比如 act（n. 法案），observe（v. 遵守法律）等。因此书中整理了从 OG 到可汗，从 PSAT 到 2018 年的所有的历史文章中比较常考的或者比较熟词僻义的历史词汇，好让大家集中歼灭。

历史词	中文释义	英文释义
abdicate	v. 正式放弃	give up
abject	adj. 悲惨的	terrible and without hope
abolish	v. 废除	to officially end a law, a system or an institution
abridge	v. 删减	to shorten in duration or extent
abuse	v. 滥用	improper or excessive use or treatment
account	n. 描述	a written or spoken description of sth that has happened
accrue to	v. 增加	to accumulate or be added periodically
acknowledgement	n. 承认	an act of accepting that sth exists or is true, or that sth is there
acquisition	n. 获得；贪欲	the act of getting sth, especially knowledge, a skill, etc.; the act of getting land, power, money etc.
actuate	v. 促使	to put into mechanical action or motion
addict	v. 使沉溺	to devote or surrender (oneself) to something habitually or obsessively
adduce	v. 举证	to provide evidence, reasons, facts, etc. in order to explain sth or to show that sth is true
administer	v. 管理	to manage and organize the affairs of a company, an organization, a country, etc.

历史词	中文释义	英文释义
affection	n. 爱	the feeling of liking or loving sb/sth very much and caring about them
affirmative	adj. 赞成的	showing that you mean yes
affix	v. 附加	to attach in any way
aggrandize	v. 夸大	to make great or greater
agitate	v. 使激动	to excite and often trouble the mind or feelings of : DISTURB
Alas	interj. 唉	used to show you are sad or sorry
alienate	v. 剥夺（权利）	to convey or transfer (as property or a right) usually by a specific act rather than the due course of law
alimony	n. 赡养费	money that a court orders someone to pay regularly to their former wife or husband after their marriage has ended
allegation	n. 断言	a positive assertion
allegiance	n. 忠诚	a person's continued support for a political party, religion, ruler, etc.
altar	n. 圣坛	a holy table or surface used in religious ceremonies
ambassador	n. 大使	an authorized representative or messenger
ambition	n. 雄心	an ardent desire for rank, fame, or power
amendment	n.（宪法）修正案	a statement of a change to the CONSTITUTION of the US
anarchy	n. 无政府主义	absence of government
annexation	n. 附加	to attach
annihilation	n. 毁灭	to destroy something or someone completely
anthem	n. 圣歌	a song or hymn of praise or gladness
appall	v. 惊骇	to shock or offend someone very much
appeal to	v. 上诉	to make a formal request to a court of law or to sb in authority for a judgement or a decision to be changed

历史词	中文释义	英文释义
appoint	v. 任命	to name officially
apprehend	v. 理解；担忧	to become aware of ; to anticipate especially with anxiety, dread, or fear
approbation	n. 许可	approval or agreement
arbitrary	adj. 专制的	not restrained or limited in the exercise of power
archbishop	n. 大主教	a bishop at the head of an ecclesiastical province or one of equivalent honorary rank
arrest	v. 阻止	to bring to a stop
article	n. 条款	a stipulation in a document (as a contract or a creed)
ascertain	v. 确定	to make certain, exact, or precise
aspiration	n. 渴望	a strong desire to have or do sth
assail	v. 质问	to attack violently with blows or words
assemble	v. 集会	to bring together
Assembly	n. 议会	a group of people who have been elected to meet together regularly and make decisions or laws for a particular region or country
assert	v. 主张拥有	to state or declare positively and often forcefully or aggressively
association	n. 协会	a connection or relationship between people or organizations
assumption	n. 假设	a belief or feeling that sth is true or that sth will happen, although there is no proof
asunder	adv. 成碎片	into pieces ; apart
asylum	n. 避难所	a place of retreat and security : SHELTER
attain	v. 达成	to succeed in getting sth, usually after a lot of effort
attend	v. 出席	to be present at an event
attribute to	v. 归因于	to believe or say that a situation or event is caused by something

历史词	中文释义	英文释义
authorize	v. 授权给	to give official permission for sth, or for sb to do sth
avow	v. 承认	to say firmly and often publicly what your opinion is, what you think is true, etc.
banish	v. 流放	to require by authority to leave a country
baronage	n. 男爵的总称	the whole body of barons or peers : NOBILITY
base	adj. 卑鄙的	not moral
bayonet	n. 刺刀	a long, sharp knife that is fastened onto the end of a RIFLE and used as a weapon in battle
be concerned in	v. 关注	involved/affected
bear	v. 有	to have
beckon	v. 吸引	to give sb a signal using your finger or hand, especially to tell them to move nearer or to follow you
benefactor	n. 捐助者	someone who helps a person or organization by giving them money
benefit	n. 利益	something that promotes well-being : ADVANTAGE
benevolence	n. 善意	an act of kindness
bestow	v. 给予	to give sth to sb, especially to show how much they are respected
bias	n. 偏见	a strong feeling in favour of or against one group of people, or one side in an argument, often not based on fair judgement
bill	n. 法案	a written suggestion for a new law that is presented to a country's parliament so that its members can discuss it
black code	n. 黑人法典	restricting African Americans' freedom and of compelling them o work in a labor economy based on low wages or debt
blest	adj. 保佑的	a past tense and a past participle of bless
bond	n. 契约	a binding agreement : COVENANT
bondage	n. 奴役	the state of being a slave or prisoner

历史词	中文释义	英文释义
brethren	n. 同胞	used to talk to people in church or to talk about the members of a male religious group
burden	n. 负担	a duty, responsibility, etc. that causes worry, difficulty or hard work
burthen	n. 负担	burden
cabinet	n. 内阁	a group of the most important government ministers, or ADVISERS to a president, responsible for advising and deciding on government policy
calamity	n. 灾难	an event that causes great harm or damage
calculate	v. 深思熟虑	to reckon by exercise of practical judgment : ESTIMATE
call upon	v. 要求	REQUIRE, OBLIGE
candid	adj. 公平的	free from bias, prejudice, or malice : FAIR
caprice	n. 反复无常	a sudden, impulsive, and seemingly unmotivated notion or action
cause	n. 原因；事业	a reason for an action or condition : MOTIVE ; a principle or movement militantly defended or supported
cavalier	adj. 漫不经心的	not caring enough about sth important or about the feelings of other people
cement	v. 巩固	to make a relationship, an agreement, etc. stronger
censure	v. 谴责	strong criticism
champion	v. 支持	to act as militant supporter of : UPHOLD, ADVOCATE
chaos	n. 混乱	a state of complete confusion and disorder
character	n. 个性	a feature used to separate distinguishable things into categories also
charge	v. 指控	to accuse sb publicly of doing sth wrong or bad
charity	n. 慈善	an organization for helping people in need
check	v. 阻止	to control sth ; to stop sth from increasing or getting worse

历史词	中文释义	英文释义
cherish	v. 怀有	to entertain or harbor in the mind deeply and resolutely
claim	v. 要求权利	to ask for especially as a right
cleave to	v. 使分开	to separate into distinct parts and especially into groups having divergent views
cloak	v. 遮掩	to cover or hide sth
cloture	n. 讨论终结	a legislative procedure for ending a debate and taking a vote
code	n. 法典	a system of laws or written rules that state how people in an institution or a country should behave
coerce	v. 强迫	to force sb to do sth by using threats
command	n. 命令	an order given
commend	v. 表扬	to praise sb/sth, especially publicly
commit	v. 犯罪	do something illegal/wrong
commodity	n. 商品	an economic good
Commonwealth	n. 共和国	used in the official names of, and to refer to, some states of the US (Kentucky, Massachusetts, Pennsylvania and Virginia)
commotion	n. 暴乱	sudden noisy confusion or excitement
compassion	n. 同情	sympathetic consciousness of others' distress together with a desire to alleviate it
compendium	n. 摘要	a brief summary of a larger work or of a field of knowledge : ABSTRACT
complacency	n. 自满	self-satisfaction especially when accompanied by unawareness of actual dangers or deficiencies
compromise	n. 妥协	an agreement made between two people or groups in which each side gives up some of the things they want so that both sides are happy at the end
compulsion	n. 强迫	a legal or other obligation to do something
concede	v. 让步	to accept as true, valid, or accurate

170

历史词	中文释义	英文释义
concentration	n. 专心	the ability to direct all your effort and attention on one thing, without thinking of other things
conduct	n. 行为	a person's behaviour in a particular place or in a particular situation
confederation	n. 邦联	an organization consisting of countries, businesses, etc. that have joined together in order to help each other
confer on	v. 授予	to give sb an award, a university degree or a particular honour or right
confess	v. 忏悔	to admit sth that you feel ashamed or embarrassed about
confided	adj. 信任的	to have confidence : TRUST
confound	v. 使混淆	to confuse and surprise sb
confrontation	n. 对抗	a situation in which there is an angry disagreement between people or groups who have different opinions
congress	n. 议会	the name of the group of people who are elected to make laws, in the US consisting of the SENATE and the HOUSE OF REPRESENTATIVES
conjecture	v. 猜测	an opinion or idea that is not based on definite knowledge and is formed by guessing
conquest	v. 征服	the act or process of conquering
conscience	n. 良心	the part of your mind that tells you whether your actions are right or wrong
conscientious	adj. 有责任心的	taking care to do things carefully and correctly
consecration	n. 神圣化	to officially state in a special religious ceremony that a place or building is holy and can be used for religious purposes
consign	v. 委托	to give, transfer, or deliver into the hands or control of another
consolidated	adj. 统一的	to join together into one whole : UNITE
constituent	n. 选民	a person who lives, and can vote in a constituency

历史词	中文释义	英文释义
constitute	v. 制定	SET UP, ESTABLISH: as a: ENACT
constitution	n. 宪法；体质	the system of laws and basic principles that a state, a country or an organization is governed by; the physical makeup of the individual especially with respect to the health, strength, and appearance of the body
consult	v. 查阅	seek
contend	v. 竞争	to strive in debate: ARGUE
contract	n. 契约	to make a legal agreement with sb for them to work for you or provide you with a service
contribution	n. 捐助	something that you do that helps to achieve something or to make it successful
convenient	adj. 方便的	useful, easy or quick to do
conviction	n. 坚信	a strong opinion or belief
convulsion	n. 动乱	a sudden important change that happens to a country or an organization
cordial	adj. 热忱的	pleasant and friendly
Coronation	n. 王冠（上帝）	a ceremony at which a CROWN is formally placed on the head of a new king or queen
corruption	n. 腐败	dishonest or illegal behaviour, especially of people in authority
counsellor	n. 顾问	a person who has been trained to advise people with problems, especially personal problems
countenance	n. 面容；v. 支持	a person's face or their expression; to support sth or agree to sth happening
course	n. 行动	progression through a development or period or a series of acts or events
cradle	n. 摇篮	a small bed for a baby which can be pushed gently from side to side
Creator	n. 上帝	God
Crown	n. 上帝	God
culpability	n. 有罪	GUILTY, CRIMINAL

历史词	中文释义	英文释义
custom	n. 风俗	an accepted way of behaving or of doing things in a society or a community
dainty	adj. 优雅的	small and attractive in a delicate way
deceive	v. 欺骗	CHEAT
declamation	n. 激情演说	to speak loudly, sometimes with actions, so that people notice you
declaration	n. 宣告	an official or formal statement, especially about the plans of a government or an organization
declare	v. 宣布	to say sth officially or publicly
decline	v. 婉拒	to refuse politely to accept or to do sth
decree	v. 裁定	to decide, judge or order sth officially
dedication	n. 奉献	an act or rite of dedicating to a divine being or to a sacred use
defend	v. 辩护	to say or write sth in support of sb/sth that has been criticized
degenerate	v. 堕落	one degraded from the normal moral standard
degradation	n. 堕落	decline to a low, destitute, or demoralized state
delegate	v. 委派 ... 为代表	to give part of your work, power or authority to sb in a lower position than you
delicate	adj. 脆弱的	easily damaged or broken
delinquent	n. 流氓	sb showing a tendency to commit crimes
demand	n. 要求	to ask for sth very firmly
democracy	n. 民主	a system of government in which all the people of a country can vote to elect their representatives
demoralize	v. 使士气低落	to make sb lose confidence or hope
depredation	n. 掠夺	acts that cause harm or damage
depress	v. 使沮丧	to make sb sad and without enthusiasm or hope
designate	v. 任命	to choose or name sb for a particular job or position
desolate	adj. 荒凉的	empty and without people, making you feel sad or frightened

历史词	中文释义	英文释义
despoil	v. 掠夺	to strip of belongings, possessions, or value : PILLAGE
despotism	n. 独裁	a system of government in which the ruler has unlimited power : ABSOLUTISM
destined to	adj. 命中注定的	certain to do something or certain to happen in the future
destiny	n. 命运	what happens to sb or what will happen to them in the future, especially things that they cannot change or avoid
destitute	adj. 困穷的	without money, food and the other things necessary for life
devote	v. 致力于	to spend a lot of time or effort doing something: DEDICATE
devout	adj. 虔诚的	devoted to religion or to religious duties or exercises
dictate	v. 命令	to tell sb what to do, especially in an annoying way
dictator	n. 独裁者	a person granted absolute emergency power
dignity	n. 尊严	a calm and serious manner that deserves respect
disappoint	v. 使失望	to fail to meet the expectation or hope of : FRUSTRATE
discipline	n. 纪律	the ability to control your behaviour or the way you live, work, etc.
discord	n. 不一致	disagreement ; quarrelling
discretion	n. 慎重	care in what you say or do, in order to keep sth secret or to avoid causing embarrassment or difficulty for sb
discriminate	v. 区别对待	to distinguish by discerning or exposing differences
dissent	v. 不同意	to have or express opinions that are different from those that are officially accepted
disenthrall	v. 释放	make free
disfranchise	v. 剥夺 ... 的投票权	to deprive of a privilege, an immunity, or a right of citizenship, especially the right to vote

历史词	中文释义	英文释义
dispose of	v. 处理掉	to get rid of
disposed to	v. 倾向于	to make someone more likely to have particular feelings or thoughts
disposition	n. 性情	the natural qualities of a person's character
disproportion	n. 不均衡	lack of proportion, symmetry, or proper relation : DISPARITY
disputable	adj. 可被质疑的	that can or should be questioned or argued about
dissipate	v. 驱散	to gradually become or make sth become weaker until it disappears
dissolve	v. 终止	to officially end a marriage, business agreement or parliament
divine	v. 预言	to find out sth by guessing
doctrine	n. 教条	a belief or set of beliefs held and taught by a Church, a political party, etc.
domestic	adj. 家庭的	used in the home ; connected with the home or family
dominion	n. 主权	authority to rule ; control
downtrodden	adj. 被践踏的	suffering oppression
draft	n. 草案	a rough written version of sth that is not yet in its final form
drudgery	n. 苦差事	hard boring work
due	adj. 应该的	owed sth ; deserving sth
duty	n. 责任	something that you feel you have to do because it is your moral or legal responsibility
educe	v. 引出	to bring out
egotist	n. 自大者	an exaggerated sense of self-importance
emancipation	n. 解放	the process of giving freedom and rights to someone: LIBERATION
embitter	v. 使受苦	to make sb feel angry or disappointed about sth over a long period of time

历史词	中文释义	英文释义
embody	v. 具体表达	to be the best possible example of a particular idea, quality, or principle
embroil	v. 使卷入	to involve sb/yourself in an argument or a difficult situation
empress	n. 女皇	a woman who is the ruler of an empire
enclave	n. 被包围的领土	an area of a country or city where the people have a different religion, culture or NATIONALITY from those who live in the country or city that surrounds it
encomium	n. 赞美	glowing and warmly enthusiastic praise
encroachment	n. 侵蚀	to enter by gradual steps or by stealth into the possessions or rights of another
end	n. 目标	an aim or a purpose
endeavor to	v. 努力	to strive to achieve or reach
endow	v. 赋予	to naturally have a particular feature, quality, etc.
enfranchisement	n. 授予选举权	to give a group of people the right to vote
enjoin	v. 命令	to order or strongly advise sb to do sth
enmity	n. 敌意	feelings of hatred towards sb
enterprise	n. 企业	a company or business
entertain	v. 怀有	to keep, hold, or maintain in the mind
enthrone	v. 加冕	to make someone the new king, queen, or BISHOP in a formal ceremony
entitle to	v. 给予名称	to give a title to : DESIGNATE
entreat	v. 恳求	to ask sb to do sth in a serious and often emotional way
epoch	n. 新纪元	a period of time in history, especially one during which important events or changes happen
equality	n. 平等	the fact of being equal in rights, status, advantages, etc.
erect	v. 建立	to create or establish sth

历史词	中文释义	英文释义
espouse	v. 支持	to give your support to a belief, policy etc.
esteem	v. 尊敬	great respect and admiration
eternity	n. 不朽	time without end, especially life continuing without end after death
evade	v. 躲避	escape
evangel	n. 福音	the Christian gospel
evil	n. 邪恶	enjoying harming others
evince	v. 表明	to display clearly : REVEAL
exaction	n. 勒索	excessive or unjust demand ; extortion
Excellency	n. 阁下	a title used when talking to or about sb who has a very important official position, especially an AMBASSADOR
exclaim	v. 呼喊	to say sth suddenly and loudly, especially because of strong emotion or pain
execrate	v. 憎恨	to detest utterly
executioner	n. 刽子手	a public official whose job is to execute criminals
exercise	v. 运用	to use your power, rights or personal qualities in order to achieve sth
exert	v. 发挥	to use power or influence to affect sb/s
exertion	n. 运用	the use of power to make sth happen
expatriate	v. 流放	BANISH, EXILE
expedient	n. 权宜之计	an action that is useful or necessary for a particular purpose, but not always fair or right
exempt	v. 豁免	allowed to ignore something such as a rule, obligation, or payment
extenuation	n. 减轻	to lessen or attempt to lessen the magnitude or seriousness of, especially by providing partial excuses
faction	n. 派别	party spirit especially when marked by dissension

历史词	中文释义	英文释义
factious	adj. 好搞派系的	of, relating to, produced by, or characterized by internal dissension
faculty	n. 能力	any of the physical or mental abilities that a person is born with
fallacious	adj. 谬误的	wrong; based on a false idea
fancy	v. 想象	to believe or imagine sth
fealty	n. 忠诚	a promise to be loyal to sb, especially a king or queen
feeble	adj. 微弱的	very weak
felicity	n. 快乐	great happiness
feminity	n. 女权	FEMININITY
fetter	v. 束缚；n. 脚镣	to restrict sb's freedom to do what they want; chains that are put around a prisoner's feet
Flag	n. 旗帜	used to refer to a particular country or organization and its beliefs and values
flagrant	adj. 恶名昭著的	shocking because it is done in a very obvious way and shows no respect for people, laws, etc.
folly	n. 愚蠢	lack of good sense or normal prudence and foresight
foothold	n. 立足点	a position usable as a base for further advance
formidable	adj. 可怕的	causing fear, dread, or apprehension
frame	v. 制定	to put or make a frame or border around sth
free	v. 使自由	to allow sb to leave prison or somewhere they have been kept against their WILL
freeholder	n. 不动产的终身保有者	a person who owns the freehold of a building or piece of land
Freudian	adj. 弗洛伊德学说的	connected with the ideas of Sigmund Freud about the way the human mind works, especially his theories of SUBCONSCIOUS sexual feelings
functionary	n. 官员	a person with official duties
general government	n. 联合政府	federacy

历史词	中文释义	英文释义
give me leave to	v. 请允许我…	
gloom	v. 忧沉	a feeling of being sad and without hope
gospel	n. 福音	one of the four books in the Bible about the life and teaching of Jesus
grand council	n. 议会	
grant	v. 允许	to agree to give sb what they ask for, especially formal or legal permission to do sth
gratify	v. 使满足	to please or satisfy sb
gratitude	n. 感谢	the feeling of being grateful and wanting to express your thanks
gravitation	n. 重力	a force of attraction that causes objects to move towards each other
grievance	n. 抱怨	the formal expression of a grievance : COMPLAINT
gross	adj.（罪行）严重的	very obvious and unacceptable
guarantee	v. 保证	to promise to do sth ; to promise sth will happen
haggard	adj. 野性的	wild in appearance
headlong	adj. 鲁莽的	without thinking carefully before doing sth
heat	n. 狂热	strong feelings, especially of anger or excitement
heedless	adj. 不谨慎的	not paying careful attention to sb/sth
hereafter	adv. 此后	from this time ; in future
heretic	n. 异端者	a dissenter from established religious dogma
hither	adv. 向此处	to this place
hitherto	adv. 至今	until now
hold	v. 持有	to have possession or ownership of or have at one's disposal
House of Commons	n. 议会	
House of representative	n. 议会	

历史词	中文释义	英文释义
idle	adj. 闲散的	not spent doing work or sth particular
ignorance	n. 无知	a lack of knowledge or information about sth
illuminate	v. 阐明	to make sth clearer or easier to understand
imbecility	n. 智力低下者	something that is foolish or nonsensical
inflammatory	adj. 煽动的	intended to cause very strong feelings of anger
immure	v. 监禁	IMPRISON
impartiality	n. 公正	not partial or biased
imperial	adj. 帝国的	connected with an empire
impose	v. 出台（法律）；把 ... 强加于	to introduce a new law, rule, tax, etc. ; to force sb/sth to have to deal with sth that is difficult or unpleasant
imposition	n. 课税	the act of introducing sth such as a new law or rule, or a new tax
imputation	n. 归罪	to say, often unfairly, that someone is responsible for something bad or has bad intentions
in vain	adv. 徒劳	no end
inalienable	adj. 不能剥夺的	incapable of being alienated, surrendered, or transferred
incantation	n. 咒语	a use of spells or verbal charms spoken or sung as a part of a ritual of magic
incidental	adj. 偶然的	being likely to ensue as a chance or minor consequence
inclination	n. 倾向	natural disposition
inculcate	v. 反复灌输	to cause sb to learn and remember ideas, moral principles, etc.
indebted	adj. 感激的	grateful to sb for helping you
independent	adj. 不受约束的	not subject to control by others
indispensable	adj. 不可缺少的	essential ; too important to be without
indissoluble	adj. 坚固的	incapable of being annulled, undone, or broken : PERMANENT

历史词	中文释义	英文释义
indulgent	adj. 纵容的	allowing some to do or have what they want
inequality	n. 不平等	the quality of being unequal or uneven
inexcusable	adj. 不可宽赦的	too bad to accept or forgive
infallible	adj. 绝无错误的	never wrong ; never making mistakes
infiltrate	v. 渗透	to cause (as a liquid) to permeate something by penetrating its pores or interstices
inflict	v. 折磨	to cause something unpleasant to happen
ingenuity	n. 创造力	the ability to solve problems in new and clever ways
inhabitant	n. 居住者	one that occupies a particular place regularly, routinely, or for a period of time
injustice	n. 不公平	unfair
inquisition	n. 质问	a series of questions that sb asks you, especially when they ask them in an unpleasant way
insolent	adj. 无礼的	extremely rude and showing a lack of respect
inspire	v. 激发	to give sb the desire, confidence or enthusiasm to do sth well
institute	v. 制定	to establish in a position or office
institution	n. 机构	an established organization or corporation (as a bank or university) especially of a public character
institutionalize	v. 使制度化	to make sth become part of an organized system, society or culture, so that it is considered normal
insulate	v. 隔离	to place in a detached situation : ISOLATE
insurrection	n. 叛乱	a situation in which a large group of people try to take political control of their own country with violence
integrity	n. 诚实	the quality of being honest and having strong moral principles
intelligible	adj. 易理解的	that can be easily understood
intercourse	v. 交流	exchange especially of thoughts or feelings : COMMUNION

历史词	中文释义	英文释义
interfere with	v. 妨碍	to interpose in a way that hinders or impedes
interposition	n. 介入	to place in an intervening position
intervene	v. 阻碍；干涉	to come in or between by way of hindrance or modification
inventiveness	n. 有创造力	adept or prolific at producing inventions : CREATIVE
inveteracy	n. 根深蒂固	the quality or state of being obstinate or persistent : TENACITY
invidious	adj. 惹人不快的	unpleasant and unfair ; likely to offend sb or make them jealous
invoke	v. 祈求	to petition for help or support
issue	n. 话题	an important topic that people are discussing or arguing about
jeopardize	v. 危害	to risk harming or destroying sth/sb
jesuitically	adv. 上帝地	a member of the Roman Catholic Society of Jesus founded by St. Ignatius Loyola in 1534 and devoted to missionary and educational work
jubilee	n. 纪念日	a special anniversary of an event, especially one that took place 25 or 50 years ago ; the celebrations connected with it
judge	v. 判断	to form an opinion about through careful weighing of evidence and testing of premises
judicial	adj. 审判上的	connected with a court of law, a judge or legal judgement
judiciary	n. 司法制度	a system of courts of law
justice	n. 正义	the fair treatment of people
justify	v. 证明合法	to show that sb/sth is right or reasonable
lamentable	adj. 哀伤的	expressing grief : MOURNFUL
lay down	v. 放弃；规定	to give up ; to assert or command dogmatically
layoff	n. 解雇	the act of laying off an employee or a workforce also : SHUTDOWN

历史词	中文释义	英文释义
legacy	n. 遗产	a gift by will especially of money or other personal property : BEQUEST
legal	adj. 合法的	allowed or required by law
legislation	n. 立法	a law or set of laws
legislative	adj. 有立法权的	connected with the act of making and passing laws
legislature	n. 立法机关	a group of people who have the power to make and change laws
legitimacy	n. 合法	the fact that something is legal
let	v. 允许	allow
libber	n. 解放论者	a person who supports a liberation movement especially for women
libel	n./v. 诽谤	the illegal act of writing things about someone that are not true
liberal	adj. 自由的	supporting or allowing gradual political and social changes
liberator	n. 解放者	to set at liberty : FREE
liberty	n. 自由	the quality or state of being free
licentious	adj. 淫荡的	behaving in a way that is considered sexually immoral
liken	v. 比作	to compare one person or thing to another and say they are similar
Lord	n. 上帝	a title used to refer to Christ
mainspring	n. 主要原因	the chief or most powerful motive, agent, or cause
malignant	adj. 有恶意的	having or showing a strong desire to harm sb
manifest	v. 证明	to make evident or certain by showing or displaying
masculine	adj. 男性的	having qualities appropriate to or usually associated with a man
maternal	adj. 母系的	inherited or derived from the female parent

183

历史词	中文释义	英文释义
maxim	n. 格言	a general truth, fundamental principle, or rule of conduct
means	n. 方式	a method for doing or achieving something: WAY
measure	n. 措施	an official action that is done in order to achieve a particular aim
menial	adj. 卑微的	not skilled or important, and often boring or badly paid
militate	v. 产生作用	to have weight or effect
militia	n. 民兵	a group of ordinary people who are trained as soldiers to fight in an emergency
mission	n. 使命	particular work that you feel it is your duty to do
mold	n. 模式	distinctive nature or character : TYPE
monarch	n. 君主	a person who rules a country or an empire, for example a king or a queen
monopoly	n. 独裁	exclusive possession or control
morality	n. 道德	principles concerning right and wrong or good and bad behaviour
mourn	v. 哀悼	to feel or express grief or sorrow
municipal	adj. 市政的	connected with or belonging to a town, city or district that has its own local government
nature	n. 本性	the usual way that a person or an animal behaves that is part of their character
nebulous	adj. 朦胧的	not developed or clear enough to describe: VAGUE
nomination	n. 提名	the act of officially suggesting someone or something for a position, duty, or prize, or the fact of being suggested for it
obdurate	adj. 顽固的	stubbornly persistent in wrongdoing
obedient	adj. 顺从的	submissive to the restraint or command of authority : willing to obey
objection	n. 反对	a feeling or expression of disapproval

历史词	中文释义	英文释义
obliged to	adj. 感激的	used when you are expressing thanks
observe	v. 遵守	to obey rules，laws，etc.
obstinacy	n. 顽固	determined not to change your ideas，behaviour，opinions etc.，even when other people think you are being unreasonable
occupation	n. 职业	a job or profession
offensive	adj. 冒犯的	rude in a way that causes you to feel upset，insulted or annoyed
onerous	adj. 繁重的	needing great effort；causing trouble or worry
opulence	n. 富裕	wealth；affluence
orate	v. 演讲	to speak in a formal，often pompous manner.
ordain	v. 规定	to officially order that something should be done
ordinance	n. 法令	an authoritative decree or direction：ORDER
outlaw	v. 宣告非法	to make sth no longer legal
overpower	v. 压倒	to defeat or gain control over sb completely by using greater strength
overthrow	v. 推翻	to cause the downfall of：BRING DOWN，DEFEAT
overwhelm	v. 战胜	to defeat sb completely
palpable	adj. 明显的	capable of being touched or felt：TANGIBLE
pamphlet	n. 小册子	a very thin book with a paper cover，containing information about a particular subject
papistical	adj. 天主教的	an offensive word for a Roman Catholic，used by some Protestants
paramount	adj. 最重要的	superior to all others：SUPREME
parliament	n. 国会	the group of people who are elected to make and change the laws of a country
partisanship	n. 党派性	a firm adherent to a party，faction，cause，or person especially：one exhibiting blind，prejudiced，and unreasoning allegiance

历史词	中文释义	英文释义
partnership	n. 合伙人	a relationship between two people, organizations, etc.
party	n. 党派	a group of people who are doing sth together such as travelling or visiting somewhere
paternalism	n. 家长式的作风	the system in which a government or an employer protects the people who are governed or employed by providing them with what they need, but does not give them any responsibility or freedom of choice
patriotism	n. 爱国精神	love for or devotion to one's country
penury	n. 贫穷	the state of being very poor
perception	n. 知觉	the ability to understand the true nature of sth
perchance	adv. 可能	PERHAPS, POSSIBLY
perilous	adj. 危险的	very dangerous
perish	v. 死亡	to die
perpetuate	v. 使永存	to make sth such as a bad situation, a belief, etc. continue for a long time
persecute	v. 迫害	to treat sb in a cruel and unfair way, especially because of their race, religion or political beliefs
persecution	n. 迫害	extremely bad treatment of someone, especially because of their race, religion, or political beliefs
piety	n. 虔诚	the quality or state of being pious
pilgrim	n. 朝圣者	one who travels to a shrine or holy place as a devotee
pious	adj. 虔诚的	having or showing a deep respect for God and religion
plague	v. 使苦恼	to cause worry or distress to : HAMPER, BURDEN
plain	adj. 没装饰的	lacking ornament : UNDECORATED
plea	n./v. 恳求	an urgent emotional request
plead	v. 辩护	to argue a case or cause in a court of law

历史词	中文释义	英文释义
pledge	v. 誓言	a serious promise
plume	v. 自夸	to indulge (oneself) in pride with an obvious or vain display of self–satisfaction
policy	n. 政策	definite course or method of action selected from among alternatives and in light of given conditions to guide and determine present and future decisions
pomp	n. 壮丽	a show of magnificence : SPLENDOR
Pope	n. 教皇	the leader of the Roman Catholic Church, who is also the Bishop of Rome
prodigal	adj. 浪费的	characterized by profuse or wasteful expenditure : LAVISH
position	n. 立场	an opinion on or an attitude towards a particular subject
posterity	n. 子孙	the offspring of one progenitor to the furthest generation
practice	n./v. 实践	action rather than ideas
preach	v. 布道	to give a religious talk in a public place, especially in a church during a service
precedent	n. 先例	a similar action or event that happened earlier
preceptress	n. 女教师	
predilection	n. 偏爱	an established preference for something
predisposition	n. 易患病的体质	to make susceptible
preeminently	adv. 卓越地	having paramount rank, dignity, or importance
prejudice	n. 偏见	an unreasonable dislike
prevail through	v. 战胜	to defeat an opponent, especially after a long struggle
privilege	n. 特权	a special right or advantage
probity	n. 诚实	the quality of being completely honest
procession	n. 游行	a group of individuals moving along in an orderly often ceremonial way

历史词	中文释义	英文释义
proclaim	v. 宣告	to publicly and officially tell people about sth important
procure	v. 获得	to obtain sth, especially with difficulty
prod	v. 刺激	to incite to action : STIR
profess	v. 公开宣称	to state openly that you have a particular belief, feeling, etc.
promptitude	n. 敏捷	being ready and quick to act as occasion demands
property	n. 财产	a thing or things that are owned by sb
prophet	n. 预言者	one who foretells future events : PREDICTOR
proposition	n. 提议	something offered for consideration or acceptance : PROPOSAL
proprietor	n. 所有者	the owner of a business, a hotel, etc.
prospect	n. 前景	an extensive view
protégé	n. 门徒	a young person who receives help or training from an older experienced person
Protestant	n. 新教徒	a member of any Christian church that is not Roman Catholic
Providence	n. 上帝	God
province	n. 个人（狭隘）观点	a person's particular area of knowledge, interest or responsibility
provision	n. 供给；临时条款	the act or process of providing ; a measure taken beforehand to deal with a need or contingency : PREPARATION
proxy	n. 代议制	the agency, function, or office of a deputy who acts as a substitute for another
pulpit	n. 讲道坛	a small platform in a church that is like a box and is high above the ground, where a priest, etc. stands to speak to the people
purport	v. 声称	to claim to be or do something, even if this is not true
ratify	v. 批准	to approve and sanction formally

历史词	中文释义	英文释义
rebellion	n. 叛乱	opposition to one in authority or dominance
reckon	v. 猜想	to think sth or have an opinion about sth
recognition	n. 承认	the act of accepting that sth exists, is true or is official
rectitude	n. 正直	moral integrity
redress	n./v. 纠正	to correct
reflection	n. 反思	careful thought about sth, sometimes over a long period of time
reflective	adj. 熟虑的	thinking deeply about things
regard of	v. 留意	ATTENTION, CONSIDERATION
regiment	n. 团	a large group of soldiers that is commanded by a COLONEL
reign	v. 统治	a protest or complaint
remonstrance	n. 抗议	a protest or complaint
render	v. 导致	to cause sb/sth to be in a particular state or condition
repeal	v. 撤销	to state officially that a law no longer has legal authority and has ended
repose	v. 使安静	to remain still or concealed
representative	n. 代表（特指议会）	a person who has been chosen to speak or vote for sb else or on behalf of a group
reproach	v. 斥责	blame or criticism for sth you have done
republic	n. 共和国	a government having a chief of state who is not a monarch and who in modern times is usually a president
republican	n. 共和党	a member or supporter of the Republican Party
repudiate	v. 否定	to refuse to accept sth
repute	n. 名誉	the state of being favorably known, spoken of, or esteemed
resolution	n. 决心；解决；正式决定	the quality of being resolute or determined ; the act of answering : SOLVING ; a formal statement of an opinion agreed on by a committee or a council, especially by means of a vote

历史词	中文释义	英文释义
resolve	v. 解决	to find a satisfactory solution to a problem or difficulty
responsibility	n. 责任	a duty to deal with or take care of sb/sth, so that you may be blamed if sth goes wrong
retain	v. 保持	to keep sth; to continue to have sth
retaliation	n. 报复	action that a person takes against sb who has harmed them in some way
revolution	n. 革命，改变	a great change in conditions, ways of working, beliefs, etc. that affects large numbers of people
righteousness	n. 正直	acting in accord with divine or moral law
rock	v. 摇	to move gently backwards and forwards or from side to side
rue	v. 遗憾	REGRET, SORROW
sacred	adj. 神圣的	connected with God or a god; considered to be holy
sacrifice	v. 牺牲	an act of offering to a deity something precious especially: the killing of a victim on an altar
salutary	adj. 有益的	producing a beneficial effect
sanction	v. 批准	to give permission for sth to take place
sanctuary	n. 避难所	a consecrated place
sanguine	adj. 怀着希望的	cheerful and confident about the future
scepticism	n. 怀疑论	an attitude of doubting that claims or statements are true or that sth will happen
scrupulous	adj. 小心谨慎的	careful about paying attention to every detail
seditious	adj. 煽动性的	encouraging people to oppose the government or not obey the law
segregation	n. 隔离	the act or policy of separating people of different races, religions or sexes and treating them differently
self-evident	adj. 不言而喻的	evident without proof or reasoning
senate	n. 参议院	an assembly or council usually possessing high deliberative and legislative functions

历史词	中文释义	英文释义
senator	n. 参议院议员	a member of a senate
sensation	n. 轰动的事件	very great surprise, excitement, or interest among a lot of people
sensible	adj. 有判断力的	able to make good judgements based on reason and experience rather than emotion
sentiment	n. 感情，观点	a feeling or an opinion, especially one based on emotions
servitude	n. 奴役	a condition in which one lacks liberty especially to determine one's course of action or way of life
setting	n. 环境	surroundings
shackle	v. 束缚	to prevent sb from behaving or speaking as they want
sham	v. 欺骗	a trick that deludes
shed	v. 脱离	to set apart : SEGREGATE
sine qua non	n. 要素	essential
situated	adj. 处于 … 境遇的	in a particular situation
slack	adj. 松懈的	not using due diligence, care, or dispatch
slander	v. 诽谤	the utterance of false charges or misrepresentations which defame and damage another's reputation
slaughter	n. 大屠杀	killing of great numbers of human beings
slaveholder	n. 奴隶主	an owner of slaves
slumber	v. 睡眠	to sleep lightly
solemn	adj. 严肃的	not happy or smiling ; looking very serious
solemnize	v. 庄重地举行	to perform a religious ceremony, especially a marriage
solicitude	n. 挂念	anxious care for sb's comfort, health or happiness
solitude	n. 孤独	alone
sophistry	n. 诡辩	the use of clever arguments to persuade people that sth is true when it is really false

历史词	中文释义	英文释义
sovereignty	n. 君主制	complete power to govern a country
speculation	n. 思考	contemplation or consideration of a subject ; meditation
stagnation	n. 停滞	a situation in which there is no progress or development
at stake	在危急关头	at issue : in jeopardy
stalemate	v. 使陷入困境	a situation in a dispute or competition in which neither side is able to win or make any progress
stamina	n. 精力	the physical or mental strength that enables you to do sth difficult for long periods of time
stand	n. 立场	an attitude towards sth or an opinion that you make clear to people
station	n. 阶层	your social position
statute	n. 法律	a law
stern	adj. 严厉的	having a definite hardness or severity of nature or manner : AUSTERE
stolid	adj. 神经麻木的	not showing much emotion or interest
strenuous	adj. 费力的	needing great effort and energy
stretch	v. 伸展	to make sth longer, wider or looser, for example, by pulling it
strife	n. 冲突	bitter sometimes violent conflict or dissension
striker	n. 罢工者	a worker who has stopped working because of a disagreement over pay or conditions
struggle	v. 挣扎	to try very hard to do sth when it is difficult or when there are a lot of problems
subdivide	v. 把 ... 再分	to divide sth into smaller parts
subdue	v. 征服	to bring sb/sth under control, especially by using force
subject	n. 主题	a thing or person that is being discussed, described or dealt with
subjoin	v. 附加	to add at the end ; append

历史词	中文释义	英文释义
subjugate	v. 征服	to defeat sb/sth
subordinate	adj. 附属的	less important than sth else
subsist	v. 活下去	to exist
subtlety	n. 微妙	the quality that something has when it has been done in a clever or skilful way, with careful attention to small details
subversion	n. 颠覆	the action of trying to destroy a government or an established belief, especially by attacking it indirectly in written or spoken material
subvert	v. 颠覆	to try to destroy the authority of a political, religious, etc. system by attacking it secretly or indirectly
succour	n. 帮助	to give help and sympathy someone
sufferance	n. 忍受	patient endurance
suffice to	v. 足够	to be enough for sb/sth
suffrage	n. 选举权	the right to vote in political elections
summon	v. 召唤	to call upon for specified action
sunder	v. 分开	to split or break sth/sb apart, especially by force
superstition	n. 迷信	a belief or practice resulting from ignorance, fear of the unknown, trust in magic or chance, or a false conception of causation
supremacist	n. 种族优越论者	a person who believes that their own race is better than others and should be in power
supreme	adj. 至高的	highest in rank or position
sweeping	adj. 广泛的	having an important effect on a large part of sth
take up	v. 开始从事	to begin to occupy
temporal	adj. 短暂的	of or relating to time as opposed to eternity
tenacity	n. 固执	determined to do something and unwilling to stop trying even when the situation becomes difficult
tenant	n. 租客	a person who pays rent for the use of a room, building, land, etc. to the person who owns it

历史词	中文释义	英文释义
tenet	n. 原则	a principle, belief, or doctrine generally held to be true
term	n. 专业术语	a word or phrase used as the name of sth
terrify	v. 恐吓	to make sb feel extremely frightened
territory	n. 领土	land that is under the control of a particular country or ruler
testify	v. 作证	to make a statement based on personal knowledge or belief
toil	n. 苦差事	to work very hard and/or for a long time
tongue	n. 语言	a spoken language
traitor	n. 背叛者	a person who betrays their friends, their country, etc.
trample	v. 践踏	to ignore sb's feelings or rights and treat them as if they are not important
tranquil	adj. 平静的	quiet and peaceful
transaction	n. 办理	the process of doing sth
transgress	v. 违法	to violate a command or law : SIN
transient	adj. 短暂的	continuing for only a short time
treaty	n. 条约	a formal agreement between two or more countries
trembling	adj. 战栗的	to be affected with great fear or anxiety
tribunal	n. 法院	a court or forum of justice
tribute	n. 贡品	a payment by one ruler or nation to another in acknowledgment of submission or as the price of protection
triumph	n. 胜利	a great success, achievement or victory
tumult	n. 骚动	disorderly agitation or milling about of a crowd usually with uproar and confusion of voices : COMMOTION
turbulence	n. 骚乱	a situation in which there is a lot of sudden change, confusion, disagreement and sometimes violence

历史词	中文释义	英文释义
turmoil	n. 骚动	a state of great anxiety, confusion and uncertainty
tyranny	n. 暴政	oppressive power
unanimity	n. 一致同意	complete agreement about sth among a group of people
unbridled	adj. 放肆的	not controlled and therefore extreme
unshackle	v. 使获自由	to free from shackles
undertake	v. 承担	to make yourself responsible for sth and start doing it
uniform	adj. 统一的	having always the same form, manner, or degree
union	n. 工会	an association or a club for people or organizations with the same interest
unionism	n. 工会主义	the principle or policy of forming or adhering to a union
uphold	v. 赞成	to support sth
upright	adj. 正直的	marked by strong moral rectitude
usurp	v. 篡夺	to take sb's position and/or power without having the right to do this
venality	n. 贪赃枉法	willing to use power and influence in a dishonest way in return for money
vicious	adj. 邪恶的	having the nature or quality of vice or immorality : DEPRAVED
victim	n. 受害人	a person who has been attacked, injured or killed as the result of a crime, a disease, an accident, etc.
vigor	n. 活力	mental energy, enthusiasm, and determination
vile	adj. 卑鄙的	extremely unpleasant or bad
vice	n. 恶习	evil or immoral behaviour
volubility	n. 健谈	characterized by ready or rapid speech
voluntary	adj. 自愿的	done willingly, not because you are forced
want	n. 缺乏，需要	to need，lack

历史词	中文释义	英文释义
weight	n. 权重	importance, influence or strength
whence	adv. 从何处	from where
wherefore	adv. 为何	for what reason or purpose：WHY
whim	n. 反复无常	a sudden wish to do or have sth, especially when it is sth unusual or unnecessary
whither	adv. 到哪里	to what place
wisdom	n. 智慧	the ability to make sensible decisions and give good advice because of the experience and knowledge that you have
woe	n. 悲痛	to express grief, regret, or distress
worse off	v. 恶化	in a worse situation than you were before, or than someone else is now
wretch	n. 可怜的人；卑鄙的人	a miserable person；an evil, unpleasant or annoying person
wrought	v. 工作	the past tense of work

抽 象 词 汇

　　抽象词汇（725 个），全部是从 100 套老 SAT 阅读中约 4800 道选项和 55 套新 SAT 中约 2800 道选项总结而成，非常具有代表性，几乎可以代表英语中常见的绝大部分抽象词，因此这些词有很大的概率会继续出现在以后的新 SAT 考试中，认识它们，对于以后你们做选项分析和排除非常有帮助。尤其是对主旨题、双篇题和目的题特别有效。这些单词也经常出现在词汇题里，说明美国出题人对这些抽象词有比较强烈的考察要求。

　　由于这些词都非常难以理解和把握，即使背诵了中文意思，也不一定知道具体是什么意思，比如 claim（宣称）和 proclaim（声称），这两个单词大家可能都认识，但中文是什么意思，它们有什么区别，大家不一定特别清晰。所以，大家一定要认真"体会"这些单词的英文释义。这些中英文释义全部是我根据 SAT 选型里常考的、精神层面的意思精心挑选的，最能代表 SAT 考试选项中出现的意思。

　　使用方法：希望同学们每个单词无论认识与否，都要把英文释义读一遍，仔细"体会"这些单词的英文释义。如果和你想象的一样，才算真正认识；如果不一样，请做好标记，多读几遍。这些单词也经常在词汇题里被考到，希望大家重视！

抽象词	中文释义	英文释义
abate	v. 减轻	to become less strong
ability	n. 能力	someone's level of skill at doing something
abstract	n. 摘要	a statement summarizing the important points of a text
accentuate	v. 强调	emphasize sth or make it more noticeable
accept	v. 接受	take willingly sth that is offered
accident	n. 事故；意外	an unpleasant event, especially in a vehicle, that happens unexpectedly and causes injury or damage; something that happens unexpectedly and is not planned in advance
acclaim	v. 称赞	praise someone or something publicly

抽象词	中文释义	英文释义
accomplishment	v. 成就	an impressive thing that is done or achieved after a lot of work
account	n. 解释	an explanation or a description of an idea, a theory or a process
accountability	n. 有义务	the quality or state of being accountable especially: an obligation or willingness to accept responsibility or to account for one's actions
accusation	n. 控告	a statement saying that someone is guilty of a crime or of doing something wrong
accustom	v. 使习惯于	make yourself/sb familiar with sth or become used to it
achieve	v. 实现	succeed in reaching a particular goal, status or standard, especially by making an effort for a long time
acknowledge	v. 承认	admit or accept that something is true or that a situation exists
acquaintance	n. 熟人	a person that you know but who is not a close friend
acquire	v. 获得	gain sth by your own efforts, ability or behaviour
acquisition	n. 获得	the process by which you gain knowledge or learn a skill
act	n. 行动	the process of doing or performing something
action	n. 行动	the state or process of acting or doing
activity	n. 活动	things that people do in order to achieve a particular aim
address	v. 演说	to make a formal speech to a group of people
admission	n. 承认	a statement in which you admit that something is true or that you have done something wrong
admit	v. 承认	agree, often unwillingly, that sth is true
adopt	v. 采用	start to use a particular method or to show a particular attitude towards sb/sth
advance	v. 提出	to suggest an idea, a theory, or a plan for other people to discuss

抽象词	中文释义	英文释义
advantage	n. 优势	a thing that helps you to be better or more successful than other people
advice	n. 忠告	an opinion or a suggestion about what sb should do in a particular situation
advocate	v. 支持	support sth publicly
affair	n. 事务	events that are of public interest or political importance
affect	v. 影响	produce a change in sb/sth
affection	n. 喜爱	the feeling of liking or loving sb/sth very much and caring about them
affinity	n. 密切关系	a strong feeling that you like and understand someone or something
affirm	v. 坚称	to state firmly or publicly that sth is true or that you support sth strongly
aftermath	n. 后果	the effects and results of something bad or important
agenda	n. 议程	a list of problems or subjects that a government, organization etc. is planning to deal with
aggravation	n. 恶化	the process of making a situation or medical condition worse
agree	v. 同意	have the same opinion as sb
allegation	n. 断言	a public statement that is made without giving proof, accusing sb of doing sth that is wrong or illegal
allow	v. 允许	let someone do or have something, or let something happen
allude	v. 暗指	mention sth in an indirect way
allusion	v. 暗示	something said or written that mentions a subject, person etc. indirectly
alteration	n. 改变	a change to sth that makes it different
altitude	n. 高度	the height of an object or place above the sea
ambition	n. 雄心	an ardent desire for rank, fame, or power

抽象词	中文释义	英文释义
amount	n. 数量	a quantity of sth
analogy	n. 类比	a comparison of one thing with another thing that has similar features
analyze	v. 对 ... 进行分析	to study or examine something in detail in order to understand or explain it
anecdote	n. 轶事	short, interesting or amusing story about a real person or event
announce	v. 宣布	officially tell people about something, especially about a plan or a decision
answer	n./v. 回答	something that you say, write or do to react to a question or situation
anticipate	v. 预期	to guess that something will happen, and be ready to deal with it
appeal to	v. 请求；吸引；上诉	to make a formal request to a court of law or to sb in authority for a judgement or a decision to be changed ; to attract or interest sb ; to call upon another for corroboration, vindication, or decision
applaud	v. 赞同	express praise for sb/sth because you approve of them or it
application	n. 应用	the practical use of sth, especially a theory, discovery, etc.
apply	v. 应用	use sth or make sth work in a particular situation
appoint	v. 任命	choose sb for a job or position of responsibility
apprise	v. 通知	tell or inform sb of sth
approach	n. 方法	a way of dealing with sb/sth ; a way of doing or thinking about sth such as a problem or a task
approbation	n. 赞许	official praise or approval
approve	v. 赞成	to officially agree to a plan, proposal, request, etc.
area	n. 范围	a particular subject or activity, or an aspect of it
argue	v. 争论	speak angrily to sb because you disagree with them

抽象词	中文释义	英文释义
argument	n. 争论	a set of reasons that show that something is true or untrue, right or wrong etc.
arouse	v. 唤起	make you become interested, expect something etc.
articulate	v. 清晰表达	pronounce what you are saying in a clear and careful way
ascertain	v. 查明	find out the true or correct information about sth
ascribe	v. 归因于	consider that sth is caused by a particular thing or person
aspect	n. 方面	one part of a situation, idea, plan etc. that has many parts
aspire	v. 渴望	have a strong desire to achieve or to become sth
assert	v. 断言	to state or declare positively and often forcefully or aggressively
assertion	n. 断言	a statement saying that you strongly believe sth to be true
assess	v. 评估	make a judgement about the nature or quality of sb/sth
assuage	v. 缓和	make an unpleasant feeling less severe
assume	v. 假定	think or accept that sth is true but without having proof of it
assumption	n. 假定	something that you think is true although you have no definite proof
atmosphere	n. 气氛	the feeling that an event or place gives you
attack	v. 抨击	criticize sb/sth severely
attain	v. 实现	succeed in getting sth, usually after a lot of effort
attempt	n./v. 试图	an act of trying to do something, especially something difficult
attention	n. 注意力	concentration of the mental powers upon an object
attitude	n. 态度	the way that you think and feel about sb/sth, the way that you behave towards sb/sth that shows how you think and feel

抽象词	中文释义	英文释义
attribute	v. 归因于	to say or believe that sb is responsible for doing sth, especially for saying, writing or painting sth
augment	v. 增大	increase the amount, value, size, etc. of sth
authenticate	v. 证明 ... 是真的	prove that something is true or real
authenticity	n. 真实	the quality of being genuine or true
authority	n. 权威	the power to give orders to people
availability	n. 有效性	the state of being able to be obtained or used
avenue	n. 方法	a choice or way of making progress towards sth
avoid	v. 避免	prevent sth bad from happening
awareness	n. 察觉	knowledge or understanding of a particular subject or situation
background	n. 背景	the circumstances or past events which help explain why sth is how it is
balance	n./v. 平衡	to bring into harmony or proportion
base	n. 基础	an idea, a fact, a situation, etc. from which sth is developed
basis	n. 基础	the principal component of something
behavior	n. 行为	the manner of conducting oneself
belief	n. 信任	an opinion about sth ; sth that you think is true
believe	v. 相信	feel certain that sth is true or that sb is telling you the truth
benefit	n. 利益	a helpful and useful effect that sth has
bestow	v. 授予	give someone something of great value or importance
bias	n. 偏见	unfairly influence sb's opinions or decisions
bolster	v. 支持	improve sth or make it stronger
breakthrough	n. 突破	an important development that may lead to an agreement or achievement
calculation	n. 深思熟虑	careful planning for yourself without caring about other people

抽象词	中文释义	英文释义
call for	v. 要求	to require as necessary or appropriate
call into question	v. 怀疑	to doubt sth or make others doubt sth
campaign	n. 运动	a series of planned activities that are intended to achieve a particular social, commercial or political aim
capacity	n. 能力	someone's ability to do something
capture	v. 获取	succeed in accurately expressing a feeling, an atmosphere, etc. in a picture, piece of writing, film/movie, etc.
case	n. 案件	an example of a particular situation or of something happening
cast	v. 怀疑	to say, do or suggest sth that makes people doubt sth or think that sb is less honest, good, etc.
cast doubt on	v. 怀疑	to doubt sth or make others doubt sth
catalog	n./v. 列举	to become listed in a catalog at a specified price
cause	v. 导致	make something happen, especially something bad
caution	n./v. 谨慎；警告	careful forethought to avoid danger or harm ; to warn sb officially that anything they say may be used as evidence against them in a court of law
celebrate	v. 赞扬	to praise sb/sth
certainty	n. 确定	something that will definitely happen or that you feel very sure about
challenge	v. 挑战	to question whether a statement or an action is right, legal, etc. ; to refuse to accept sth
champion	v. 支持	fight for or speak in support of a group of people or a belief
chance	n. 机会	how possible or likely it is that something will happen, especially something that you want
character	n. 性格；人物	all the qualities and features that make a person, groups of people, and places different from others ; an interesting or unusual person
characterize	v. 描绘 ... 的特性	to give sth its typical or most noticeable qualities or features

抽象词	中文释义	英文释义
choice	n. 选择	selected with care
circumstance	n. 环境	the conditions and facts that are connected with and affect a situation, an event or an action
cite	v. 引用	mention sth as a reason or an example, or in order to support what you are saying
civilization	n. 文明	an advanced state of intellectual, cultural, and material development in human society, marked by progress in the arts and sciences, the extensive use of record-keeping, including writing, and the appearance of complex political and social institutions.
claim	v. 声称	say that sth is true although it has not been proved and other people may not believe it
clarification	n. 澄清	the act of making something clearer or easier to understand, or an explanation that makes something clearer
clarify	v. 澄清	make sth clearer or easier to understand
command	v. 命令	to tell sb to do sth
commemorate	v. 纪念	do something to show that you remember and respect someone important or an important event in the past
commend	v. 称赞	praise sb/sth, especially publicly
comment	n./v. 评论	something that you say or write which gives an opinion on or explains sb/sth
commentary	n. 评论	a spoken description of an event
commit	v. 使 ... 承担义务	promise sincerely that you will definitely do sth, keep to an agreement or arrangement, etc.
compare	v. 比较	to examine people or things to see how they are similar and how they are different
complication	n. 复杂	a thing that makes a situation more complicated or difficult
comply	v. 遵守	obey a rule, an order
comprehend	v. 理解	understand sth fully

抽象词	中文释义	英文释义
concede	v. 让步	to acknowledge, often reluctantly, as being true, just, or proper
conceive	v. 设想	form an idea, a plan, etc. in your mind
concentrate	v. 全神贯注	give all your attention to sth
concept	n. 概念	an idea or a principle that is connected with sth
concern	n. 焦虑；关心	a feeling of worry, especially one that is shared by many people; to be a care, trouble, or distress to
conclude	v. 总结	decide or believe sth as a result of what you have heard or seen
conclusion	n. 结论	something that you decide when you have thought about all the information connected with the situation
concur	v. 同意	agree
condemn	v. 谴责	say very strongly that you do not approve of something or someone, especially because you think it is morally wrong
condemnation	n. 谴责	say very strongly that you do not approve of something or someone, especially because you think it is morally wrong
condescend	v. 屈尊	to behave in a way that shows that you think you are more important or more intelligent than other people
condition	n. 情况	the situation in which people live or work, especially the physical things that affect the quality of their lives
condone	v. 宽恕	accept behaviour that is morally wrong or to treat it as if it were not serious
conduct	n. 行为	a person's behaviour in a particular place or in a particular situation
confession	n. 认罪	a statement that a person makes, admitting that they are guilty of a crime
confirm	v. 证实	show that something is definitely true, especially by providing more proof

抽象词	中文释义	英文释义
conflict	n./v. 冲突	a state of disagreement or argument between people, groups, countries etc.
confrontation	n. 对抗	a situation in which there is an angry disagreement between people or groups who have different opinions
congratulate	v. 祝贺	tell someone that you are happy because they have achieved something or because something nice has happened to them
conscience	n. 责任心	the sense or consciousness of the moral goodness or blameworthiness of one's own conduct, intentions, or character together with a feeling of obligation to do right or be good
consciousness	n. 觉悟	the state of being able to use your senses and mental powers to understand what is happening
consensus	n. 一致	an opinion that all members of a group agree with
consequence	n. 结果	something that happens as a result of a particular action or set of conditions
conservation	n. 保护	the protection of the natural environment
consider	v. 考虑	think about sth carefully, especially in order to make a decision
contend	v. 主张	argue or state that something is true
context	n. 上下文	the words that come just before and after a word, phrase or statement and help you to understand its meaning
contextualization	n. 根据上下文	to place (as a word or activity) in a context
contradict	v. 反驳	express the opposite of (a statement)
contrast	n./v. 对比	the fact of comparing two or more things in order to show the differences between them
contribute	v. 贡献	give sth, especially money or goods, to help sb/sth
controversy	n. 争论	public discussion and argument about sth that many people strongly disagree about, disapprove of, or are shocked by

抽象词	中文释义	英文释义
convert	v. 改变	to change or make sth change from one form, purpose, system, etc. to another
convey	v. 表达	communicate or express something, with or without using words
conviction	n. 坚信	a very strong belief or opinion
convince	v. 说服	make sb/yourself believe that sth is true
correlation	n. 关联	a connection between two ideas, facts etc., especially when one may be the cause of the other
correspond	v. 符合	be the same as or match sth
counter	v. 反对	reply to sb by trying to prove that what they said is not true
counteract	v. 抵消	reduce or prevent the bad effect of something, by doing something that has the opposite effect
counterargument	n. 反论点	an argument in opposition to another
counterbalance	v. 抵消	have an equal and opposite effect to something such as a change, feeling etc.
counterclaim	v. 反诉	claim made in reply to another claim and different from it
counterpoint	n. 对应物	a complementing or contrasting item
course	n. 路线	of sth the way sth develops or should develop
create	v. 创造	make something exist that did not exist before
credibility	n. 可信性	the quality that sb/sth has that makes people believe or trust them
credit	v. 信任	to believe sth, especially sth surprising or unexpected
criteria	n. 标准	standards that are used for judging something or making a decision about something
critic	n. 批评家	a person who expresses opinions about the good and bad qualities of books, music, etc.
criticism	n. 批评	express your disapproval of someone or something, or to talk about their faults

抽象词	中文释义	英文释义
criticize	v. 批评	express your disapproval of someone or something, or to talk about their faults
critique	n. 批评	a piece of written criticism of a set of ideas, a work of art, etc.
cultivate	v. 培养	to develop an attitude, a way of talking or behaving
culture	n. 文化	the beliefs, way of life, art, and customs that are shared and accepted by people in a particular society
curiosity	n. 好奇心	a strong desire to know about sth
custom	n. 风俗，习惯	something that is done by people in a particular society because it is traditional
dare	v. 挑战	to challenge to perform an action especially as a proof of courage
deal with	v. 处理	to take action with respect to someone or something
debate	n. 辩论	a formal discussion of an issue at a public meeting or in a parliament
debunk	v. 揭穿	show that an idea, a belief, etc. is false, to show that sth is not as good as people think it is
deception	n. 欺骗	the act of deliberately making someone believe something that is not true
decide	v. 决定	think carefully about the different possibilities that are available and choose one of them
decision	n. 决定	a choice or judgement that you make after thinking and talking about what is the best thing to do
declaration	n. 宣布	an official or formal statement, especially about the plans of a government or an organization
decline	v. 婉拒	express polite refusal
decry	v. 谴责	state publicly that you do not approve of something
dedication	n. 奉献	the hard work and effort that sb puts into an activity or purpose because they think it is important

抽象词	中文释义	英文释义
deed	n. 行为	a thing that sb does that is usually very good or very bad
defend	v. 辩护	to say or write sth in support of sb/sth that has been criticized
defense	n. 辩护	the act of protecting something or someone from attack
defiance	n. 挑战	behaviour that shows you refuse to do what someone tells you to do, especially because you do not respect them
define	v. 定义	describe something correctly and thoroughly, and to say what standards, limits, qualities etc. it has that make it different from other things
definition	n. 定义	an explanation of the meaning of a word or phrase, especially in a dictionary
defy	v. 公然反抗	refuse to obey a law or rule, or refuse to do what someone in authority tells you to do
degree	n. 程度	the amount or level of sth
deliberate	v. 仔细考虑，权衡	think very carefully about sth, usually before making a decision
delineate	v. 描绘，描写	describe or draw something carefully so that people can understand it
deliver	v. 发表	give a speech, talk, etc. or other official statement
demand	n./v. 要求	a very firm request for sth
demean	v. 贬低 … 的身份	do something that makes people lose respect for someone or something
demonstrate	v. 证明	show sth clearly by giving proof or evidence
demonstration	n. 证明	the act of showing or making evident
demystify	v. 去神秘化	make a subject that seems difficult or complicated easier to understand, especially by explaining it in simpler language
denounce	v. 谴责	express strong disapproval of someone or something, especially in public

抽象词	中文释义	英文释义
deny	v. 否定	say that sth is not true
depict	v. 描述	to describe sth in words, or give an impression of sth in words or with a picture
depiction	n. 描述	to describe sth in words, or give an impression of sth in words or with a picture
describe	v. 描绘	say what something or someone is like by giving details about them
description	n. 描写	say what something or someone is like by giving details about them
designate	v. 指定	choose someone or something for a particular job or purpose
desire	n. 渴望	a strong wish to have or do sth
destine	v. 命中注定	do sth having a future which has been decided or planned at an earlier time, especially by fate
destiny	n. 命运	what happens to sb or what will happen to them in the future, especially things that they cannot change or avoid
detail	n. 细节	the small facts or features of sth
determine	v. 坚决	decide definitely to do sth
devalue	v. 降低...的价值	reduce the value of one country's money when it is exchanged for another country's money
develop	v. 发展	to think of or produce a new idea, product, etc. and make it successful
development	n. 发展	the process of producing or creating sth new or more advanced
differentiate	v. 区分	recognize or express the difference between things or people
digress	v. 使离题	start to talk about sth that is not connected with the main point of what you are saying
dilemma	n. 进退两难	a situation which makes problems, often one in which you have to make a very difficult choice between things of equal importance
dimension	n. 方面	a part of a situation or a quality involved in it

抽象词	中文释义	英文释义
direction	n.方向	the way something or someone moves, faces, or is aimed
disagree	v.不同意	have an opinion that is different from the opinion that another person has
disapprove	v.不赞成	think that sb/sth is not good or suitable
disbelief	n.怀疑	the feeling of not being able to believe sth
discern	v.识别	notice or understand something by thinking about it carefully
discipline	n.科目；纪律	an area of knowledge; the ability to control your behaviour or the way you live, work, etc.
discourage	v.使气馁	try to prevent sth or to prevent sb from doing sth, especially by making it difficult to do or by showing that you do not approve of it
discourse	n./v.论述	a long and serious treatment or discussion of a subject in speech or writing
discover	v.发现	find sb/sth that was hidden or that you did not expect to find
discovery	n.发现	find sb/sth that was hidden or that you did not expect to find
discredit	v.不信；使丢脸	to cause disbelief in the accuracy or authority of; damage to sb's reputation
discriminate	v.区别	show a difference between people or things
discuss	v.讨论	talk about something with another person or a group in order to exchange ideas or decide something
discussion	n.讨论	talk about something with another person or a group in order to exchange ideas or decide something
disillusionment	n.醒悟	to make someone realize that something which they thought was true or good is not really true or good
dismay	v.使沮丧	make sb feel shocked and disappointed
dismiss	v.不予理会	decide that sb/sth is not important and not worth thinking or talking about

抽象词	中文释义	英文释义
disparage	v. 蔑视	suggest that sb/sth is not important or valuable
display	v. 显示	show something to people, or put it in a place where people can see it easily
disposition	n. 性情	the natural qualities of a person's character
disprove	v. 证明…是虚假的	show that something is wrong or not true
dispute	n./v. 争论	to argue or disagree strongly with sb about sth, especially about who owns sth
disregard	v. 忽视	ignore something or treat it as unimportant
dissent	v. 不同意	have or express opinions that are different from those that are officially accepted
dissolve	v. 使终止	to officially end a marriage, business agreement or parliament
dissuade	v. 劝阻	persuade sb not to do sth
distinction	n. 不同	a clear difference or contrast especially between people or things that are similar or related
distinguish	v. 区分	recognize the difference between two people or things
distort	v. 扭曲	to change a situation from the way it would naturally be
domain	n. 领域	an area of knowledge or activity, especially one that sb is responsible for
downplay	v. 轻视	make people think that sth is less important than it really is
dramatize	v. 戏剧化	make a situation seem more exciting, terrible etc. than it really is
drawback	n. 缺点	a disadvantage or problem that makes sth a less attractive idea
duty	n. 责任	something that you feel you have to do because it is your moral or legal responsibility
effect	n. 结果	a change that sb/sth causes in sb/sth else, a result
effort	n. 努力，尝试	an attempt to do something, especially when this involves a lot of hard work or determination

抽象词	中文释义	英文释义
elaborate	v. 详细阐述	explain or describe sth in a more detailed way
element	n. 要素	a necessary or typical part of sth
elicit	v. 引出	to draw forth or bring out (something latent or potential)
embodiment	n. 具体化	sth a person or thing that represents or is a typical example of an idea or a quality
embolden	v. 使大胆	to make sb feel braver or more confident
embrace	v. 接受	to accept an idea, a proposal, a set of beliefs, etc., especially when it is done with enthusiasm
emotion	n. 情感	a strong human feeling such as love, hate, or anger
emphasize	v. 强调	give special importance to sth
employ	v. 使用	use a particular object, method, skill etc. in order to achieve something
emulate	v. 模仿	to try to do sth as well as sb else because you admire them
encourage	v. 鼓励	to give sb support, courage or hope
endeavor	n. 努力	an attempt to do sth, especially sth new or difficult
endorse	v. 支持	say publicly that you support a person, statement or course of action
endure	v. 忍耐	experience and deal with sth that is painful or unpleasant, especially without complaining
engage	v. 从事	be doing or to become involved in an activity
engender	v. 引起	to cause to exist or to develop
ensure	v. 使确信	to make sure that sth happens or is definite
enumerate	v. 列举	name things on a list one by one
environment	n. 环境	the circumstances, objects, or conditions by which one is surrounded
envision	v. 想象	imagine what a situation will be like in the future, especially a situation you intend to work towards

抽象词	中文释义	英文释义
episode	n. 插曲	an event, a situation, or a period of time in sb's life, a novel, etc. that is important or interesting in some way
epitomize	v. 具体化	be a very typical example of something
espouse	v. 支持	support an idea, belief etc., especially a political one
essence	n. 本质	the most basic and important quality of something
establish	v. 建立	to start or create an organization, a system, etc. that is meant to last for a long time
estimate	v. 估计	try to judge the value, size, speed, cost etc. of something, without calculating it exactly
ethics	n. 道德	moral beliefs and rules about right and wrong
euphemism	n. 委婉语	an indirect word or phrase that people often use to refer to sth embarrassing or unpleasant, sometimes to make it seem more acceptable than it really is
evaluate	v. 评估	judge how good, useful, or successful something is
evaluation	n. 评估	judge how good, useful, or successful something is
event	n. 事件	something that happens, especially something important, interesting or unusual
evidence	n. 证据	facts or signs that show clearly that something exists or is true
evoke	v. 引起	produce a strong feeling or memory in someone
evolution	n. 进化	the gradual development of plants, animals, etc. over many years, from simple to more complicated forms
evolve	v. 进化	develop gradually, especially from a simple to a more complicated form
exaggerate	v. 夸大	make sth seem longer, better, worse or more important than it really is
examination	n. 检测	the act of looking at or considering sth very carefully

抽象词	中文释义	英文释义
examine	v. 检查	to consider or study an idea, a subject, etc. very carefully
example	n. 例子	something such as an object, a fact or a situation that shows, explains or supports what you say
exception	n. 例外	a person or a thing that is not included in a general statement
excuse	n. 借口	a reason, either true or invented, that you give to explain or defend your behaviour
execution	n. 执行	a process in which you do something that has been carefully planned
exemplify	v. 例证	be a typical example of sth
exercise	v. 运用	to use your power, rights or personal qualities in order to achieve sth
exert	v. 运用（权威）	use your power, influence etc. in order to make something happen
expand	v. 扩展	to become greater in size, number or importance; to make sth greater in size, number or importance
expect	v. 预料	think that something will happen because it seems likely or has been planned
expectation	n. 预料	a belief that sth will happen because it is likely
experience	n./v. 经历	have a particular situation affect you or happen to you
experiment	n. 实验	a scientific test that is carried out in order to study what happens and to gain new knowledge
explain	v. 解释	tell someone about something in a way that is clear or easy to understand
explanation	n. 解释	a statement, fact, or situation that tells you why sth happened; a reason given for sth
explicate	v. 详细说明	to explain an idea or a work of literature in a lot of detail
exploration	n. 探索	the act of travelling through a place in order to find out about it or look for sth in it

抽象词	中文释义	英文释义
expose	v. 使暴露	to show sth that is usually hidden
exposure	n. 暴露	the state of having the true facts about sb/sth told after they have been hidden because they are bad, immoral or illegal
express	v. 表达	show or make known a feeling, an opinion, etc. by words, looks or actions
expression	n. 表达	things that people say, write or do in order to show their feelings, opinions and ideas
extent	n. 范围	how large, important, serious, etc. sth is
fact	n. 事实	something demonstrated to exist or known to have existed
factor	n. 因素	one of several things that influence or cause a situation
feasibility	n. 可行性	capable of being done or carried out
feature	n. 特征	something important, interesting or typical of a place or thing
feedback	n. 反馈	advice, criticism or information about how good or useful sth or sb's work is
feel	v. 感到	experience a particular physical feeling or emotion
feeling	n. 感情；观点	something that you feel through the mind or through the senses; the idea or belief that a particular thing is true or a particular situation is likely to happen
field	n. 领域	a particular subject or activity that sb works in or is interested in
figure	n. 人物	a person, thing, or action representative of another
finding	n. 发现	information that is discovered as the result of research into sth
flashback	n. 倒叙	a sudden, very clear, strong memory of sth that happened in the past that is so real you feel that you are living through the experience again
focus on	v. 聚焦	to give attention, effort, etc. to one particular subject, situation or person rather than another

抽象词	中文释义	英文释义
foreboding	n. 凶兆	a strong feeling that sth unpleasant or dangerous is going to happen
foreshadow	v. 凶兆	be a sign of sth that will happen in the future
foresight	n. 远见	the ability to imagine what is likely to happen and to consider this when planning for the future
forestall	v. 预先阻止	to prevent sth from happening or sb from doing sth by doing sth first
forewarn	v. 预先警告	warn someone about something dangerous, unpleasant, or unexpected before it happens
foster	v. 鼓励	encourage sth to develop
foundation	n. 基础	a principle, an idea or a fact that sth is based on and that it grows from
function	n. 功能	a special activity or purpose of a person or thing
in general terms	adv. 概括地	not specific
generalization	n. 概括	a general statement that is based on only a few facts or examples ; the act of making such statements
generalize	v. 概括	form a general principle or opinion after considering only a small number of facts or examples
goal	n. 目标	something that you hope to achieve
ground	n. 范围	an area of interest, knowledge or ideas
group	n. 组	a number of people or things that are together in the same place or that are connected in some way
highlight	v. 强调	emphasize sth, especially so that people give it more attention
hint	n./v. 暗示	something that you say or do to suggest something to someone, without telling them directly
honor	v. 尊敬	respect for what you do
humor	n. 幽默	the quality that makes something laughable or amusing

抽象词	中文释义	英文释义
hyperbole	n. 夸张法	a way of describing something by saying it is much bigger, smaller, worse etc. than it actually is
hypothesis	n. 假设	an idea or explanation of sth that is based on a few known facts but that has not yet been proved to be true or correct
hypothesize	v. 假设	suggest a way of explaining sth when you do not definitely know about it
idea	n. 想法	a plan, thought or suggestion, especially about what to do in a particular situation
idealize	v. 使理想化	imagine or represent something or someone as being perfect or better than they really are
identification	n. 鉴定	the process of showing, proving or recognizing who or what sb/sth is
identify	v. 鉴定	recognize sb/sth and be able to say who or what they are
identity	n. 身份	who or what sb/sth is
ignite	v. 激起	arouse the passions of
ignore	v. 忽视	pay no attention to sth
illuminate	v. 阐明	make sth clearer or easier to understand
illusion	n. 错觉	an idea or opinion that is wrong, especially about yourself
illustrate	v. 举例说明	to make the meaning of sth clearer by using examples, pictures, etc.
imagine	v. 想象	form a picture in your mind of what sth might be like
impact	n. 影响	the powerful effect that sth has on sb/sth
implication	n. 结果	a possible effect or result of an action or a decision
imply	v. 暗示	suggest that sth is true or that you feel or think sth, without saying so directly
impression	n. 印象	idea, a feeling or an opinion that you get about sb/sth, or that sb/sth gives you

抽象词	中文释义	英文释义
impulse	n. 冲动	a sudden strong desire to do something without thinking about whether it is a sensible thing to do
incident	n. 事故	something that happens, especially sth unusual or unpleasant
inclination	n. 倾向	a feeling that makes you want to do sth
inconsistency	n. 前后矛盾	a situation in which two statements are different and cannot both be true
indicate	v. 表明	show that sth is true or exist
indication	n. 指示	a remark or sign that shows that sth is happening or what sb is thinking or feeling
influence	n./v. 影响	the effect that sb/sth has on the way a person thinks or behaves or on the way that sth works or develops
inform	v. 通知	formally or officially tell someone about something or give them information
information	n. 信息	facts or details about sb/sth
inquiry	n. 质询	a question intended to get information about someone or something
insight	n. 洞察力	the ability to see and understand the truth about people or situations
instance	n. 例子	a particular example or case of sth
intention	n. 意图	a plan or desire to do something
interaction	n. 相互作用	mutual or reciprocal action or influence
interest	n. 兴趣	the feeling that you have when you want to know or learn more about sb/sth
interpretation	n. 解释	the particular way in which sth is understood or explained
introduce	v. 介绍	make sb learn about sth or do sth for the first time
introduction	n. 介绍	the act of bringing sth into use or existence for the first time, or of bringing sth to a place for the first time

抽象词	中文释义	英文释义
invite	v. 招致（尤指坏事）	to make sth, especially sth bad or unpleasant, likely to happen
invoke	v. 引起	make a particular idea, image, or feeling appear in people's minds by describing an event or situation, or by talking about a person
involve	v. 包含	include or affect someone or something
involvement	n. 卷入	to engage as a participant
irony	n. 反讽	the use of words that say the opposite of what you really mean, often as a joke and with a tone of voice that shows this
issue	n. 话题	an important topic that people are discussing or arguing about
item	n. 项目	a single thing, especially one thing in a list, group, or set of things
judgment	n. 判断	the formation of an opinion after consideration or deliberation
justice	n. 正义	the quality of being right and deserving fair treatment
justification	n. 辩护	a good reason why sth exists or is done
justify	v. 证明 ... 是正当的	give an acceptable explanation for something that other people think is unreasonable
knowledge	n. 知识	the information, understanding and skills that you gain through education or experience
level	n. 水平	the amount of sth that exists in a particular situation at a particular time
limitation	n. 限制	the act or process of limiting or controlling sb/sth
link	n. 连接	a connection between two or more people or things
logic	n. 逻辑	the study of the principles of reasoning, especially of the structure of propositions as distinguished from their content and of method and validity in deductive reasoning
look forward to	v. 期望	expect

抽象词	中文释义	英文释义
magnitude	n. 量级	the great size or importance of sth ; the degree to which sth is large or important
manifestation	n. 证明	an event, action or thing that is a sign that sth exists or is happening ; the act of appearing as a sign that sth exists or is happening
manipulate	v. 操纵	to control or influence sb/sth, often in a dishonest way so that they do not realize it
manner	n. 方式	the way that sth is done or happens
matter-of-fact	n. 事实	said or done without showing any emotion, especially in a situation in which you would expect sb to express their feelings
means	n. 方式	an action, an object or a system by which a result is achieved ; a way of achieving or doing sth
measurement	n. 措施	an official action that is done in order to achieve a particular aim
method	n. 方法	a well-organized and well-planned way of doing something
methodology	n. 方法学	the set of methods and principles that you use when studying a particular subject or doing a particular kind of work
mind	n. 理智	the part of a person that makes them able to be aware of things, to think and to feel
misapplication	n. 误用	the use of sth for the wrong purpose or in the wrong way
misbehave	v. 行为不端	behave badly
misconception	n. 误解	a belief or an idea that is not based on correct information, or that is not understood by people
misinterpretation	n. 曲解	to explain wrongly
mission	n. 使命	particular work that you feel it is your duty to do
mistake	n. 错误	an action or an opinion that is not correct, or that produces a result that you did not want
misunderstand	v. 误解	don't understand someone or something correctly

抽象词	中文释义	英文释义
misunderstanding	n. 误解	a situation in which a comment, an instruction, etc. is not understood correctly
motivate	v. 刺激	make sb want to do sth, especially sth that involves hard work and effort
motivation	n. 动机	a feeling of enthusiasm or interest that makes you determined to do something
motive	n. 动机	a reason for doing sth
nature	n. 本性	the inherent character or basic constitution of a person or thing
note	v. 注意	notice or pay careful attention to sth
notice	v. 注意到	pay attention to sb/sth
notion	n. 概念	an idea, belief, or opinion
objection	n. 反对	a reason why you do not like or are opposed to sth
objective	n. 目标；adj. 客观的	something that you are trying to achieve; not influenced by personal feelings or opinions; considering only facts
objectivity	n. 客观性	a state or situation in which something is based only on facts and evidence
obligation	n. 义务	a moral or legal duty to do something
observation	n. 观察	the act of watching sb/sth carefully for a period of time, especially to learn sth
occasion	n. 场合	a time when something happens
offer	v. 提供	make sth available or to provide the opportunity for sth
opinion	n. 观点	your ideas or beliefs about a particular subject
opportunity	n. 机会	a chance to do something or an occasion when it is easy for you to do something
oppose	v. 反对	disagree with something such as a plan or idea and try to prevent it from happening or succeeding
opposition	n. 反对	the act of strongly disagreeing with sb/sth, especially with the aim of preventing sth from happening

抽象词	中文释义	英文释义
option	n. 选择	something that you can choose to have or do
outcome	n. 结果	the final result of a meeting, discussion, war etc. – used especially when no one knows what it will be until it actually happens
outline	v. 概述	give a description of the main facts or points involved in sth
overcome	v. 克服	succeed in dealing with or controlling a problem that has been preventing you from achieving sth
overlook	v. 忽略	fail to see or notice sth
overstate	v. 夸张	to say sth in a way that makes it seem more important than it really is
overview	n. 概要	a general description or an outline of sth
parallel	n./v. 并列	two or more lines that are parallel to each other are the same distance apart at every point
paraphrase	v. 释义	express what sb has said or written using different words, especially in order to make it easier to understand
parody	n. 恶搞	a piece of writing, music, acting, etc. that deliberately copies the style of sb/sth in order to be amusing
passion	n. 激情	a very strong feeling of love, hatred, anger, enthusiasm, etc.
perceive	v. 意识到	notice or become aware of sth
perception	n. 知觉	an idea, a belief or an image you have as a result of how you see or understand sth
permit	v. 允许	allow sb to do sth or to allow sth to happen
personality	n. 人格	the various aspects of a person's character that combine to make them different from other people
perspective	n. 角度	a particular attitude towards sth ; a way of thinking about sth
persuade	v. 劝说	make sb do sth by giving them good reasons for doing it

抽象词	中文释义	英文释义
phenomenon	n. 现象	something that happens or exists in society, science, or nature, especially something that is studied because it is difficult to understand
plan	n. 计划	something you have decided to do
plea	n./v. 恳求	a request that is urgent or full of emotion
point	n. 观点	the main or most important idea in sth that is said or done
point out	v. 指出	some economists have pointed out that low inflation is not necessarily a good thing
ponder	v. 沉思	think about sth carefully for a period of time
portray	v. 描绘	describe or show sb/sth in a particular way, especially when this does not give a complete or accurate impression of what they are like
portrayal	n. 描绘	the act of showing or describing sb/sth in a picture, play, book, etc. ; a particular way in which this is done
pose	v. 造成（威胁、问题）	create a threat, problem, etc. that has to be dealt with
position	n. 观点	an opinion on or an attitude towards a particular subject
possibility	n. 可能性	the fact that sth might exist or happen, but is not certain to
postulate	v. 假定	suggest or accept that sth is true so that it can be used as the basis for a theory, etc.
practical	adj. 实际的	connected with real situations rather than with ideas or theories
practicality	n. 实际	the quality of being suitable, or likely to be successful
practice	n. 实践	action rather than ideas
praise	n./v. 赞扬	say that you admire and approve of someone or something, especially publicly
preconceive	v. 预想	form (as an opinion) prior to actual knowledge or experience

抽象词	中文释义	英文释义
predict	v. 预言	say that something will happen, before it happens
prediction	n. 预言	a statement that says what you think will happen; the act of making such a statement
prefer	v. 更喜欢	choose one thing rather than sth else because you like it better
preference	n. 偏爱	a greater interest in or desire for sb/sth than sb/sth else
prefigure	v. 预想	suggest or show sth that will happen in the future
premise	n. 前提	a statement or an idea that forms the basis for a reasonable line of argument
preoccupation	n. 全神贯注	something that you give all your attention to
present	v. 提出	show or offer sth for other people to look at or consider
presentation	n. 展示	the act of showing sth or of giving sth to sb
presume	v. 假定	think that something is true, although you are not certain
presuppose	v. 假定	accept sth as true or existing and act on that basis, before it has been proved to be true
principle	n. 原则	a moral rule or a strong belief that influences your actions
privilege	n. 特权	a special advantage that is given only to one person or group of people
problem	n. 难题	a situation that causes difficulties
procedure	n. 过程	a way of doing something, especially the correct or usual way
process	n. 过程	a series of actions that are done in order to achieve a particular result
proclaim	v. 公开宣告	say publicly or officially that something important is true or exists
profile	n. 轮廓	the general impression that sb/sth gives to the public and the amount of attention they receive

抽象词	中文释义	英文释义
project	n. 项目	a set of aims, ideas or activities that sb is interested in or wants to bring to people's attention
promise	n./v. 承诺	tell sb that you will definitely do or not do sth, or that sth will definitely happen
promote	v. 促进	help something to develop or increase
proof	n. 证据	information, documents, etc. that show that sth is true
property	n. 性质	a quality or characteristic that sth has
proposal	n. 建议	a plan or suggestion which is made formally to an official person or group, or the act of making it
propose	v. 建议	suggest something as a plan or course of action
prospect	n. 前景	the possibility that sth will happen
prove	v. 证明	use facts, evidence, etc. to show that sth is true
provoke	v. 激起	to arouse to a feeling or action
pun	n. 双关语	the clever or humorous use of a word that has more than one meaning, or of words that have different meanings but sound the same
purpose	n. 目的	the intention, aim or function of sth, the thing that sth is supposed to achieve
pursue	v. 追求	to do sth or try to achieve sth over a period of time
qualification	n. 限制	a restriction in meaning or application
query	n./v. 质问	express doubt about whether sth is correct or not
quest	n./v. 寻求	a long search for sth, especially for some quality such as happiness
question	n./v. 怀疑	have or express doubts or suspicions about sth
quotation	n. 引用	repeat the exact words that another person has said or written
quote	v. 引用	repeat the exact words that another person has said or written

抽象词	中文释义	英文释义
raise	v. 提出	mention sth for people to discuss or sb to deal with
range	n. 范围	the limits between which sth varies
rationale	n. 基本原理	the principles or reasons which explain a particular decision, course of action, belief, etc.
rationalize	v. 使……合理化	find or try to find a logical reason to explain why sb thinks, behaves, etc. in a way that is difficult to understand
reaction	n. 反应	(to sb/sth) what you do, say or think as a result of sth that has happened
reality	n. 现实	the true situation and the problems that actually exist in life, in contrast to how you would like life to be
reason	n. 理由	a cause or an explanation for sth that has happened or that sb has done
reasoning	n. 推理	the process of thinking about things in a logical way; opinions and ideas that are based on logical thinking
reassess	v. 再评价	think again about sth to decide if you need to change your opinion of it
reassure	v. 使…安心	say or do sth that makes sb less frightened or worried
rebuke	v. 指责	speak to someone severely about something they have done wrong
rebut	v. 反驳	say or prove that a statement or criticism is false
recall	v. 回想起	remember a particular fact, event, or situation from the past
receive	v. 收到	get or accept sth that is sent or given to you
reception	n. 欢迎	a formal social occasion to welcome sb or celebrate sth
reciprocate	v. 互换	behave or feel towards sb in the same way as they behave or feel towards you

抽象词	中文释义	英文释义
reclaim	v. 收回	claim back
recognition	n. 认出	the act of remembering who sb is when you see them, or of identifying what sth is
recognize	v. 承认	admit or to be aware that sth exists or is true
recollection	n. 回忆	the ability to remember sth
recommend	v. 推荐	tell sb that sth is good or useful, or that sb would be suitable for a particular job, etc.
reconcile	v. 使和解	have a good relationship again with someone after you have quarrelled with them
record	n./v. 记录	a writtenaccount of sth that is kept so that it can be looked at and used in the future
recount	v. 叙述	tell sb about sth, especially sth that you have experienced
rectify	v. 纠正	to put right sth that is wrong
refer	v. 提到	mention or speak about someone or something
reference	n. 提及	a thing you say or write that mentions sb/sth else ; the act of mentioning sb/sth
reflect	v. 反思	to think carefully and deeply about sth
refrain	v. 克制	stop yourself from doing sth, especially sth that you want to do
refuse	v. 拒绝	say that you will not do sth that sb has asked you to do
refutation	n. 反驳	the act of proving that a statement or idea is not correct
refute	v. 反驳	prove that a statement or idea is not correct
regard	v. 认为	think about sb/sth in a particular way
regulation	n. 规章	an official rule made by a government or some other authority
reinforce	v. 强化	make a feeling, an idea, etc. stronger

抽象词	中文释义	英文释义
reiterate	v. 重申	say or do again or repeatedly
rejection	n. 拒绝	to refuse to accept or consider sth
relate	v. 使有联系	bring into or link in logical or natural association
relationship	n. 关系	the way in which two people, groups or countries behave towards each other or deal with each other
relevance	n. 相关	relation to the matter at hand
relief	n. 减轻	remove or reduce an unpleasant feeling or pain
relieve	v. 减轻	remove or reduce an unpleasant feeling or pain
remind	v. 使想起	make someone remember something that they must do
reminisce	v. 回忆	talk or think about pleasant events in your past
remorse	n. 懊悔	the feeling of being extremely sorry for sth wrong or bad that you have done
render	v. 致使 ... 到某种境地	cause sb/sth to be in a particular state or condition
renounce	v. 宣布放弃	state officially that you are no longer going to keep a title, position, etc.
report	n./v. 报告	to give people information about sth that you have heard, seen, done, etc.
represent	v. 代表	be a member of a group of people and act or speak on their behalf at an event, a meeting, etc.
representation	n. 代表	the act of presenting sb/sth in a particular way; something that shows or describes sth
reproach	v. 责备	to blame or criticize sb for sth that they have done or not done, because you are disappointed in them
repudiate	v. 否认	to refuse to accept sth
reputation	n. 名声	the general estimation in which a person is held by the public

抽象词	中文释义	英文释义
request	v. 请求	ask for sth or ask sb to do sth in a polite or formal way
require	v. 要求	to make sb do or have sth, especially because it is necessary according to a particular law or set of rules
research	n. 研究	a careful study of a subject, especially in order to discover new facts or information about it
reservation	n. 保留	a feeling of doubt about a plan or an idea
resolution	n. 决心；解决；正式决定	the quality of being resolute or determined；the act of answering：SOLVING；a formal statement of an opinion agreed on by a committee or a council, especially by means of a vote
resolve	v. 解决（难题）；下决心	to find a satisfactory solution to a problem or difficulty；to make a firm decision to do sth
respond to	v. 作出反应	do something as a reaction to something that has been said or done
response	n. 回应	something that is done as a reaction to something that has happened or been said
responsibility	n. 责任	a duty to be in charge of someone or something, so that you make decisions and can be blamed if something bad happens
restate	v. 重申	say sth again or in a different way, especially so that it is more clearly or strongly expressed
result	n. 结果	something that happens or exists because of something that happened before
reveal	v. 透露	make known something that was previously secret or unknown
review	n./v. 回顾	an examination of sth, with the intention of changing it if necessary
revive	v. 使复兴	bring something back after it has not been used or has not existed for a period of time
reward	v. 奖励	give sth to sb because they have done sth good, worked hard, etc.
right	n. 权利	power or privilege to which one is justly entitled

抽象词	中文释义	英文释义
role	n. 角色	the function or position that sb has or is expected to have in an organization, in society or in a relationship
romance	n. 浪漫史	an exciting, usually short, relationship between two people who are in love with each other
romanticism	n. 浪漫主义	the quality of seeing people, events and situations as more exciting and interesting than they really are
rouse	v. 激起	make someone start doing something, especially when they have been too tired or unwilling to do it
sacrifice	n./v. 牺牲	the fact of giving up sth important or valuable to you in order to get or do sth that seems more important, sth that you give up in this way
sake	n. 缘由	a reason for wanting something done
scale	n. 范围	the size or extent of sth, especially when compared with sth else
scenario	n. 设想；剧本	a description of how things might happen in the future; a written outline of what happens in a film/movie or play
sensation	n. 感觉	a feeling that you get from one of your five senses, especially the sense of touch
sensationalism	n. 哗众取宠	a way of getting people's interest by using shocking words or by presenting facts and events as worse or more shocking than they really are
sense	n./v. 感觉	one of the five powers (sight, hearing, smell, taste and touch) that your body uses to get information about the world around you
sentiment	n. 感情，观点	a feeling or an opinion, especially one based on emotions
sequence	n. 系列事件	a set of events, actions, numbers, etc. which have a particular order and which lead to a particular result
series	n. 系列	several events or things of a similar kind that happen one after the other

抽象词	中文释义	英文释义
setting	n. 环境	a set of surroundings
severity	n. 严厉	strict in judgment, discipline, or government
shift	n./v. 转换	to move, or move sth, from one position or place to another
shortcoming	n. 缺点	a fault in sb's character, a plan, a system, etc.
show	v. 显示	provide facts or information that make it clear that something is true, that something exists, or that something has happened
situation	n. 情况	a combination of all the things that are happening and all the conditions that exist at a particular time in a particular place
sketch	n./v. 描绘	to give a general description of sth, giving only the basic facts
solution	n. 解决方案	a way of solving a problem or dealing with a difficult situation
solve	v. 解决	find a way of dealing with a problem or difficult situation
sophistication	n. 成熟老练	having a lot of experience of life, and good judgment about socially important things such as art, fashion etc.
source	n. 来源	a place, person or thing that you get sth from
specialize	v. 使专门化	limit all or most of your study, business etc. to a particular subject or activity
specify	v. 指定	state sth, especially by giving an exact measurement, time, exact instructions, etc.
speculate	v. 推断	form an opinion about sth without knowing all the details or facts
speculation	n. 思考	the act of forming opinions about what has happened or what might happen without knowing all the facts
speech	n. 演讲	a talk, especially a formal one about a particular subject, given to a group of people

抽象词	中文释义	英文释义
spirit	n. 精神	the part of a person that includes their mind, feelings and character rather than their body
stage	n. 阶段	a particular time or state that something reaches as it grows or develops
stance	n. 立场	the opinions that sb has about sth and expresses publicly
standard	n. 标准	a level of quality, especially one that people think is acceptable
standpoint	n. 立场	a way of thinking about people, situations, ideas etc.
state	v. 陈述	formally write or say sth, especially in a careful and clear way
statement	n. 声明	something you say or write, especially publicly or officially, to let people know your intentions or opinions, or to record facts
status	n. 地位	the legal position of a person, group or country
stimulate	v. 刺激；鼓舞	encourage or help an activity to begin or develop further
stir	v. 激起	make sb excited or make them feel sth strongly
strain	v. 努力	to make an effort to do sth, using all your mental or physical strength
strategy	n. 策略	a planned series of actions for achieving something
strength	n. 强度	the quality of being physically strong
strengthen	v. 加强	become stronger or make something stronger
stress	v. 强调	emphasize a statement, fact, or idea
strive	v. 努力	make a great effort to achieve something
structure	n. 结构	the way in which the parts of sth are connected together, arranged or organized; a particular arrangement of parts
struggle	v. 挣扎	try very hard to do sth when it is difficult or when there are a lot of problems

抽象词	中文释义	英文释义
study	n./v. 研究	examine sth carefully in order to understand it
subject	n. 主题	the thing you are talking about or considering in a conversation, discussion, book, film etc.
submit	v. 服从	accept the authority, control or greater strength of sb/sth
substance	n. 实质	the most important or main part of sth
substantiate	v. 证实	to provide information or evidence to prove that sth is true
success	n. 成功	the fact that you have achieved sth that you want and have been trying to do or get
suggest	v. 建议；暗示	put forward an idea or a plan for other people to think about; to make evident indirectly; intimate or imply
suggestion	n. 建议；暗示	put forward an idea or a plan for other people to think about; to make evident indirectly; intimate or imply
summarize	v. 总结	make a short statement giving only the main information and not the details of a plan, event, report etc.
summary	n. 总结	a short statement that gives only the main points of sth, not the details
support	n./v. 支持	say that you agree with an idea, group, or person, and usually to help them because you want them to succeed
suppose	v. 假设	assume to be true or real for the sake of argument or explanation
supposition	n. 假定	an idea that you think is true although you may not be able to prove it
survey	n. 调查	an investigation of the opinions, behaviour, etc. of a particular group of people, which is usually done by asking them questions
susceptibility	n. 敏感	the state of being very likely to be influenced, harmed or affected by sth

抽象词	中文释义	英文释义
symbol	n. 象征	a person, an object, an event, etc. that represents a more general quality or situation
system	n. 系统	a group of related parts that work together as a whole for a particular purpose
take for granted	v. 理所当然	to assume as true, real, or expected
take issue with	v. 与…争论	argue with
target	n. 目标	a result that you try to achieve
task	n. 任务	a piece of work that sb has to do, especially a hard or unpleasant one
taste	n. 品味	a person's ability to choose things that people recognize as being of good quality or appropriate
technology	n. 技术	scientific knowledge used in practical ways in industry, for example in designing new machines
tendency	n. 趋势	predisposition to think, act, behave, or proceed in a particular way
term	n. 术语	a word or phrase used as the name of sth, especially one connected with a particular type of language
terminology	n. 术语	the set of technical words or expressions used in a particular subject
theme	n. 主题	the subject or main idea in a talk, piece of writing or work of art
theorem	n. 定理	a rule or principle, especially in mathematics, that can be proved to be true
theory	n. 理论	a formal set of ideas that is intended to explain why sth happens or exists
thought	n. 思想	a person's ideas or opinions about something
tolerate	v. 忍受	allow sb to do sth that you do not agree with or like
tone	n. 语气	the general character and attitude of sth such as a piece of writing, or the atmosphere of an event

抽象词	中文释义	英文释义
topic	n. 主题	a subject that you talk, write or learn about
tradition	n. 传统	a belief, custom or way of doing sth that has existed for a long time among a particular group of people
trait	n. 特征	a particular quality in your personality
transition	n. 过渡	passage from one form, state, style, or place to another
treatment	n. 处置	a particular way of behaving towards someone or of dealing with them
trend	n. 趋势	a general tendency in the way a situation is changing or developing
trigger	v. 引发	make something happen very quickly, especially a series of events
triumph	n. 胜利	an important victory or success after a difficult struggle
trivia	n. 琐事	detailed facts about history, sport, famous people etc.
trivialize	v. 使不重要	make sth seem less important, serious, difficult, etc. than it really is
truth	n. 事实	the true facts about sth, rather than the things that have been invented or guessed
unconcern	n. 不感兴趣	a lack of care, interest or worry about sth that other people would care about
underestimate	v. 低估	think or guess that something is smaller, cheaper, easier etc. than it really is
undergo	v. 经受	experience something, especially something that is unpleasant but necessary
underlie	v. 成为…的基础	be the basis or cause of sth
undermine	v. 渐渐破坏	make sth, especially sb's confidence or authority, gradually weaker or less effective
underscore	v. 强调	emphasize something or show that it is important

抽象词	中文释义	英文释义
understand	v. 理解	know or realize the meaning of words, a language, what sb says, etc.
understanding	n. 理解	the knowledge that sb has about a particular subject or situation
understate	v. 轻描淡写	describe something in a way that makes it seem less important or serious than it really is
understatement	n. 轻描淡写	the practice of making things seem less impressive, important, serious, etc. than they really are
undertake	v. 承担	make yourself responsible for sth and start doing it
undertaking	n. 承担	a task or project, especially one that is important and/or difficult
uneasiness	n. 不安	feeling worried or unhappy about a particular situation
uphold	v. 赞成	support sth that you think is right, fair, etc. and make sure that it continues to exist
urge	v. 催促	strongly suggest that someone does something
utilize	v. 利用	use sth, especially for a practical purpose
validate	v. 证实	prove that sth is true
validity	n. 有效性	the state of being legally or officially acceptable
value	v. 重视	consider important
verification	n. 核实	the act of verifying or the state of being verified
view	n. 观点	what you think or believe about something
viewpoint	n. 观点	a way of thinking about a subject
vindicate	v. 证明…正确	prove that sth is true or that you were right to do sth, especially when other people thought differently
virtue	n. 美德	behaviour or attitudes that show high moral standards
visualize	v. 想象	form a picture of someone or something in your mind

抽象词	中文释义	英文释义
voice	n. 观点	a particular attitude, opinion or feeling that is expressed
vulnerability	n. 易受伤	a place, thing, or idea that is vulnerable is easy to attack or criticize
warn	v. 警告	tell sb about sth, especially sth dangerous or unpleasant that is likely to happen, so that they can avoid it
way	n. 方法	a method, style or manner of doing sth
weakness	n. 弱点	lack of strength, power or determination
weigh	v. 权衡	consider sth carefully before making a decision
wisdom	n. 智慧	good sense and judgment, based especially on your experience of life
withstand	v. 禁得起	be strong enough to remain unharmed by something such as great heat, cold, pressure etc.
witness	n. 证人	someone who sees a crime or an accident and can describe what happened
wonder	v. 想知道	to feel curiosity or doubt
worry	n. 担心	keep thinking about unpleasant things that might happen or about problems that you have
worsen	v. 使恶化	become or make sth worse than it was before
yearn	v. 渴望	want sth very much, especially when it is very difficult to get
yield	v. 产生；屈服	to produce something useful such as information or evidence; to stop resisting sth/sb

态 度 词 汇

态度词汇（598 个），全部是从 100 套老 SAT 阅读中约 4800 道选项里和新 SAT55 套阅读中约 2800 道选项总结而成，非常具有代表性，几乎可以代表了英语中常见的绝大部分态度词，因此这些词有很大的概率会继续出现在以后的新 SAT 考试中，尤其是在小说文章中。认识它们，对于以后你们做选项分析和排除非常有帮助。

与抽象词类似，态度词也都非常难以理解和把握，即使背诵了中文意思，也不一定知道具体是什么意思。所以，大家一定要认真"体会"这些单词的英文释义。这些中英文释义全部是笔者根据 SAT 选型里常考的、精神层面的意思精心挑选的，最能代表 SAT 考试选项中出现的意思。

使用方法：希望同学们，每个单词无论认识与否，都要把英文释义读一遍，仔细"体会"这些单词的英文释义。如果和你想象的一样，才算真正认识；如果不一样，请做好标记，多读几遍。这些单词也经常在词汇题里被考到，希望大家重视！

态度词	中文释义	英文释义	态度
abashed	adj. 羞愧的	embarrassed and ashamed because of sth that you have done	负
abhorrence	n. 痛恨	a feeling of strong hatred, especially for moral reasons	负
abject terror	n. 不幸的恐怖	terrible and without hope ; a feeling of extreme fear	负
absolute neutrality	n. 绝对中立	the state of not supporting either side in a disagreement, competition or war	中
absurd	adj. 荒谬的	completely ridiculous ; not logical and sensible	负
accepting	adj. 可接受的	tolerating without protest	正
accusatory	adj. 指责的	intended to show someone that you think they have done something wrong	负

态度词	中文释义	英文释义	态度
acquisitive	adj. 贪得无厌的	trying to get things, especially because you want them, rather than because you need them	负
acrimonious	adj. 刻薄的	bitter and sharp in language or tone	负
adamant	adj. 坚定不移的	determined not to change your mind or to be persuaded about sth	正
admirable	adj. 令人钦佩的	having many good qualities that you respect and admire	正
admiration	n. 钦佩	a feeling of respect and liking for sb/sth	正
affecting	adj. 令人感动（伤心）的	producing strong feelings of sadness and sympathy	负
affectionate	adj. 温柔亲切的	showing caring feelings and love for sb	正
aggressive	adj. 侵略性的	behaving in an angry, threatening way, as if you want to fight or attack someone	负
agitated	adj. 焦虑的	showing in your behaviour that you are anxious and nervous	负
agreement	n. 同意	the state of sharing the same opinion or feeling	正
alarm	n. 惊慌	fear and anxiety that sb feels when sth dangerous or unpleasant might happen	负
aloof	adj. 冷淡的	someone who is aloof, or who remains or stays aloof from something, is not friendly or does not want to be involved in something	负
altruistic	adj. 利他的	thinking or behaving in a way that shows you care about other people and their interests more than you care about yourself	正
amazement	n. 惊异	a feeling of great surprise	负
ambiguous	adj. 模糊不清的	open to more than one interpretation	中
ambivalence	n. 矛盾情绪	The coexistence of opposing attitudes or feelings, such as love and hate, toward a person, object, or idea.	中
ambivalent	adj. 矛盾的	feeling two different things about something at the same time, for example that you like it and dislike it	中

态度词	中文释义	英文释义	态度
amiable	adj. 和蔼可亲的	friendly and easy to like	正
amused	adj. 被逗乐的	entertained or interested by something	正
amused disbelief	n. 被逗乐的怀疑	the feeling of not being able to believe sth	负
analytical	adj. 客观的	using a logical method of thinking about sth in order to understand it，especially by looking at all the parts separately	中
angry	adj. 愤怒的	feeling or showing anger	负
annoyance	n. 烦恼	a slightly angry or impatient feeling	负
annoyed	adj. 恼怒的	aroused to impatience or anger	负
anticipatory	adj. 期待的	a feeling of excitement about sth (usually sth good) that is going to happen	正
anxious	adj. 焦虑的	feeling worried or nervous	负
apathetic	adj. 冷漠的	feeling or showing a lack of interest or concern；indifferent	中
apologetic	adj. 道歉的	showing that you are sorry for doing something wrong or causing a problem	负
appreciate	v. 欣赏	to recognize the good qualities of sb/sth	正
apprehension	n. 恐惧	worry or fear that sth unpleasant may happen	负
apprehensive	adj. 忧虑的	worried or frightened that sth unpleasant may happen	负
approval	n. 批准	the feeling that sb/sth is good or acceptable	正
arbitrary	adj. 武断的	determined by chance，whim，or impulse，and not by necessity，reason，or principle	负
argumentative	adj. 争辩的	a person who is argumentative likes arguing or often starts arguing	负
arrogant	adj. 傲慢的	behaving in an unpleasant or rude way because you think you are more important than other people	负

态度词	中文释义	英文释义	态度
ashamed	adj. 惭愧的	feeling guilty or embarrassed because you have done something wrong, or think that you have not reached a standard that people expect	负
assured	adj. 自信的	confident in yourself and your abilities	正
astonishment	n. 惊讶	a feeling of very great surprise	负
athletic	adj. 体格健壮的	physically strong, fit and active	正
attractive	adj. 吸引人的	pleasant to look at	正
auspicious	adj. 吉兆的	showing signs that sth is likely to be successful in the future	正
awe	n. 敬畏	feelings of respect and slight fear	中
awestruck	adj. 惊奇不已的	feeling great respect for the importance, difficulty, or seriousness of someone or something	正
bafflement	n. 迷惑	if something baffles you, you cannot understand or explain it at all	负
balanced	adj. 平衡的	giving equal attention to all sides or opinions	中
baseless	adj. 无根据的	not supported by good reasons or facts	负
bashful	adj. 害羞的	shy and easily embarrassed	负
bemusement	n. 困惑	confusion resulting from failure to understand	负
beneficial	adj. 有益的	something that is beneficial has a good effect or influence on someone or something	正
bewilderment	n. 困惑	a feeling of being completely confused	负
biased	adj. 有偏见的	having a tendency to show favour towards or against one group of people or one opinion for personal reasons ; making unfair judgements	负
bitter disappointment	n. 大失所望	a feeling of dissatisfaction that results when your expectations are not realized	负
blatantly	adv. 喧闹地	noisy especially in a vulgar or offensive manner : CLAMOROUS	负

态度词	中文释义	英文释义	态度
blissful	adj. 极其喜悦的	extremely happy or enjoyable	正
blunt	adj. 直言不讳的	very direct；saying exactly what you think without trying to be polite	负
boredom	n. 厌倦	the feeling of being bored	负
boring	adj. 无聊的	not interesting；making you feel tired and impatient	负
calculated	adj. 深思熟虑的	carefully planned to get what you want	中
calm	adj. 平静的	not excited, nervous or upset	正
candid	adj. 坦白的	telling the truth, even when the truth may be unpleasant or embarrassing	正
capricious	adj. 反复无常的	likely to change your mind suddenly or behave in an unexpected way	负
captivate	v. 迷住	to influence and dominate by some special charm, art, or trait and with an irresistible appeal	正
carefree	adj. 无忧无虑的	having no worries or responsibilities	正
casual	adj. 非正式的	not formal	中
casual acceptance	n. 非正式的接受	the act of agreeing with sth and approving of it, not formal	正
cataclysmic	adj. 大灾难的	changing a situation in a sudden, violent, and unpleasant way	负
catharsis	n. 感情宣泄	the process of releasing strong feelings, for example through plays or other artistic activities, as a way of providing RELIEF from anger, suffering, etc.	正
caustic	adj. 刻薄的	a caustic remark criticizes someone in a way that is unkind but often cleverly humorous	负
cautious	adj. 谨慎的	being careful about what you say or do, especially to avoid danger or mistakes；not taking any risks	正
cautious optimism	n. 谨慎的乐观	a feeling that good things will happen and that sth will be successful	正

态度词	中文释义	英文释义	态度
cavalier	adj. 傲慢的	not caring enough about sth important or about the feelings of other people	负
celebratory	adj. 庆贺的	celebrating sth or marking a special occasion	正
cheerful optimism	n. 愉快的乐观	a feeling that good things will happen and that sth will be successful ; the tendency to have this feeling	正
cheerfulness	n. 高兴	happy, or behaving in a way that shows you are happy	正
civil	adj. 有礼貌的	adequate in courtesy and politeness : MANNERLY	正
clumsy	adj. 笨拙的	moving or doing things in a very awkward way	负
combative	adj. 好战的	ready and willing to fight or argue	负
comforting	adj. 令人欣慰的	making you feel calmer and less worried or unhappy	正
comical	adj. 滑稽的	behaviour or situations that are comical are funny in a strange or unexpected way	正
commendable	adj. 值得赞美的	deserving praise or admiration	正
compassion	n. 同情	a strong feeling of sympathy for people who are suffering and a desire to help them	正
complacent	adj. 自满的	too confident and relaxed because you think you can deal with something easily, even though this may not be true	负
complete agreement	n. 完全赞同	the fact of sb approving of sth and allowing it to happen	正
complimentary	adj. 问候的	saying that you admire someone or something	正
concerned	adj. 焦虑的	feeling or showing worry or solicitude	负
conciliatory	adj. 调和的	having the intention or effect of making angry people calm	正
condescending	adj. 故意屈尊的	behaving as though you think you are better, more intelligent, or more important than other people	负

态度词	中文释义	英文释义	态度
confessional	adj. 忏悔的	admitting to bad or embarrassing things that you have done	负
confident	adj. 自信的	sure that something will happen in the way that you want or expect	正
confiding	adj. 坦白的	behaving in a way that shows you want to tell someone about something that is private or secret	负
conflicted	adj. 矛盾的	unable to decide what your feelings or opinions are about something	中
confrontational	adj. 对抗的	behaving in a way that shows you want to have an argument or fight with someone	负
confused	adj. 困惑的	unable to understand or think clearly what someone is saying or what is happening	负
confusion	n. 困惑	a state of uncertainty about what is happening, what you should do, what sth means, etc.	负
conjectural	adj. 猜测的	the development of a theory or guess based on information that is not complete	负
conscientious	adj. 尽责的	careful to do everything that it is your job or duty to do	正
considerable	adj. 可观的	great in amount, size, importance, etc.	正
considerable surprise	n. 极度吃惊	an event, a piece of news, etc. that is unexpected or that happens suddenly	负
consternation	n. 惊愕	a feeling of great surprise, shock or anxiety	负
constrained	adj. 不自然的	not natural ; forced or too controlled	负
constructive	adj. 有助益的	having a useful and helpful effect rather than being negative or with no purpose	正
contempt	n. 轻视，蔑视	lack of respect accompanied by a feeling of intense dislike	负
contemptuous	adj. 轻蔑的	feeling or showing that you have no respect for sb/sth	负
contented	adj. 满足的	showing or feeling happiness or satisfaction, especially because your life is good	正

态度词	中文释义	英文释义	态度
contentious	adj. 引起争论的	causing a lot of argument and disagreement between people	负
contentment	n. 满意	a feeling of happiness or satisfaction	正
contrite	adj. 后悔的	very sorry for sth bad that you have done	负
controversial	adj. 有争议的	causing a lot of disagreement，because many people have strong opinions about the subject being discussed	负
convoluted	adj. 复杂的	extremely complicated and difficult to follow	负
corrupt	adj. 腐败的	willing to use their power to do dishonest or illegal things in return for money or to get an advantage	负
courageous	adj. 勇敢的	brave	正
cramped	adj. 限制的	writing that is cramped is very small and difficult to read	负
crass	adj. 愚钝的	very stupid and showing no sympathy or understanding	负
credible	adj. 可信的	able to be believed or trusted	正
credulous	adj. 轻信的	too ready to believe things and therefore easy to deceive	负
critical	adj. 批评的	expressing disapproval of sb/sth and saying what you think is bad about them	负
cryptic	adj. 神秘的	with a meaning that is hidden or not easily understood	负
cunning	adj. 狡猾的	someone who is cunning is clever and good at deceiving people in order to get what they want	负
curiosity	n. 好奇心	a desire to know or learn	正
curious	adj. 好奇的	having a strong desire to know about sth	正
cynical	adj. 讽刺的	expressing jaded or scornful skepticism or negativity	负
cynical mistrust	n. 愤世嫉俗的不信任	a feeling that you cannot trust sb/sth	负

态度词	中文释义	英文释义	态度
dark foreboding	n. 不祥的预感	a strong feeling that sth unpleasant or dangerous is going to happen	负
deceitful	adj. 欺骗的	behaving in a dishonest way by telling lies and making people believe things that are not true	负
deceptive	adj. 欺诈的	likely to make you believe sth that is not true	负
decisive	adj. 果断的	able to decide sth quickly and with confidence	正
dedication	n. 奉献	hard work or effort that someone puts into a particular activity because they care about it a lot	正
defensive	adj. 防御用的	protecting sb/sth against attack	正
deferential	adj. 恭顺的	respect and esteem due a superior or an elder	正
defiant	adj. 挑衅的	openly refusing to obey sb/sth，sometimes in an aggressive way	负
dejected	adj. 沮丧的	unhappy and disappointed	负
delicate	adj. 敏感的	marked by keen sensitivity or fine discrimination	负
delighted	adj. 高兴的	very pleased	正
demeaning	adj. 降低身份的	putting sb in a position that does not give them the respect that they should have	负
deplorable	adj. 可叹的	extremely bad and shocking	负
depressed	adj. 沮丧的	very sad and without hope	负
derisive	adj. 嘲笑的	showing that you think someone or something is stupid or silly	负
despair	n. 绝望	the feeling of having lost all hope	负
despondent	adj. 沮丧的	extremely unhappy and without hope	负
destructive	adj. 破坏的	causing destruction or damage	负
detached	adj. 客观的	not feeling involved with someone or something in a close or emotional way	中

态度词	中文释义	英文释义	态度
detachment	n. 客观	the state of not being involved in sth in an emotional or personal way	中
deteriorating	adj. 恶化的	become worse	负
determination	n. 决心	the quality of trying to do something even when it is difficult	正
determined	adj. 坚决的	firmly resolved	正
detrimental	adj. 有害的	harmful	负
didactic	adj. 说教的	designed to teach people sth, especially a moral lesson	负
diffident	adj. 缺乏自信的	not having much confidence in yourself ; not wanting to talk about yourself	负
disapproving	adj. 不赞成的	showing that you do not approve of sb/sth	负
disbelief	n. 怀疑	the feeling of not being able to believe sth	负
discerning	adj. 有辨识能力的	able to show good judgement about the quality of sb/sth	正
discreet	adj. 谨慎的	careful about what you say or do, so that you do not offend, upset, or embarrass people or tell secrets	正
disdain	v. 鄙弃	to think that someone or something is not important and does not deserve any respect	负
disdainful	adj. 轻蔑的	showing that you do not respect someone or something, because you think that they are not important or good enough	负
disgruntled	adj. 不高兴的	annoyed or disappointed because sth has happened to upset you	负
disgust	n./v. 厌恶	a strong feeling of dislike or disapproval for sb/sth that you feel is unacceptable, or for sth that looks, smells, etc. unpleasant	负
disillusioned	adj. 幻想破灭的	disappointed because the person you admired or the idea you believed to be good and true now seems without value	负

态度词	中文释义	英文释义	态度
dismay	n. 沮丧	the worry, disappointment, or unhappiness you feel when something unpleasant happens	负
dismissal	n. 放弃	the failure to consider sth as important	负
dismissive	adj. 表示轻视的	showing that you do not believe a person or thing to be important or worth considering	负
disobedient	adj. 不服从的	refusing or neglecting to obey	负
disparaging	adj. 轻蔑的	criticizing someone or something, and showing that you do not think they are very good or important	负
dispirited	adj. 沮丧的	having no hope or enthusiasm	负
dissatisfaction	n. 不满	a feeling of not being satisfied	负
distant	adj. 冷漠的	not friendly; not wanting a close relationship with sb	负
distress	n. 悲痛	a feeling of great worry or unhappiness; great suffering	负
disturbing	adj. 令人不安的	making you feel anxious and upset or shocked	负
divisive	adj. 造成不和的	causing a lot of disagreement between people	负
doleful	adj. 悲哀的	very sad	负
doubt	n./v. 怀疑	to feel uncertain about sth; to feel that sth is not true, will probably not happen, etc.	负
doubtful	adj. 可疑的	not sure that something is true or right	负
dramatic anticipation	戏剧性的期待	a feeling of excitement about something enjoyable that is going to happen soon	正
dread	n. 恐惧	a strong fear of something that is going to happen or may happen	负
dreary	adj. 沉闷的	dull and making you feel sad or bored	负
droll	adj. 滑稽的	funny in an unusual way	正
dubious	adj. 可疑的	probably not honest, true, right etc.	负

态度词	中文释义	英文释义	态度
duplicitous	adj. 奸诈的	dishonest behaviour that is intended to deceive someone	负
dynamic	adj. 有活力的	full of energy and new ideas, and determined to succeed	正
eager	adj. 渴望的	very interested and excited by sth that is going to happen or about sth that you want to do	正
eagerness	n. 渴望	positive feeling of wanting to push ahead with something	正
earnest	adj. 诚恳的	serious, determined, and meaning what you say	正
eccentric	adj. 古怪的	considered by other people to be strange or unusual	负
ecstatic	adj. 狂喜的	very happy, excited and enthusiastic	正
elated	adj. 兴高采烈的	very happy and excited because of sth good that has happened, or will happen	正
embarrassment	n. 窘迫	shy, awkward or guilty feelings ; a feeling of being embarrassed	负
emotional	adj. 情感的	determined or actuated by emotion rather than reason	中
empathetic	adj. 同理心的	the ability to understand other people's feelings and problems	正
emphatic	adj. 断然的	expressing an opinion, idea etc. in a clear, strong way to show its importance	正
engaging	adj. 迷人的	interesting or pleasant in a way that attracts your attention	正
entertaining	adj. 令人愉快的	interesting and amusing	正
enthusiasm	n. 热情	a strong feeling of interest and enjoyment about something and an eagerness to be involved in it	正
enthusiastic	adj. 热情的	feeling or showing a lot of excitement and interest about sb/sth	正

态度词	中文释义	英文释义	态度
envious	adj. 嫉妒的	unhappy because you want very much to do something that someone else does or have something that they have	负
envy	n. 嫉妒	a feeling of discontent and resentment aroused by and in conjunction with desire for the possessions or qualities of another	负
equivocal	adj. 模棱两可的	uncertain as an indication or sign	中
erroneous	adj. 错误的	not correct ; based on wrong information	负
euphoric	adj. 欣快的	feeling very happy and excited	正
evenhanded	adj. 公平的	showing no partiality ; fair	正
evocative	adj. 唤起的	making you think of or remember a strong image or feeling, in a pleasant way	正
exaggeration	n. 夸张	a statement or description that makes sth seem larger, better, worse or more important than it really is	负
exasperated	adj. 激怒的	extremely annoyed, especially if you cannot do anything to improve the situation	负
exasperation	n. 恼怒	when you feel annoyed because someone continues to do something that is upsetting you	负
excited	adj. 兴奋的	feeling or showing happiness and enthusiasm	正
excusable	adj. 可原谅的	if something bad is excusable, you can understand why someone did it and forgive them	正
exhausted	adj. 疲惫的	extremely tired	负
exhilarated	adj. 高兴的	feeling extremely happy, excited, and full of energy	正
extravagant	adj. 奢侈的	spending a lot more money or using a lot more of sth than you can afford or than is necessary	负
exuberant	adj. 生机勃勃的	full of energy, excitement and happiness	正
fair	adj. 公平的	treating all equally	正

态度词	中文释义	英文释义	态度
fallacious	adj.谬误的	wrong ; based on a false idea	负
fascinated	adj.着迷的	intensely interested in or attracted	正
fascination	n.魅力	a very strong attraction, that makes sth very interesting	正
fatalistic	adj.宿命论的	showing a belief in fate and feeling that you cannot control events or stop them from happening	负
fear	n.害怕	the bad feeling that you have when you are in danger, when sth bad might happen, or when a particular thing frightens you	负
fearful	adj.可怕的	frightened that something might happen	负
feigned innocence	n.假装无辜	pretended to be not guilty of a crime, etc.	负
flattery	n.奉承	praise that you do not really mean	负
flawed	adj.有缺陷的	spoiled by having mistakes, weaknesses, or by being damaged	负
flawless	adj.完美的	being entirely without flaw or imperfection	正
flippant	adj.轻率的	showing that you do not take sth as seriously as other people think you should	负
fickle	adj.变幻无常的	changing often and suddenly	负
foolish	adj.愚蠢的	lacking in sense, judgment, or discretion	负
formulaic	adj.刻板的	containing or made from ideas or expressions that have been used many times before and are therefore not very new or interesting	负
forthright	adj.直率的	direct and honest in manner and speech	正
foul	adj.邪恶的	very evil or wicked	负
frank	adj.坦白的	open and sincere in expression ; straightforward	正
frantic	adj.疯狂的	extremely worried and frightened about a situation, so that you cannot control your feelings	负

态度词	中文释义	英文释义	态度
fraudulent	adj. 欺骗性的	made with the intention of tricking someone, especially illegally	负
friendly	adj. 友好的	behaving towards someone in a way that shows you like them and are ready to talk to them or help them	正
frightened	adj. 害怕的	thrown into a state of intense fear or desperation	负
frivolous	adj. 无价值的	unworthy of serious attention; trivial	负
frugality	n. 节俭	careful to buy only what is necessary	正
frustration	n. 挫折	the feeling of being annoyed, upset, or impatient, because you cannot control or change a situation, or achieve something	负
furious	adj. 狂怒的	very angry	负
futile	adj. 无用的	having no purpose because there is no chance of success	负
generosity	n. 慷慨	kindness, especially in giving things to people	正
genial	adj. 友好的	friendly and cheerful	正
genuine	adj. 诚恳的	a genuine feeling, desire etc. is one that you really feel, not one you pretend to feel	正
gifted	adj. 有天赋的	having a natural ability to do one or more things extremely well	正
grandiose	adj. 浮夸的	seeming very impressive but too large, complicated, expensive, etc. to be practical or possible	负
grateful	adj. 感谢的	feeling that you want to thank someone because of something kind that they have done, or showing this feeling	正
gratifying	adj. 令人满足的	pleasing and giving satisfaction	正
gratitude	n. 感谢	the feeling of being grateful and wanting to express your thanks	正
groundless	adj. 无理由的	not based on facts or reason	负

态度词	中文释义	英文释义	态度
grudging	adj. 勉强的	done, given, or allowed unwillingly, reluctantly, or sparingly	中
grudging acceptance	n. 勉强的接受	general agreement that something is true, reasonable, or cannot be changed unwillingly	正
guarded	adj. 谨慎的	careful; not showing feelings or giving much information	正
guarded skepticism	n. 有点儿怀疑	a doubting or questioning attitude or state of mind	负
guilty	adj. 内疚的	feeling very ashamed and sad because you know that you have done something wrong	负
gullible	adj. 易受骗的	too willing to believe or accept what other people tell you and therefore easily tricked	负
haughty	adj. 傲慢的	proud and unfriendly	负
headstrong	adj. 顽固的	a headstrong person is determined to do things their own way and refuses to listen to advice	负
heartening	adj. 鼓舞人心的	encouraging	正
heartfelt	adj. 真诚的	showing strong feelings that are sincere	正
heartless	adj. 无情的	cruel and not feeling any pity	负
heavy-handed	adj. 无同理心的	not showing a sympathetic understanding of the feelings of other people	负
heightened	adj. 气势高涨的	to make brighter or more intense :DEEPEN	正
hilarious	adj. 喜不自禁的	extremely funny	正
hopeful	adj. 有希望的	believing that what you hope for is likely to happen	正
hostile	adj. 敌对的	very unfriendly or aggressive and ready to argue or fight	负
hostility	n. 敌意	unfriendly or threatening behavior or feelings toward someone	负
humble	adj. 谦逊的	not considering yourself or your ideas to be as important as other people's	正

态度词	中文释义	英文释义	态度
humility	n. 谦逊	the quality of not thinking that you are better than other people ; the quality of being humble	正
humor	n. 幽默	The quality that makes something laughable or amusing ; funniness	正
humorous	adj. 幽默的	funny and entertaining ; showing a sense of humour	正
hyperbolic	adj. 夸张的	a way of describing something by saying it is much bigger, smaller, worse etc. than it actually is	负
hypocrite	n. 伪君子	a person who pretends to have moral standards or opinions that they do not actually have	负
idealistic	adj. 空想的	having a strong belief in perfect standards and trying to achieve them, even when this is not realistic	负
idyllic	adj. 田园诗的	extremely beautiful and peaceful	正
ill-tempered	adj. 坏脾气的	angry and rude or irritated, especially when this seems unreasonable	负
imaginative	adj. 富于想象的	having or showing new and exciting ideas	正
impartial	adj. 中立的	not partial or biased ; unprejudiced	中
impassive	adj. 冷漠的	not showing any feeling or emotion	负
impatience	n. 无耐心	annoyance at having to accept delays, other people's weaknesses etc.	负
impatient	adj. 不耐心的	annoyed because of delays, someone else's mistakes etc.	负
impersonal	adj. 没人情味的	lacking friendly human feelings or atmosphere ; making you feel unimportant	负
impetuous	adj. 鲁莽的	tending to do things very quickly, without thinking carefully first, or showing this quality	负
impressive	adj. 印象深刻的	making a strong or vivid impression ; striking or remarkable	正

态度词	中文释义	英文释义	态度
incapable	adj. 不能胜任的	not able to do sth	负
incensed	adj. 愤怒的	very angry	负
incomprehensible	adj. 费解的	impossible to understand	负
inconclusive	adj. 不确定的	not leading to a clear decision or result	负
inconsequential	adj. 不重要的	not important	负
incredible	adj. 难以置信的	surprising or difficult to believe	负
incredulity	n. 怀疑	a feeling that you cannot believe something	负
incredulous	adj. 怀疑的	not able to believe something or not wanting to believe it	负
indifference	n. 漠不关心	lack of interest or concern	中
indifferent	adj. 漠不关心的	having or showing no interest in sb/sth	中
indignant	adj. 愤怒的	feeling or showing anger and surprise because you think that you have been treated unfairly	负
indignation	n. 愤怒	a feeling of anger and surprise caused by sth that you think is unfair or unreasonable	负
indulgent	adj. 放纵的	willing to allow someone, especially a child, to do or have whatever they want, even if this is not good for them	负
industrious	adj. 勤勉的	always working very hard	正
inflammatory	adj. 煽动性的	intended to cause very strong feelings of anger	负
influential	adj. 有影响的	having a lot of influence on sb/sth	正
informal	adj. 非正式的	not following strict rules of how to behave or do sth	中
infuriate	v. 激怒	to make sb extremely angry	负
ingenious	adj. 有独创性的	having a lot of clever new ideas and good at inventing things	正
ingrained	adj. 根深蒂固的	ingrained attitudes or behaviour are firmly established and therefore difficult to change	负

态度词	中文释义	英文释义	态度
innovative	adj.创新的	an innovative idea or way of doing something is new, different, and better than those that existed before	正
inquisitive	adj.好奇的	very interested in learning about many different things	正
insane	adj.极愚蠢的	completely stupid or crazy, often in a way that is dangerous	负
insecure	adj.不安全的	not safe or protected	负
insidious	adj.阴险的	something that is insidious is dangerous because it seems to be harmless or not important but in fact causes harm or damage	负
insightful	adj.有洞察力的	showing a very good understanding of a person or a complicated situation	正
insolent	adj.傲慢的	extremely rude and showing a lack of respect	负
inspirational	adj.鼓舞人心的	giving you the enthusiasm to do or create something	正
inspiring	adj.鼓舞人心的	giving people a feeling of excitement and a desire to do something great	正
instructive	adj.有益的	giving a lot of useful information	正
instrumental	adj.有帮助的	to be important in making something happen	正
intelligent	adj.聪明的	good at learning, understanding and thinking in a logical way about things ; showing this ability	正
intimidating	adj.令人生畏的	making you feel worried and not confident	负
intolerable	adj.无法忍受的	too difficult, bad, annoying etc. for you to accept or deal with	负
intolerant	adj.无法忍受的	unable or unwilling to endure	负
intoxicating	adj.令人头脑迷糊的	making you feel excited so that you cannot think clearly	负
intrigued	adj.好奇的	very interested in sth/sb and wanting to know more about it/them	正

态度词	中文释义	英文释义	态度
invigorating	adj. 精力充沛的	making you feel healthy and giving you a lot of energy	正
irate	adj. 盛怒的	very angry	负
ironic	adj. 反讽的	showing that you really mean the opposite of what you are saying ; expressing IRONY	负
ironic detachment	n. 具有讽刺意味的客观	the state of not being involved in sth in an emotional or personal way, using words that are the opposite of what you really mean, often in a joking way	负
irony	n. 讽刺	when you use words that are the opposite of what you really mean, often in order to be amusing	负
irrefutable	adj. 无可辩驳的	that cannot be proved wrong and that must therefore be accepted	正
irreverent	adj. 不敬的	not showing respect to sb/sth that other people usually respect	负
irritation	n. 激怒	the feeling of being annoyed about something, especially something that happens repeatedly or for a long time	负
jaded dismissal	n. 无聊的放弃	tired and bored, usually because you have had too much of sth; the failure to consider sth as important	负
jealous	adj. 嫉妒的	feeling angry or unhappy because you wish you had sth that sb else has	负
jocular	adj. 诙谐的	enjoying making people laugh	正
jocularity	n. 幽默	activity characterized by good humor	正
jovial	adj. 善良快活的	friendly and happy	正
jubilation	n. 喜欢	a feeling of great happiness because of a success	正
judgmental	adj. 妄下判断的	criticizing people very quickly	负
lamentable	adj. 令人哀悼的	so bad that you feel disappointed or angry	负
laudatory	adj. 赞美的	expressing praise or admiration	正

态度词	中文释义	英文释义	态度
lighthearted	adj. 心情愉快的	happy and not worried about anything	正
ludicrous	adj. 荒唐的	laughable or hilarious because of obvious absurdity or incongruity	负
magnanimous	adj. 宽宏大量的	willing to forgive people or willing to be kind and fair	正
malicious	adj. 恶毒的	having or showing hatred and a desire to harm sb or hurt their feelings	负
manipulative	adj. 幕后操纵的	clever at controlling or deceiving people to get what you want	负
maudlin	adj. 感情脆弱的	talking in a silly, emotional way, often full of pity for yourself, especially when drunk	负
measured	adj. 慎重的	slow and careful; controlled	正
mediocre	adj. 平庸的	not very good; of only average standard	负
melancholy	adj. 使人悲伤的	a deep feeling of sadness that lasts for a long time and often cannot be explained	负
menacing	adj. 威胁的	seeming likely to cause you harm or danger	负
mercenary	adj. 唯利是图的	only interested in making or getting money	负
merriment	n. 欢喜	happy talk, laughter and enjoyment	正
mild	adj. 温和的	not severe or harsh	正
mirthful	adj. 愉快的	full of gladness and gaiety	正
mischievous	adj. 淘气的	enjoying playing tricks and annoying people	负
misguided	adj. 被误导的	a misguided idea or action is based on judgments or opinions that are wrong	负
misleading	adj. 令人误解的	giving the wrong idea or impression and making you believe sth that is not true	负
mockery	n. 嘲弄	the remarks or behavior intended to make someone seem stupid	负
mocking	adj. 嘲弄的	showing that you think sb/sth is ridiculous	负
modest	adj. 谦虚的	not talking much about your own abilities or possessions	正

态度词	中文释义	英文释义	态度
moody	adj. 易郁闷的	subject to depression : GLOOMY	负
momentous	adj. 重要的	very important because of having an effect on future events	正
moral	adj. 道德的	following the standards of behaviour considered acceptable and right by most people	正
moralistic	adj. 说教的	expressing strong ideas about what is right or wrong and trying to make other people behave according to them	负
morose	adj. 郁闷的	unhappy, bad-tempered and not talking very much	负
mundane	adj. 平凡的	not interesting or exciting	负
naive	adj. 幼稚的	a naive person lacks experience of life and tends to trust other people and believe things too easily	负
naked ambition	n. 赤裸的雄心	an eager or strong desire to achieve something, such as fame or power	正
narrow-minded	adj. 心胸狭窄的	not willing to listen to new ideas or to the opinions of others	负
nervous apprehension	n. 紧张的忧惧	worry or fear that sth unpleasant may happen	负
neutral	adj. 中立的	belonging to neither side in a controversy	中
neutrality	n. 中立	the state of not supporting either side in a disagreement, competition or war	中
nonchalance	n. 冷淡	the trait of remaining calm and seeming not to care	中
nonchalant	adj. 漠不关心的	behaving calmly and not seeming interested in anything or worried about anything	中
nonplussed	adj. 困惑的	so surprised and confused that you do not know what to do or say	负
nostalgia	n. 怀旧	a feeling of sadness mixed with pleasure and affection when you think of happy times in the past	负

态度词	中文释义	英文释义	态度
nostalgic	adj. 怀旧的	a wistful or excessively sentimental yearning for return to or of some past period or irrecoverable condition	负
nostalgic regret	n. 怀旧的遗憾	a feeling of sadness or disappointment that you have because of sth that has happened or sth that you have done or not done	负
objective	adj. 客观的	not influenced by personal feelings or opinions ; considering only facts	中
obsequious	adj. 奉承的	very eager to please or agree with people who are powerful	负
offended	adj. 冒犯的	hurt or upset	负
offensive	adj. 冒犯的	unpleasant or insulting, and likely to make people upset or embarrassed	负
ominous	adj. 不吉利的	making you feel that something bad is going to happen	负
open amusement	n. 极度逗乐	the feeling that you have when sth is funny or amusing, or it entertains you	正
open contempt	n. 极度蔑视	the feeling that sb/sth is without value and deserves no respect at all	负
open-minded	adj. 思想开明的	willing to consider and accept other people's ideas and opinions	正
opposition	n. 反对	strong disagreement with, or protest against, something such as a plan, law, or system	负
optimism	n. 乐观	a feeling that good things will happen and that sth will be successful ; the tendency to have this feeling	正
optimistic	adj. 乐观的	expecting good things to happen or sth to be successful	正
outrage	n. 愤怒	a strong feeling of shock and anger	负
outright disapproval	n. 完全不赞同	a feeling that you do not like an idea, an action or sb's behaviour because you think it is bad, not suitable or going to have a bad effect on sb else	负

态度词	中文释义	英文释义	态度
outspoken condemnation	n.直言不讳的谴责	an expression of very strong disapproval	负
overbearing	adj.专横的	trying to control other people in an unpleasant way	负
overpowering	adj.无法控制的	an overpowering feeling is so strong you cannot control it	负
overwhelming	adj.势不可挡的	very great or very strong ; so powerful that you cannot resist it or decide how to react	正
pampered	adj.放纵的	receiving a lot of care and attention, often so much that it spoils your character	负
patronizing	adj.摆出恩赐态度的	behaving or speaking in a way that shows you think you are more intelligent or important than someone	负
paradoxical	adj.矛盾的	consisting of two parts that seem to mean the opposite of each other	中
paranoid	adj.妄想狂的	worrying that people do not like you and are trying to harm you, although you have no proof of this	负
partial acceptance	n.部分接受	the act of agreeing with sth and approving of it, not complete or whole	正
passionate	adj.热情的	having or showing strong feelings of enthusiasm for sth or belief in sth	正
patriotic	adj.爱国的	having or expressing a great love of your country	正
pensive	adj.哀思的	thinking deeply about sth, especially because you are sad or worried	负
perplexed	adj.困惑的	confused and anxious because you are unable to understand sth	负
perplexity	n.困惑	the feeling of being confused or worried by something you cannot understand	负
persuasive	adj.有说服力的	able to persuade sb to do or believe sth	正
pessimistic	adj.悲观的	thinking that the worst thing will happen in every situation	负

态度词	中文释义	英文释义	态度
placid	adj. 平静的	not easily excited or irritated	正
plausible	adj. 可信的	reasonable and likely to be true	正
playful	adj. 幽默的	full of fun and high spirits	正
pleased	adj. 高兴的	experiencing or manifesting pleasure	正
polite	adj. 有礼貌的	someone who is polite behaves toward other people in a pleasant way that follows all the usual rules of society	正
possessive	adj. 占有欲强的	not willing to share things	负
poignant	adj. 辛辣的	having a strong effect on your feelings, especially in a way that makes you feel sad	负
precarious	adj. 危险的	not safe or certain ; dangerous	负
precocious	adj. 太早熟的	(sometimes disapproving) (of a child) having developed particular abilities and ways of behaving at a much younger age than usual	负
preoccupation	n. 全神贯注	a mood created by thinking or worrying about sth and ignoring everything else	负
pretentious	adj. 自命不凡的	if someone or something is pretentious, they try to seem more important, intelligent, or high class than they really are in order to be impressive	负
pride	n. 自豪	a feeling of pleasure or satisfaction that you get when you or people who are connected with you have done sth well or own sth that other people admire	正
profound	adj. 有深度的	having intellectual depth and insight	正
proud	adj. 自豪的	feeling pleased and satisfied about sth that you own or have done, or are connected with	正
provocative	adj. 激怒的	intended to make people angry or upset ; intended to make people argue about sth	负
prudent	adj. 谨慎的	sensible and careful when you make judgements and decisions ; avoiding unnecessary risks	正

态度词	中文释义	英文释义	态度
puzzled	adj. 困惑的	confused and unable to understand something	负
puzzlement	n. 迷惑	the state of being confused or baffled ; perplexity	负
qualified admiration	n. 有保留的赞扬	a feeling of respect and liking for sb/sth, limited in some way	正
qualified appreciation	n. 有点儿欣赏	limited pleasure you feel when you realize something is good, useful, or well done	正
quarrelsome	adj. 好争论的	liking to argue with other people	负
quizzical	adj. 古怪的	comically quaint	负
reckless	adj. 鲁莽的	showing a lack of care about danger and the possible results of your actions	负
recommended	adj. 被推荐的	mentioned as worthy of acceptance	正
reflective	adj. 沉思的	thinking quietly about something	正
regretful	adj. 后悔的	feeling or showing sadness or disappointment because of sth that has happened or sth that you have done or not done	负
relief	n. 减轻	removal of anxiety / pain	正
relieved	adj.（焦虑）缓和的	feeling happy because you are no longer worried about something	正
reluctant	adj. 不情愿的	not willing to do something	负
remorseful	adj. 懊悔的	feeling sad or guilty for having done something wrong	负
reproach	v. 责备	to blame or criticize sb for sth that they have done or not done, because you are disappointed in them	负
resent	v. 怨恨	to feel bitter or angry about sth, especially because you feel it is unfair	负
resentful disappointment	n. 愤恨的不满	sadness because sth has not happened or been as good, successful, etc. as you expected or hoped	负

态度词	中文释义	英文释义	态度
resentment	n. 愤恨	a feeling of anger or unhappiness about sth that you think is unfair	负
resignation	n. 无可奈何而放弃	when someone calmly accepts a situation that cannot be changed, even though it is bad	负
resigned	adj. 放弃的	to give up deliberately	负
resolute	adj. 坚决的	extremely determined	正
respectful	adj. 恭敬的	feeling or showing respect	正
retaliation	n. 报复	action that a person takes against sb who has harmed them in some way	负
reticence	n. 沉默寡言	restrained in expression, presentation, or appearance	负
reverent	adj. 恭敬的	feeling or expressing a lot of respect and admiration	正
rewarding	adj. 有益的	worth doing ; that makes you happy because you think it is useful or important	正
righteous	adj. 正义的	morally right and good	正
saccharine	adj. 甜得发腻的	too romantic in a way that seems silly and insincere	负
sanguine	adj. 乐观的	cheerful and confident about the future	正
sarcasm	n. 反讽	a way of using words that are the opposite of what you mean in order to be unpleasant to sb or to make fun of them	负
sarcastic	adj. 反讽的	saying things that are the opposite of what you mean, in order to make an unkind joke or to show that you are annoyed	负
sardonic	adj. 讽刺的	showing that you think that you are better than other people and do not take them seriously	负
satiric	adj. 讽刺的	a way of criticizing something such as a group of people or a system, in which you deliberately make them seem funny so that people will see their faults	负

态度词	中文释义	英文释义	态度
satirical	adj. 讽刺性的	a way of criticizing something such as a group of people or a system, in which you deliberately make them seem funny so that people will see their faults	负
satisfactory	adj. 满意的	good enough to be accepted in a particular situation	正
scholarly	adj. 博学的	someone who is scholarly spends a lot of time studying, and knows a lot about a particular subject	正
scorn	v. 轻蔑	to show that you think that something is stupid, unreasonable, or not worth accepting	负
scornful	adj. 轻蔑的	feeling or expressing scorn	负
seductive	adj. 引人注意的	something that is seductive is very interesting or attractive to you, in a way that persuades you to do something you would not usually do	正
self-centered	adj. 自我中心的	limited to or caring only about yourself and your own needs	负
self-congratulatory	adj. 自满的	showing you are very proud of what you have done, in a way that annoys other people	负
self-critical	adj. 自我批评的	critical of oneself and one's faults and weaknesses	正
self-effacing	adj. 不出风头的	not wanting to attract attention to yourself or your abilities	正
self-important	adj. 妄自尊大的	thinking that you are more important than other people	负
self-indulgent	adj. 放纵的	allowing yourself to have or do something special that you like very much, often something you should not have or do	负
self-interested	adj. 自私的	when you only care about what is best for you, and do not care about what is best for other people	负
selfish	adj. 自私的	caring only about yourself rather than about other people	负

态度词	中文释义	英文释义	态度
self-sacrificing	adj. 自我牺牲的	when you decide not to do or have something you want or need, in order to help someone else	正
self-satisfied	adj. 自鸣得意的	too pleased with yourself or your own achievements	负
self-serving	adj. 自私自利的	interested only in gaining an advantage for yourself	负
sensible	adj. 有判断力的	able to make good judgements based on reason and experience rather than emotion	正
sensitive	adj. 敏感的	easily upset or offended by events or things that people say	负
sentimental	adj. 多愁善感的	someone who is sentimental is easily affected by emotions such as love, sympathy, sadness etc., often in a way that seems silly to other people	负
sentimental reminiscence	adj. 感伤的回忆	a spoken or written description of sth that sb remembers about their past life	负
shame	n. 羞愧	the feelings of guilt, sadness and embarrassment that you have when you know that sth you have done is wrong or stupid	负
sheepish	adj. 羞怯的	looking or feeling embarrassed because you have done sth silly or wrong	负
shock	n./v. 震惊	to surprise and upset sb	负
shocked	adj. 震惊的	very surprised and upset by something bad that happens unexpectedly	负
shortsighted	adj. 目光短浅的	lacking foresight	负
showy	adj. 炫耀的	so bright, colourful, large or exaggerated that it attracts a lot of attention	负
shrewd	adj. 敏锐的	able to judge people and situations very well and make good decisions	正
shy	adj. 害羞的	nervous or embarrassed about meeting and speaking to other people	负

态度词	中文释义	英文释义	态度
sincere	adj. 真诚的	a feeling, belief, or statement that is sincere is honest and true, and based on what you really feel and believe	正
sincerely	adv. 真诚地	in a way that shows what you really feel or think about sb/sth	正
sinister	adj. 凶兆的	making you feel that something evil, dangerous, or illegal is happening or will happen	负
skeptic	n. 怀疑论者	one who instinctively or habitually doubts, questions, or disagrees with assertions or generally accepted conclusions.	负
skeptical	adj. 怀疑的	having doubts about something that other people think is true or right	负
skepticism	n. 怀疑论	a doubting or questioning attitude or state of mind	负
smitten	adj. 被重击的	seriously affected by something such as an illness or emotion	负
smug	adj. 自鸣得意的	showing too much satisfaction with your own cleverness or success	负
smugness	n. 自鸣得意	an excessive feeling of self-satisfaction	负
snide	adj. 暗讽的	criticizing sb/sth in an unkind and indirect way	负
softhearted	adj. 心软的	easily moved to pity or sorrow	正
solemn	adj. 沉重的	not happy or smiling ; looking very serious	负
solicitous	adj. 热切关心的	being very concerned for sb and wanting to make sure that they are comfortable, well or happy	正
somber	adj. 忧郁的	sad and serious	负
soothing	adj. 抚慰的	to make someone feel calmer and less anxious, upset, or angry	正
sophisticated	adj. 经验丰富的	having a lot of experience of the world and knowing about fashion, culture and other things that people think are socially important	正

态度词	中文释义	英文释义	态度
sorrow	n. 悲伤	a feeling of great sadness, usually because someone has died or because something terrible has happened to you	负
speculative	adj. 猜测的	based on guessing or on opinions that have been formed without knowing all the facts	负
spellbound	adj. 被迷住的	with your attention completely held by what you are listening to or watching	正
spirited	adj. 生机勃勃的	full of or characterized by animation, vigor, or courage	正
spiteful	adj. 怀有恶意的	behaving in an unkind way in order to hurt or upset sb	负
startle	v. 使吓一跳	to make a person or animal feel suddenly frightened or surprised by doing something they do not expect	负
staunch advocacy	n. 坚定的支持	strong and loyal in your opinions and attitude; strong public support for something	正
straightforward	adj. 坦率的	clear and honest	正
strained	adj. 焦虑的	showing the effects of worry or pressure	负
striking	adj. 引人注目的	interesting and unusual enough to attract attention	正
stubborn	adj. 顽固的	determined not to change your opinion or attitude	负
studied	adj. 深思熟虑的	deliberate and carefully planned	正
studied interest	n. 深思熟虑的兴趣	the feeling that you have when you want to know or learn more about sb/sth	正
studious	adj. 好学的	giving a lot of attention and care to what you are doing or learning	正
stylish	adj. 时髦的	fashionable; elegant and attractive	正
stymied	adj. 妨碍的	to present an obstacle to	负
substantial	adj. 实质的	large in amount or value; important	正
sullen	adj. 不高兴的	angry and silent, especially because you feel life has been unfair to you	负

态度词	中文释义	英文释义	态度
superficial	adj. 肤浅的	not studying or looking at sth thoroughly ; seeing only what is obvious	负
supportive	adj. 支持的	giving help, encouragement or sympathy to sb	正
surreal	adj. 超现实主义的	marked by the intense irrational reality of a dream	负
surprise	n. 惊奇	an event, a piece of news, etc. that is unexpected or that happens suddenly	负
surprised disbelief	n. 吃惊的难以置信	the feeling of not being able to believe sth	负
suspicion	n. 怀疑	a feeling that you do not trust someone	负
suspicious	adj. 可疑的	feeling that sb has done sth wrong, illegal or dishonest, without having any proof	负
sympathetic	adj. 有同情心的	caring and feeling sorry about someone's problems	正
sympathy	n. 同情	the feeling of being sorry for someone who is in a bad situation	正
tactful	adj. 机智委婉的	careful not to say or do anything that will annoy or upset other people	正
teasing	adj. 嘲弄的	the act of harassing someone playfully or maliciously (especially by ridicule)	负
tedious	adj. 冗长乏味的	lasting or taking too long and not interesting	负
tempered	adj. 缓和的	calmness of mind	中
tenacious	adj. 顽强的	determined to do something and unwilling to stop trying even when the situation becomes difficult	正
tenderness	n. 温柔	gentle and careful in a way that shows love	正
terse	adj. 简洁的	brief and to the point	正
terrified	adj. 恐惧的	very frightened	负
theatrical	adj. 夸张的	exaggerated in order to attract attention or create a particular effect	负

态度词	中文释义	英文释义	态度
thoughtful	adj. 体贴的	showing that you think about and care for other people	正
threatening	adj. 危险的	showing or saying that someone is likely to do something that will harm you	负
thrilling	adj. 令人兴奋的	exciting and enjoyable:	正
timid	adj. 羞怯的	shy and nervous ; not brave	负
tolerant	adj. 宽容的	able to accept what other people say or do even if you do not agree with it	正
treacherous	adj. 不可信的	that cannot be trusted ; intending to harm you	负
trepidation	n. 恐惧	great worry or fear about sth unpleasant that may happen	负
triumphant	adj. 胜利的	very successful in a way that causes great satisfaction	正
trivial	adj. 不重要的	of little significance or value	负
troublesome	adj. 讨厌的	causing problems , in an annoying way	负
unabashed admiration	n. 大胆的崇拜	a feeling of respect and liking for sb/sth, not ashamed, embarrassed or affected by people's disapproval, when other people would be	正
unassuming	adj. 不装腔作势的	exhibiting no pretensions, boastfulness, or ostentation ; modest	正
unbiased	adj. 无偏见的	without bias or prejudice ; impartial.	中
uncertain	adj. 迟疑不决的	feeling doubt about something	负
uncertainty	n. 不确定	the state of being uncertain	负
unconcern	adj. 不感兴趣的	a lack of care, interest or worry about sth that other people would care about	中
unconvinced	adj. 不相信的	not certain that something is true or right	负
uncouth	adj. 粗鲁的	rude or socially unacceptable	负
underhanded	adj. 狡诈的	secret and dishonest	负

态度词	中文释义	英文释义	态度
undisguisedly envy	n. 赤裸裸地嫉妒	to wish you had the same qualities, possessions, opportunities, etc. as sb else	负
uneasiness	n. 不安	worried or slightly afraid because you think that something bad might happen	负
uneasy	adj. 心神不安的	feeling worried or unhappy about a particular situation, especially because you think that sth bad or unpleasant may happen or because you are not sure that what you are doing is right	负
unequivocal	adj. 明确的	expressing your opinion or intention very clearly and firmly	正
unflattering	adj. 不奉承的	making sb/sth seem worse or less attractive than they really are	正
unintelligent	adj. 缺乏才智的	having or displaying a lack of intelligence	负
uninterested	adj. 不感兴趣的	not interested ; not wanting to know about sb/sth	中
unintimidated	adj. 毫无畏惧的	not shrinking from danger	正
uninviting	adj. 不动人的	not attractive or pleasant	负
unlifting	adj. 低沉的	to raise from a higher to a lower position	负
unmitigated greed	n. 彻头彻尾的贪婪	a strong desire for more wealth, possessions, power, etc. than a person needs	负
unrestrained joy	n. 无限制的快乐	a feeling of great happiness, free of constraint	正
unsympathetic	adj. 不同情的	not kind or helpful to someone who is having problems	负
untenable	adj.（论据等）站不住脚的	an untenable argument, suggestion etc. is impossible to defend	负
urbane	adj. 彬彬有礼的	behaving in a pleasant, relaxed, and correct way in social situations	正
urgent	adj. 紧急的	very important and needing to be dealt with immediately	负
urgent concern	n. 紧迫的焦虑	a feeling of worry, especially one that is shared by many people	负

态度词	中文释义	英文释义	态度
utopian	adj. 空想的	characterized by or aspiring to impracticable perfection	负
utter contempt	n. 全然藐视	lack of respect accompanied by a feeling of intense dislike	负
vacuous	adj. 空洞的	showing no intelligence or having no useful purpose	负
vague	adj. 模糊的	unclear because someone does not give enough detailed information or does not say exactly what they mean	负
valid	adj. 合法的	that is legally or officially acceptable	正
validated	adj. 经过验证的	to support or corroborate on a sound or authoritative basis	正
vehement	adj. 激烈的（怒）	showing very strong feelings, especially anger	负
veiled distaste	n. 有点儿厌恶	a feeling of intense dislike with a concealing cover	负
vigilant	adj. 警惕的	very careful to notice any signs of danger or trouble	正
vindictive	adj. 怀恨的	trying to harm or upset sb, or showing that you want to, because you think that they have harmed you	负
vivid	adj. 生动的	vivid memories, dreams, descriptions etc. are so clear that they seem real	正
vulgar	adj. 粗俗的	rude, unpleasant, and offensive	负
wariness	n. 谨慎	the trait of being cautious and watchful	正
wary	adj. 谨慎的	careful when dealing with sb/sth because you think that there may be a danger or problem	正
weary	adj. 疲倦的	very tired or bored, especially because you have been doing something for a long time	负
weighty	adj. 重要的	important and serious	正
whimsical	adj. 反复无常的	unusual and not serious in a way that is either amusing or annoying	负

态度词	中文释义	英文释义	态度
whimsy	n. 反复无常	a way of thinking or behaving, or a style of doing sth that is unusual and not serious, in a way that is either amusing or annoying	负
wholehearted	adj. 一心一意的	complete and enthusiastic	正
wistful	adj. 怀旧（难过）的	thinking sadly about sth that you would like to have, especially sth in the past that you can no longer have	负
wistfulness	n. 怀旧（难过）	thinking sadly about something you would like to have but cannot have, especially something that you used to have in the past	负
witty	adj.（富于机智）幽默的	able to say or write clever, amusing things	正
wonder	n. 奇迹	a feeling of surprise and admiration that you have when you see or experience sth beautiful, unusual or unexpected	正
wry	adj. 讽刺的	dryly humorous, often with a touch of irony	负
wry amusement	n. 冷幽默	the feeling that you have when sth is funny or amusing, or it entertains you	中
zealous	adj. 热心的	showing great energy and enthusiasm for sth, especially because you feel strongly about it	正